Denial, Negation,
and the Forces of the Negative

SUNY SERIES IN HEGELIAN STUDIES

William Desmond, editor

DENIAL, NEGATION, AND THE FORCES OF THE NEGATIVE

Freud, Hegel, Lacan, Spitz, and Sophocles

WILFRIED VER EECKE

STATE UNIVERSITY OF NEW YORK PRESS

Published by
STATE UNIVERSITY OF NEW YORK PRESS
ALBANY

For information, address
State University of New York Press
194 Washington Avenue, Suite 305, Albany, NY 12210-2384

Production, Laurie Searl
Marketing, Susan Petrie

Library of Congress Cataloging-in-Publication Data

Ver Eecke, Wilfried.
    Denial, negation, and the forces of the negative : Freud, Hegel, Lacan, Spitz, and
Sophocles / Wilfried Ver Eecke.
        p. cm. — (SUNY series in Hegelian studies)
    Includes bibliographical references and index.
    ISBN 0-7914-6599-3 (hardcover : alk. paper)
    1. Freud, Sigmund, 1856–1939. 2. Psychoanalysis. 3. Denial (Psychology) 4. Negation
(Logic) 5. Negativity (Philosophy) 6. Hegel, Georg Wilhelm Friedrich, 1770–1831. I.
Title. II. Series.

BF175.V465 2005
121'.5—dc22

                                                                                                2004029291

                        10   9   8   7   6   5   4   3   2   1

For Josiane,
with whom I crossed an ocean
to start a family in the promised land.

Contents

Acknowledgments

This book would not have been possible without the editorial assistance of Lynn Poss and David O'Mara, supported by a Georgetown University Undergraduate Research Opportunity grant, and Lacy Baugher and Eupil Muhn, supported by the Department of Philosophy. I want to give special thanks to Devra Simiu for helping to improve the style of the whole manuscript.

Several chapters have appeared before as separate articles. All have been adapted to the interdisciplinary nature of this book. Often, I have added extensive references to the treatment of the problem in other disciplines, in particular, psychoanalysis, psychology, linguistics, and philosophy. I wish to thank the following publishers for their permission to use articles in writing some of the chapters of this book.

I made use of: Ver Eecke, W. "Ontology of Denial." *Rereading Freud: Psychoanalysis through Philosophy*. Ed. J. Mills (Albany, NY: State University of New York Press, 2004). 103–25, in writing chapter 1, "The Complex Phenomenon of Denial," with the kind permission of State University of New York Press.

I made use of: Ver Eecke, W. "Epistemological Consequences of Freud's Theory of Negation." *Man and World* 14 (1981): 111–25, in writing chapter 2, "The Epistemological Problem of Self-description in Freudian Psychoanalysis," with the kind permission of Kluwer Academic Publishers, copyright owner of *Man and World*.

I made use of: Ver Eecke, W. "Negation and Desire in Freud and Hegel." *Owl of Minerva* 15 (1983): 11–22, in writing chapter 3, "Denial and Hegel's Philosophical Anthropology," with the kind permission of Owl of Minerva.

I made use of: Ver Eecke, W. "Seeing and Saying 'No' Within the Theories of Spitz and Lacan." *Psychoanalysis and Contemporary Thought* 12:3 (1989): 383–431, in writing chapter 5, "A Child's No-Saying: A Step towards Independence," with the kind permission of International Universities Press, based upon: Copyright 1989 *Psychoanalysis and Contemporary Thought*, published by International Universities Press, Inc., Madison, CT.

Introduction

This is a book about denial, negation, and the forces of the negative. A denial is a paradoxical phenomenon. In a denial, such as "this woman in my dream is not my mother," a truth is revealed, but the revelation is done in such a way that the revelation is explicitly denied. A denial thus appears as a misleading statement. As presented, it is not true, but false. Nevertheless, the falsity of a denial does not make it worthless. A denial reveals two things to a good listener. It reveals a truth that the patient him or herself cannot yet accept. Secondly, it reveals that the patient is caught in a conflict and thus cannot see reality truthfully. One can say, therefore, that a denial is much more revealing than a simple affirmative statement. It labels the truth, while in its denial of what it labels, it gives a hint of the paralysis of the speaking subject.

Freud's therapeutic attitude towards denials and his intellectual conclusions about them give us two entirely different paths on which to evaluate the phenomenon of denial. From a therapeutic perspective, Freud suggests steps to help the patient overcome the limitations resulting from his or her conflicted situation. These steps should help the patient become a more free individual. The first step, the easiest, is the one which consists of helping the patient to intellectually accept the true revelation hidden in the denial. The therapist can let the patient reveal information which accumulatively provides evidence for the truth of what was previously denied. The patient is then forced, often reluctantly, to confess that that which was previously denied is true. Freud points out that such an intellectual acceptance of the truth, hidden in a denial, does not mean that the truth is emotionally accepted. Freud writes, "The outcome of this is a kind of intellectual acceptance of the repressed, while at the same time what is essential to the repression persists" (Freud, S.E., XIX, 236). Therefore, a second therapeutic step needs to be undertaken. The therapist must help the patient emotionally accept the truth hidden in the denial. To accept something emotionally means to accept the consequences of that truth and to undertake the rational actions implied by the

1

accepted truth. Overcoming the negative forces hidden behind the formation of a denial can thus be expected to be an arduous process.

In his theoretical reflections on denial, Freud follows a different line of reasoning. Indeed, Freud accepts the conflicted nature of a human being. He then takes this acceptance a step further by affirming that a conflicted being must have at its disposal mechanisms to bridge the conflict. Mastering a conflict requires that one first expresses the conflict. Freud points to the linguistic expression of negation as such a mechanism. Indeed, Freud writes, "But the performance of the function of judgment [acknowledging the truth] is not made possible until the creation of the symbol of negation has endowed thinking with a first measure of freedom from the consequences of repression and, with it, from the compulsion of the pleasure principle" (Ibid. 239).

The above-mentioned puzzling dimensions of a denial are presented in detail in the first chapter of this book. One important implication of the phenomenon of denial is then analyzed in chapter 2. There I argue that it is not possible to classify all false self-descriptions as lies, because such a move locates a denial in the moral domain. Classifying a statement as a lie supposes that the speaker has achieved a level of agency that is simply not achieved by someone who utters a denial. Such a person is in conflict and is thus not master in her own home. She is subject to negative forces that she does not control. A denial can therefore be better classified as a sign of deficiency in agency. It shows an anthropological weakness and not a moral failure. This ends the first part of the book, in which the text of Freud is clarified.

In chapters 3 and 4 of the book, I examine the conflicted forces that are behind the creation of negations and denials. I do so by employing Hegel's philosophy. In chapter 3, I make use of Hegel's anthropology in order to theorize about denial, making philosophical generalizations where Freud makes astute observations. In Hegel's analysis of the master-slave dialectic, Hegel demonstrates that the relationship between the body and the mind involves contradictory requirements which unavoidably lead to denial. I make that argument more general by using Hegel's claim that the road to truth is not solely a path of doubt, but more properly a highway of despair. The road towards truth changes doubt into despair whenever doubt involves one's self-conception. If doubt undermines one's self-conception, it destroys the possibility of being a desiring subject. Such a doubt makes one lose one's bearings and creates despair. Denial can thus be understood as a desiring being's defense against despair.

In chapter 4, I start from the view that a denial is a misguided effort to sustain life by avoiding despair. I try to clarify the misguided effort to sustain life, present in a denial, by appealing to Hegel's analysis of the human will. The appeal to Hegel is promising in that Hegel defines the free will as a will that relates negatively to the object of its own willing. The student, whose summer job consists of washing dishes, remains free in so far as he relates negatively to what he does by saying that he is earning his college tuition. Thus, the student is able to maintain that washing dishes is only a byproduct of his effort to earn his tuition. I then argue that in uttering a denial, a person tries to exercise the negativity, required for the will to be free, by denying an epistemological connection rather than by putting distance between the objectively given and the volition of the will.

Hegel calls the eudemonic will the will which is able to create distance between itself and the objectively given without denying epistemologically that given. It succeeds in doing so because it is able to create a norm, happiness, to which it subjects any thing that is objectively given. All that is objectively given is epistemologically recognized, but no given is allowed to make a decisive influence on what the will intends to decide. The given that is chosen as object of the will is the given that contributes to the goal of the will, say, happiness. The eudemonic will thus succeeds both in being open to the given and keeping its distance from the given when making a decision.

Where the eudemonic will succeeds, the arbitrary will fails. It is a will which exercises the necessary distance demanded by a free will by not giving enough consideration to the given. Instead, the arbitrary will is a will that reserves for itself the right to decide without having to give a reason beyond the claim: I so decided. For the arbitrary will, the given is disregarded as a legitimate input in the decision.

It looks as if someone who utters a denial tries to create the distance to the given, required to be a free will, by disregarding the epistemologically given, as does the arbitrary will, instead of creating that distance by evaluating the given in terms of its contribution to a personal goal, as does the eudemonic will. Such a Hegelian interpretation of denial allows us to understand why the therapeutic effort of patients uttering a denial consists of two steps. First, it must address the epistemological error used mistakenly to create the illusionary distance required by the logic of the will. Secondly, it must provide the will with the ability to accept the objectively given while maintaining the possibility of evaluating that given in light of one's chosen goals.

In chapters 5, 6, and 7 of the book, I address three implications of Freud's theory of denial. In chapter 5, I examine Freud's claim that the acquisition of the linguistic symbol of negation is the prerequisite for freedom of the will. I find Spitz's work to be a useful framework in which to address that question. Spitz argues that human beings, particularly children, do not show a linear development. Rather, he argues, multiple parallel developments lead to the creation of new possibilities. As examples he gives the appearance of the social smile at about two months, the eight-month anxiety—sometimes also called separation anxiety, and the no-saying at about fifteen months of age. These phenomena are indicators of the new psychic possibilities of the child. Thus, the eight-month anxiety indicates that the child establishes a deeper relationship with its caregivers. I argue that the anxiety indicates that the child is dealing with the alienating dimensions of having appropriated its body in the mirror stage. The no-saying is, according to Spitz, the first unequivocal concept used by the child. I argue that the no-saying of the child shows an irrational dimension in that the child seems to refuse that which it manifestly wants. That irrational dimension becomes supremely rational if one understands that the no-saying aims at cutting the emotional ties with the caregiver. I interpret the no-saying of the fifteen-month-old infant as her effort to establish the right to decide on her own, even if that means losing what she wants. I also argue that the use of the linguistic symbol of negation (no-saying), by itself, affirms the right to autonomy. It is not only an indicator of the autonomy of the child, it is the organizer of that autonomy. I argue that the eight-month anxiety is only an indicator, and not an organizer, of the new psychic achievements of the child at eight months. The new psychic achievement is the establishment of a deeper attachment to caregivers in order to overcome the alienating dimension of having appropriated the body.

In chapter 6, I analyze more closely the process of undoing a denial as it happens in Sophocles' tragedy *Oedipus, the King*. Freud warned us that such a process is difficult and arduous. Sophocles' tragedy allows us to illustrate the idea that a denial is connected with situations in which the self-image of a person is threatened in such a way that the possibility of desire is destroyed. *Oedipus, the King* shows how and how not to help someone undo a denial.

In chapter 7, I analyze the autobiography of Antony Moore in which the author reveals the many complex psychic acts he has undertaken to overcome a profound denial. Indeed, Moore, who lost his father in the Second World War when he was only two months old, developed unconsciously a deep identification with his dead and idealized father. At the same time, when asked if he missed his father, he replied, when growing up: "One cannot miss what one never had." He combined this primary denial with the idea that he had learned to be his own father and thus needed no substitute father, certainly not in the figure of his maternal grandfather. Finally, in his childish grandiosity, he made himself unconsciously responsible for the death of his father by the argument that his father died shortly after he was born. Therefore, there was no room in the world for both of them. Moore thus felt that in fathering a son, his father wrote his own death warrant and that if he were to father a child it would mean his own death as well. In the autobiography of Moore, more than in the article by Freud, we see that a denial is, as it were, the tip of an iceberg, covering deep tragic experiences. In that same autobiography we find a description of all the psychic work that is required to undo, not just intellectually but also emotionally, a denial. I will demonstrate that it is by means of appropriate help from others and by means of metaphoric work by himself that Moore was able to acknowledge that he deeply missed his father but could also start feeling that he was not responsible for the death of his father. Furthermore, he could start experiencing himself as the fulfillment of the promise of life, which did not come to fruition in his father but which did come to fruition in the son.

ONE

The Complex
Phenomenon of Denial

abstract: Freud drew attention to the puzzling phenomenon of denial in many passages of his work. He focused on some of the contradictory aspects of the phenomenon in an article published in 1925. In that same article Freud theorized about a number of characteristics in human beings that one must postulate in order to do justice to these many puzzling and contradictory aspects of denial. One of the strongest conclusions that Freud made was the claim that negation is a precondition for human freedom. I will present Freud's ideas, but I will also demonstrate that his analysis is incomplete. In particular, Freud, in his crucial article on denial ("Negation" 1925), did not analyze the arduous work required to undo fully a denial and its consequences. In particular Freud did not draw attention to the need for acts of separation from primary care givers and for the creation of metaphoric moves in order to free oneself from the contradictions inherent in denials.

INTRODUCTION

In this chapter I will present Freud's analysis of the puzzling phenomenon of denial, which consists of simultaneously denying and revealing the truth. Thus, when a patient answers that the female figure in his dream is not his mother, Freud interprets the answer as revealing that it really is his mother (Freud, S.E., XIX, 235).[1] Or when a patient boasts that it is pleasant not to have had her headaches for so long, Freud interprets this as signaling that the attack is not far off (Ibid. 236).

I will start by delineating the problem as Freud treated it. Next, I will show that the phenomenon of denial is part of a larger process. I will also point out that Freud refrains from fully analyzing that whole process, leaving a promising task for readers of this chapter. Third, I will describe and elaborate on three metapsychological insights of Freud, one of which, I will show, implies that realizing the truth hidden in a denial is more than an epistemological problem: it involves hard emotional work. Fourth, I will show some limitations in Freud's analysis of the phenomenon of denial. In particular, I will show that realizing the truth hidden in a denial requires more than epistemological work; it requires also acts of separation from intimate others and the mobilization of powerful aspects of language. Finally, I will briefly present and analyze an autobiography in which the author describes the undoing of a profound denial related to the death of his father on the battlefield when the author was a two-month old infant. This case will illustrate my theoretical claim that undoing a denial requires acts of separation and skillful usages of metaphors.[2]

1. DEMARCATION OF THE PROBLEM

By the examples he gives, Freud demarcates the problem he intends to discuss by means of the concept of *Verneinung*, translated in the the Standard Edition of Freud's works as "negation," but which I prefer to translate as "denial."[3] Freud's demarcation is at the same time restrictive and expansive.

Let us first look at the restrictions imposed by Freud's examples on the domain of the concept *Verneinung*. In the first example, a patient rejects an emotion that might be imputed to her, given what she intends to say. Freud presents the case in this way: "Now you'll think I mean to say something insulting, but really I've no such intention" (Ibid. 235). Freud continues by presenting what he thinks goes on in the patient: "We realize that this is a rejection, by projection, of an idea that has just come up" (Ibid.). Typical for a denial is the fact that the patient labels a phenomenon—in this case an emotion—but that the labeling is incorrectly rejected as untrue.

The second example concerns a patient who has told Freud about a dream in which there is a female figure. Freud reports the case as follows: "'You ask who this person in the dream can be. It is *not* my mother.'" Freud then continues: "We emend this to: 'So it is his mother.' In our interpretation, we take the liberty of disregarding the negation and of picking out the subject-matter alone of the association. It is as though the patient had said: 'It's true that my mother came into my mind as I thought of this person, but I don't feel inclined to let the association count'" (Ibid.). In his comments on this second example Freud is very explicit about the two dimensions he seems to consider constitutive of the phenomenon of denial. On the one hand, there is an activity of labeling. Freud describes it as an act of associating a known figure (mother) with the unknown figure in the dream. Describing what happens in the first constitutive moment of denial as an association seems to me to underplay the role of linguistically identifying the unknown phenomenon. In a denial, one does not so much associate two images—the unknown figure in the dream and the figure of the mother—as one labels a previously unknown phenomenon. The other constitutive element of a denial is the negation of the labeling activity performed by the patient. Freud interprets the negation in a denial to mean, in the first example, a rejection of an idea that has come up, and, in the second example, a disinclination "to let the association count" (Ibid.).

Freud's third example is of a neurotic who has already been informed by Freud of the workings of unconscious processes. Freud describes his patient as telling him: "'I've got a new obsessive idea, . . . and it occurred to me at once that it might mean so and so. But no; that can't be true, or it couldn't have occurred to me.'" Freud interprets the statements of his patient as follows: "What he is repudiating, on grounds picked up from his treatment, is, of course, the correct meaning of the obsessive idea" (Ibid.). In this example we have again two moments: 1) what Freud calls "the repudiation" and 2) the description of the meaning of a new obsessive idea.

In the third paragraph of his article, Freud starts to conceptualize what he thinks to be the phenomenon he wants to study. He writes: "Thus the content of a repressed image or idea can make its way into consciousness, on condition that it is negated. Negation is a way of taking cognizance of what is repressed" (Ibid.). Freud here introduces explicitly a third constitutive element of denial: repression.[4] The first constitutive moment was the correct labeling of the repressed. The second constitutive moment was the refusal of the revealed truth. A denial is then understood as a mechanism whereby an unknown repressed phenomenon "makes its way into consciousness" (Ibid.). Freud finds the mechanism of negating so essential for the result of a denial— letting the repressed make its way to consciousness—that he proposes a new technique for treating patients who have difficulty in revealing a piece of information about something that is repressed and thus unconscious. Freud writes: "'What,' we ask, 'would you consider the most unlikely imaginable thing in that situation? What do you think was furthest from your mind at that time?' If the patient falls into the trap and says what he thinks is most incredible, he almost always makes the right admission" (Ibid.). In order for Freud to invent this new technique and, even more, for this technique to be effective, it must be the case both that there are two centers of meaning creation and that the meanings created by these two centers are not compatible. Freud addresses this incompatibility between the two systems of meaning creation by giving consciousness a face-saving device. Freud asks what the most unlikely imaginable thing is or what was furthest from the patient's thought. Freud provides consciousness with a form of distance from the truth it is invited to discover or, formulated differently, he provides consciousness with the opportunity to deny what it sees. Freud observes that when a patient accepts the face-saving device and describes what he thinks is furthest from his mind, he *almost always* describes the unconscious correctly. In one of the next paragraphs, Freud calls the negation in a denial "the hall-mark of repression, a certificate of origin—like, let us say, 'Made in Germany'" (Ibid. 236).[5]

Some authors have expanded the meaning of denial to include non-verbal activities.[6] Thus Edith Jacobson uses the label 'denial' for such phenomena as amnesia (Jacobson 63, 64), disavowal or undoing of castration (Ibid. 74, 77, 83), avoidance (Ibid. 75), and wishful fantasies distorting reality when they are a means of defending against fearful objects (Ibid. 78). Such an expansion of the concept of denial omits, in my opinion, a crucial element in the phenomenon Freud wants to study: that is, a denial *correctly labels the repressed phenomenon*, even though a denial denies the correctness of the labeling. Labeling and correctly labeling that which is repressed are crucial aspects of the puzzle which Freud wants to study under the phenomenon called 'denial.'[7]

There is, however, an expanded meaning of denial which does correspond to Freud's interpretation of denial. I believe that I can argue for that expansion because Freud provided a fourth example of the kind of phenomena he was going to study. The fact that the example is mentioned not in the main text, but in a footnote, might indicate that Freud, too, felt that this example is a form of extension of the core phenomenon. He actually claims that the fourth example is using the same process; he does not claim that the process is identical with the process at work in the first three examples. Here is how Freud describes the new example, which he calls boasting: "'How nice not to have had one of my headaches for so long.' But this is in fact the first announcement of an attack, of whose approach the subject is already sensible, although he is as yet unwilling to believe it" (Freud, *S.E.*, XIX, 236). At first, one could argue that the patient in this new example does not make a false statement. It seems to be correct for the patient to say that he has not had the headaches for a long time. Therefore, this example could be said to be a misfit. It is not a proper example of the phenomenon Freud is studying, for in it nothing is falsely denied. However, when one looks in the rest of Freud's oeuvre one can notice additional similar examples.[8] Freud's explanation of these examples provides arguments for seeing the similarity between the fourth example and the other three. In the process, Freud also forces us to accept a fourth not-so-visible constituent element in the phenomenon of denial.

Freud discusses the danger of boasting in his study of Frau Emmy von N. He does so in a long footnote, having warned his readers at the beginning of his study that he will reproduce the notes that he made at night during the beginning of the treatment and will put insights acquired later in footnotes (Freud, *S.E.*, II, 48). Emmy von N. regularly had "neck-cramps." Freud describes them as consisting "in an 'icy grip' on the back of the neck, together

with an onset of rigidity and a painful coldness in all her extremities, an inca-
pacity to speak and complete prostration. They last from six to twelve hours"
(Ibid. 71). In the evening session of May 17, 1889,[9] Emmy von N. "expressed
her astonishment that it was such a long time since she had had any neck-
cramps, though they usually came on before every thunderstorm" (Ibid. 75).
The morning of May 18, Emmy von N. "complained of cold at the back of
her neck, tightness and pains in the face, hands and feet. Her features were
strained and her hands clenched" (Ibid. 75–76). In a footnote which may
have been written up to five years after the treatment, Freud writes that
Emmy von N.'s "astonishment the evening before at its being so long since
she had had a neck-cramp . . . [can be understood as] a premonition of an
approaching condition which was already in preparation at the time and was
perceived in the unconscious" (Ibid. 76, n. 1). The patient disregards the true
premonition.

Freud describes a second patient, Frau Cäcilie M., who regularly had similar premonitions. Thus, Freud writes, "while she was in the best of health,
she said to me 'It's a long time since I've been frightened of witches at night,'
or, 'how glad I am that I've not had pains in my eyes for such a long time,' I
could feel sure that the following night a severe onset of her fear of witches
would be making extra work for her nurse or that her next attack of pains in
the eyes was on the point of beginning" (Ibid. 76, n. 1). Freud provides a
beginning of a conceptualization of these phenomena. He says it this way:
"On each occasion what was already present as a finished product in the
unconscious was beginning to show through indistinctly. This idea, which
emerged as a sudden notion, was worked over by the unsuspecting 'official'
consciousness (to use Charcot's term) into a feeling of satisfaction, which
swiftly and invariably turned out to be unjustified" (Ibid. 76, n. 1). These
examples of boasting are therefore not, strictly speaking, like the other three
examples of denial. In boasting the patient does not utter a falsity. It is indeed
true that the patient has not had neck-cramp, been frightened of witches, or
had pain in the eyes. However, what the patient is reporting is naive because
it does not report the most interesting thing that could be reported. The
patient does not say that he feels that an attack, or witches, or pain in the
eyes is coming. Here we come to the essence of Freud's new insight. Freud
claims that the unconscious has a wisdom that consciousness does not have.
Freud claims that the cause for the boasting of his patients is the wisdom of
the unconscious which feels that the attack or the painful crisis is coming.
Consciousness, in its limited information capabilities, does not see the attack
on the horizon. All that consciousness can report is that it is aware that these
attacks have not occurred for some time. Freud thus tells us, on the one hand,
that the unconscious takes the initiative and formulates the truth, but that,
on the other hand, consciousness does not know what the unconscious
already knows. Freud says as much when he explains the popular warning

against boasting: "We do not boast of our happiness until unhappiness is in the offing and we become aware of our anticipation in the form of a boast" (Ibid. 76, n. 1).[10]

In boasting, as in the other examples of denials, an all too real but frightening truth is denied. The real truth is that the unconscious is aware of a coming attack. Thus, things are bad. Consciousness, on the other hand, looking only to the past, says that things are good. But notice, boasting is not without epistemological value. Just as with the other examples, boasting hits the nail on the head by correctly labeling the problem. Only, as in the other examples, boasting wrongly evaluates the problem. One can therefore formulate the similarity of boasting to examples of clear-cut denial as follows: an unknown unpleasant truth has been correctly labeled but wrongly evaluated.

Let us make a further observation about Freud's explanation of boasting. In a last attempt to clarify the superstition that boasting is bad, Freud writes: "[In boasting] the subject-matter of what we are recollecting emerges before the feeling that belongs to it—that is to say, because an agreeable contrasting idea is present in consciousness" (Ibid. 76, n. 1). We have here in Freud's analysis of boasting the first hint that the unconscious and consciousness systems obey different logics in creating statements. The unconscious is able to present something to which unpleasant feelings are attached. Consciousness seems inclined to turn to pleasant feelings. Freud will explain later in the article that the ego, as the seat of consciousness, is, at some point in its development, unable to accept anything unpleasant associated with itself. He writes: "the original pleasure-ego wants to introject into itself everything that is good and to eject from itself everything that is bad" (Ibid. 237). The ego is thus at that point of its development a narcissistic, imaginary construction.[11]

2. PHENOMENOLOGICAL ANALYSIS
OF THE PROCESS OF DENIAL

Having delineated the phenomenon that he wants to analyze (verbal denial), Freud then proceeds to unpack the background of that phenomenon. Freud teaches us that a verbal denial is part of a larger process.

First, there is a postulated prior phase: repression. Freud points out that a *Verneinung* (denial) has the effect of "taking cognizance of what is repressed" (Ibid. 235). This idea is so important to Freud that he formulates it three more times. He writes: "Thus the content of a repressed image or idea can make its way into consciousness, on condition that it is *negated*" (Ibid.). Or: "it [*Verneinung* (a denial)] is already a lifting of the repression" (Ibid.). Or finally: "[by *Verneinung* (a denial)] one consequence of the process of repression is undone—the fact, namely, of the ideational content of what is repressed not reaching consciousness" (Ibid.). As already pointed out in the analysis of the examples given by Freud, a necessary precondition for a denial thus seems to be the existence of repression. When the mechanism of repression is successful then consciousness is faced with a blank. For the patient who dreamed about a female figure, a successful repression would have resulted in her saying: "You ask me who that figure is in my dream? I do not know." We have an example in Freud's patient Emmy von N., when Freud asks her "what the stammer came from" (*S.E.*, II, 61). Freud reports that the patient reacted by silence, by giving no reply. When Freud insisted and asked: "Don't you know?" she replied "No." When Freud pressed her by asking "Why not?" the patient angrily replied: "Because I *mayn't*" (Ibid.).

Second, there is the actual phase of denial. By contrasting the phenomenon of denial with the postulated state that preceded it, Freud is able to emphasize the novelty in the phenomenon of denial. The novelty is that consciousness is now aware of a phenomenon that it was not aware of before. Further on in his reflections, Freud describes denial as contributing to freedom of thinking because it provides consciousness with content that it lacked, insofar as consciousness is now aware of that which it previously was not. Furthermore, repressed thoughts are important—Freud even claims that they are indispensable—to the patient. Freud puts it this way: "With the help of the symbol of negation [in a denial], thinking frees itself from the restrictions of repression and enriches itself with material that is indispensable for its proper functioning" (*S.E.*, XIX, 236). Again: "But the performance of the function of judgment is not made possible until the creation of the symbol of negation has endowed thinking with a first measure of freedom from the consequences of repression and, with it, from the compulsion of the pleasure principle" (Ibid. 239).

Freud, however, points out that one should not be too enthusiastic about the presumed victory of denial over repression. He describes that victory in a variety of ways. He writes that a denial is "a way of taking cognizance of what is repressed . . . though not, of course an acceptance of what is repressed" (Ibid. 235–36). Or: "With the help of negation only one consequence of repression is undone" (Ibid. 236). Or finally: "The outcome of this is a kind of intellectual acceptance of the repressed, while at the same time what is essential to the repression persists" (Ibid.). A denial is thus a very ambiguous performance.[12] It undoes one crucial aspect of repression in that a denial labels the repressed. A denial lets a careful listener know precisely what the object of an effort of repression is. On the other hand, a denial makes it clear to any listener that the patient does not accept the truth as it is labeled and thus revealed in a denial. Freud knows that the female figure represented— let us suppose as domineering—in the patient's dream is in truth the patient's mother. But the patient's denial states the contrary: that female figure is not my mother. Freud describes the ambiguity of this denial quite well when he writes: "It is as though the patient had said: 'It's true that my mother came into my mind as I thought of this person, but I don't feel inclined to let the association count'" (Ibid. 235). In a denial, a patient thus rejects or refuses to accept a true proposition.

Third, Freud informs us that therapy can promote further progress. Freud reports that it is possible to conquer "the negation as well and [bring] about a full intellectual acceptance of the repressed" (Ibid. 236). He adds, however, that in this new phase "the repressive process itself is not yet removed" (Ibid.). One can imagine that Freud asked the patient who dreamt about the female figure what eyes the female figure had, what hair, what clothes, what shoes, and so forth. If the patient was forced to recognize each time that the eyes, the hair, the clothes and the shoes of the figure all resembled those of his mother, he might then have concluded: "I guess it then must be my mother." Such an intellectual acknowledgment is clearly not a full emotional acknowledgment.[13] As in the case of denial, here too there is a split between the intellectual and the affective processes.[14]

Clearly, this latter situation suggests the expected existence of a fourth stage in the process of denial wherein that which is repressed is overcome both intellectually and affectively.[15] One can imagine that the patient who dreamt about a domineering lady and who subsequently identified her as his mother is now able to solve the emotional conflict arising from the fact that the female figure is simultaneously a domineering figure and his mother. Freud does not provide us, in his article, with any hints of the steps that will have to be taken to achieve that fourth stage.[16] In the rest of this chapter I will articulate insights derived from studying that fourth stage.[17]

3. FREUD'S META-PSYCHOLOGICAL REFLECTIONS

Having observed a difference between the emotional reaction and the intellectual attitude towards a repressed phenomenon as revealed in a denial, one would have expected that Freud would have reflected on that difference. Instead, Freud uses most of the rest of the article on denial to explain how the intellectual function, that is, judging, is similar to and possibly emerges out of the affective life.[18] He makes use of the generally accepted distinction between an attributive and an existential judgment. In an attributive judgment one is concerned with whether an object—in Freud's examples, the ego—has a particular quality. Am I a person who insults people, has bad ideas about my mother, and so forth? An existential judgment must decide whether a representation exists only in my memory or in my mind or, on the contrary, also exists in reality. Freud gives as example the child who imagines the mother's breast. An existential judgment must make the distinction between a representation to which nothing corresponds in reality and a representation that fits the reality.

In the process of reflecting on attributive judgments, Freud reminds us of a first meta-psychological thesis which will be very useful to explain a puzzling aspect of denial. It will also give us a hint of the difficult road that must be traveled to undo a denial. The piece of psychoanalytic theory that Freud reminds us of is the thesis that the ego is a narcissistic construction whose judgments, at first, follow the pleasure principle and not the reality principle. Freud writes that "the original pleasure-ego wants to introject into itself everything that is good and to eject from itself everything that is bad. What is bad, what is alien to the ego and what is external are, to begin with, identical" (Ibid. 237).

If we apply this piece of psychoanalytic theory to the person who makes a denial, one must accept the proposition that the ego of that person does not follow the logic of the reality principle in which truth is recognized even if it is unpleasant. Rather, the ego in that case follows the logic of what Freud calls the pleasure principle.[19] That logic is described as introjecting into oneself anything that is good and rejecting from oneself all that is bad. Such an explanation fits the examples given by Freud. Insulting thoughts about someone one depends upon, a negative image of one's mother, headaches: all are undesirable things and the logic of the pleasure principle demands that each of them be rejected from the original pleasure-ego. Under the logic of the pleasure principle, only elements having the narcissistically pleasing characteristics of being good and nothing else but good can be admitted.

Enlightened by this Freudian idea, one is able to predict that fully undoing a denial will involve much more than epistemological work. It will involve addressing the ego's love of a narcissistic self-image. Giving up such a narcissistic image is for the ego to accept that it is less than what it thought it was and loved thinking itself to be. The great question is then: How will the person react to such a demand? Will he react with aggression? Will he mourn? Will he look for a creative way to somehow recover that which he denied? Or finally, will he select a combination of these techniques?[20]

When reflecting on the judgment of existence, Freud develops a second meta-psychological idea. He starts by pointing out that a judgment of existence is necessary when a person has developed a more realistic ego, an ego that obeys the reality principle. Freud himself gives the example of the infant who must be interested in distinguishing an imagined breast from an imagined breast which also exists (*Project for a Scientific Psychology*, S.E., I, 327–30). An imagined breast or, more generally, a representation of something is by itself already a warrant of the existence of the represented thing because "The antithesis between subjective and objective does not exist from the first" (S.E., XIX, 237). Freud then continues his argument by claiming that the opposition between the subjective and the objective is the result of the activities of the mind. The mind can bring before itself "once more something that has once been perceived, by reproducing it as a presentation without the external object having still to be there" (Ibid.). Also "the reproduction of a perception as a presentation is not always a faithful one; it may be modified by omissions, or changed by the merging of various elements" (Ibid. 238). The judgment of existence must then verify if the object that is presented by the mind is still there in reality. Freud is now ready to make his second meta-psychological comment while reflecting on the process of denial. Freud writes: "The first and immediate aim, therefore, of reality-testing is, not to *find* an object in real perception which corresponds to the one presented, but to *refind* such an object, to convince oneself that it is still there" (Ibid. 237–38). Or "it is evident that a precondition for the setting up of reality-testing is that objects shall have been lost which once brought real satisfaction" (Ibid. 238). This line of thinking by Freud suggests that truth telling as it is conditioned by judgments of existence requires more than the acquisition of the linguistic function of negation. *It also requires a non-linguistic form of negativity.*[21] It requires that something that once provided real satisfaction has been lost. But such a loss cannot just be passively undergone. It will also have to be actively created. Some act of separation will have to be made.

Freud presents a third meta-psychological idea when he concludes his reflections on judgments. He argues that he has been able to show the psychological origin of judgments because they make moves similar to those of the primary instincts. In attributive judgments—so Freud tell us—a characteristic of a thing is to be accepted and thus affirmed or is to be rejected and thus denied. In judgments of existence one wants to know whether a presentation of a thing is only a presentation and is thus to be considered worthless or whether, on the contrary, something real corresponds to the presentation and thus the presentation is valuable because it corresponds to something that exists. Freud writes: "The polarity of judgments appears to correspond to the opposition of the two groups of instincts which we have supposed to exist. Affirmation—as a substitute for uniting—belongs to Eros; negation—the successor to expulsion—belongs to the instinct of destruction" (Ibid. 239). Freud thus makes the connection between judgments and emotions by means of three pairs of concepts. The first pair is *affirmation* and *negation*. The second pair is *substitute for uniting* and *successor to expulsion*. The third pair is *Eros* and *instinct of destruction*.

The last pair, Eros and instinct of destruction, expresses the polarity of human affectivity as Freud sees it. From early on Freud explained neurosis by means of the notion that a human being is a battlefield for different emotional forces. Originally, he thought that the basic opposition was between sexuality and ego-forces. Sexuality assured reproduction. The ego-forces assured self-preservation and expressed themselves most strongly in hunger. Freud called the sexual energy libido.[22]

When Freud analyzed the problem of narcissism he noticed that the libido was directed not only towards the sexual object but also towards the ego itself. This insight destroyed the opposition between the libido (a force for reproduction) and the "ego-force." In *Beyond the Pleasure Principle*, Freud explicitly accepts this conclusion and therefore reduces both the ego-instincts and the libido to one force, Eros (Freud, *S.E.*, XVIII, 44–61). The force opposing the libido (or love-force) is the instinct of destruction (which in its ultimate form is the death-instinct). Thus, Freud reintroduces psychological duality.

The second pair, substitute for uniting and successor to expulsion, is a strange one. The way Freud labels them indicates that the two elements of the pair are not co-equal; there is no symmetry between the two. The German word *Nachfolge* (successor) indicates that a prior action has taken place—referred to as expulsion. Freud's understanding of the way the original narcissistic ego constructs itself is consonant with the idea that it is a "successor." Indeed, Freud claims that the narcissistic ego is the result of—metaphorically—'spitting out of itself' what is considered bad (Freud, *S.E.*, XIX, 237). The German word *Ersatz* (substitute), on the other hand, is used for an object or a situation. The idea that something is a substitute presupposes that something precedes the substitute either in time or in thought. The idea of unity does not include that same suggestion of a prior state as suggested by the idea of substitute. Could this mean that, according to Freud, unity is the primary situation of the child, whereas rejection (spitting out) is a secondary reaction?[23]

The asymmetry signaled in the choice of labels for the second of the three pairs of words relating judgments and affective forces can be clarified further by reflecting on the central problem of this article: negation-denial. A denial presupposes, first, a connection between two facts, that is, a form of unity. A denial also presupposes that this connection was repressed. A negative judgment—particularly a denial—is then the expression of an original connection *and* of a trace of a prior repression, that is, a negation. An affirmative judgment expresses only a relation between the two contents. Whether or not there was a split between them is not expressed in an affirmative judgment. Thus, an affirmative judgment has less expressive potential than a negative judgment. In an affirmative judgment one only affirms a connection or a unity. What preceded the connection cannot be expressed by an affirmative judgment.

This leads us to the first pair mentioned by Freud: the affirmative and the negative judgment. This pair too must consist of parts that are not equally important. The negative judgment has more expressive potential. Thus, it is understandable that Freud finishes the paragraph by underlining the central function of the symbol of negation. Negation expresses both a connection between two concepts and a rejection of that connection. When the negative sentence is a denial, then the negation is a sign of a repression which is simultaneously overcome and maintained at a new level.

Freud uses his meta-psychological speculation on the connection between affective forces and judgments and the primacy of Eros to explain a clinical fact: the negativism of many psychotics.[24] Freud thinks the negative attitude of this type of psychotic results from a withdrawal of the libidinal components of the instincts such that too much destructivity remains. A normal person seems to need a quantity of libido. This type of psychotic is then one who lives in a degenerated situation because of a lack of sufficient libido. Psychosis is here explained as degeneration. In *The Ego and the Id* (Freud, *S.E.*, XIX, 40–47, especially 40–42), Freud talks about the mixing of the libido and the aggressive tendencies. Here, Freud takes a developmental point of view. The child's libido develops from an oral to a genital phase. This happens, says Freud, through the addition of erotic components. The regression from a genital to an anal-sadistic libido is the result of the disappearance of the erotic elements. In these reflections Freud moves from his epistemological problem of denial to anthropological concerns about the development of libidinal and aggressive tendencies. It is a connection that will prove very valuable for exploring an aspect of denial that Freud did not explicitly address: the full undoing of a denial.

4. SPECIFICATIONS AND CORRECTIONS OF FREUD'S REFLECTIONS

However influential this short paper of Freud's has been, it is important to show its limitations. First, Freud seems to have a misconception of his own analysis. Freud claims to be analyzing the function of judgments. In fact Freud is not analyzing judgments but rather is analyzing the prehistory of judgments. Using Merleau-Ponty's terminology, one could say that Freud is sketching the preverbal history of the judgment. In that preverbal history Freud emphasizes the great importance of the acquisition of the linguistic symbol of negation. In doing so he either overlooks or fails to emphasize two other dimensions in a person's preverbal history.[25] Both dimensions remain hidden behind Freud's emphasis on the importance of acquiring the linguistic symbol of negation. This dimension has to do with the human requirement to elevate thoughts and feelings to the level of language. Acceding to this requirement is not restricted to the act of repressing or negating; Lacan understood this when he interpreted Freud's concept of *Bejahung* (affirmation) in the pair *Bejahung-Verneinung* as a "saying yes" to the whole symbolic system in general.

Independent of the psychoanalytic tradition, Hegel also seems to have understood the requirement for human beings to elevate needs and feeling to the level of language. Hegel does not use the word language but points to a requirement that must produce two characteristics consonant with elevating things to the level of language. Thus, Hegel writes: "as the feeling too is itself particular and bound up with a special corporeal form, it follows that . . . the subject . . . is still susceptible of disease, so far as to remain fast in a *special* phase of its self-feeling, unable to refine it to 'ideality' and get the better of it" (Hegel, *Philosophy of Mind*, 122–23). Bringing feelings (and needs) to the level of 'ideality' allows free subjectivity to assign feelings and needs the relative places that subjectivity wants and needs to assign them. By elevating feelings and needs to 'ideality,' consciousness acquires a form of fluidity (Ibid. 124) compatible with the requirement of freedom. Such a consciousness can then proscribe to itself "behaviour which follows from its individual position and its connection with the external world, which is no less a world of laws" (Ibid. 123). If consciousness is unable to elevate a particular feeling to 'ideality,' then consciousness "is engrossed with a single phase of feeling, it fails to assign that phase its proper place and due subordination in the individual system of the world which a conscious subject is" (Ibid. 123). Consequently, such "a feeling with a fixed corporeal embodiment sets [itself] up against the whole mass of adjustments forming the concrete consciousness" (Ibid. 124).[26]

I interpret Hegel's claim that human beings must elevate feelings and needs to 'ideality' as similar to the Lacanian claim that human beings need to insert themselves with all their needs and wishes into the world of language so as to make all and each of these needs and wishes interconnected and thus relative. Failing to do so leads, according to both Lacan and to Hegel, to mental illness.[27] By overemphasizing the importance of replacing repression by a linguistic negation, Freud neglects to bring out the important point that the whole of life needs to be elevated to a linguistic world.

The second dimension hidden behind Freud's emphasis on the importance of acquiring the linguistic form of negation is the individual's prehistory of negation, with its effort at separation and the aggression involved in it. Freud does mention that the "the original pleasure-ego wants . . . to eject from itself everything that is bad. What is bad, what is alien to the ego and what is external are, to begin with, identical" (Freud, S.E., XIX, 237). Spitz does not just mention that prehistory of negation, he also analyzes it. In particular, he analyzes the function of aggression related to saying "no" (Spitz 1957, 51–52, 56–59, 130–33).

Spitz starts by pointing to the fact that prior to the acquisition of saying "no," at about fifteen months of age, the child's relation to its mother undergoes a drastic change. As the child begins to crawl and/or walk, the child moves away from the mother and does things that might endanger it. The mother, acting as the external ego of the child, constantly issues prohibitions in word and gesture. These prohibitions force the child into passivity and are experienced as frustrations. Among the most frequently returning means for the mother's expression of prohibitions is the use of the word "no." According to Spitz, the child responds to the frustrations resulting from the prohibitions in progressively more complicated ways. First, the child sides with the adult who prohibits and does what the adult wants—for example, not touch-ing an electric outlet (Ibid. 56). However, such a reaction leads to unaccept-able frustrations for the child. Furthermore, the passivity forced upon the child provokes an aggressive reaction from the unconscious. The child is thus put in a paradoxical situation: he/she is still in a very dependent relation with the maternal figure while also feeling aggression towards that same figure. Spitz believes that the child resolves this tension by identifying with its mother as an aggressor (Ibid. 56, 133).[28] By such a move the child dynami-cally satisfies both contradictory feelings. In consequence, the child acquires no-saying and is now able to use the word or gesture with all the frustration and aggression attached to it. Finally, the child can make use of the newly acquired word (or gesture) either against him or herself or against the mother. In using the no-saying against him or herself the child creates a cleavage within between him or herself as an object observed and as an observer (Ibid. 130, 133). In using the no-saying against a person with whom the child has "primary narcissistic dependent relations" (Ibid. 56), the child severs his/her dependency relations with that person (Ibid. 52) and establishes separateness (Ibid. 57). From then on the child will have to establish new kinds of rela-tions with that person. Spitz calls those new relations "highly enriched" (Ibid. 57, 129, 131).[29] By means of a case I will study in the next section, I will demonstrate that the acts of separation and severing involved in no-saying introduce a need for metaphorical relations. The linguistic form of negation will thus lead us by means of the idea of separation and the idea of aggression hidden in acts of separation to the appearance of the phenomenon of metaphor.[30]

5. COMPLETING FREUD'S REFLECTIONS

In his study on denial, Freud greatly stressed the importance for the human being of acquiring the linguistic symbol of negation. However, I claim that, in laying this stress, Freud was also undervaluing the many other functions of language, as well as undervaluing the act of separation, with its implied aggression, that is behind the no-saying. I will now illustrate my claim with a concrete case of denial and the person's successful efforts at overcoming the denial.

In *Father, Son, and Healing Ghosts*, the author, Anthony Moore, provides us with an autobiographical account of dealing with his father's death. When Moore was two months old, his father died on a battlefield in the Second World War. As a young boy, Moore developed several strategies to deal with this traumatic event. He identified with his father, the dead marine officer, so strongly and imitated him so much that the young Moore at one point felt that "he was unable to be [himself] (Moore 4).[31] At the same time, when asked about his feelings about the loss of his father, Moore had the habit, from his childhood on, of answering: "You can't miss what you never had" (Ibid. 1). Clearly this is a denial. We can see the pain of losing his father in his attempts to erase it via suffocating imitation and identification. We also find traces of young Moore's pain—some of it self-inflicted—in two fantasies related to his father's death. As he was born April 16, 1944, and his father died June 15, 1944, young Moore developed the fantasy that there must not have been space enough in the world for both of them together and that thus he was the cause of his father's death. He further fantasized that if he were to father a child that would be his own death warrant (Ibid. 3, 98).

With the help of a therapist, as in Freud's own reported examples, Moore was able to undo intellectually the denial that he did not miss his father. In the case of Moore, the therapist said: "You can also miss what you never had but know you had every right to have" (Ibid. 4). Emotionally undoing the conflict and healing the wound behind the denial is a more complicated story.

Moore's efforts at distancing himself from the idealization of his father were crucial. After years as a dedicated and enthusiastic student in a military high school, the young Moore avoided ROTC in college. He gives as his reason that he felt he "had had enough of the military" (Ibid. 2). By his senior year, Moore returned to his love for the Marines and took the entrance exam for the Marine Corps Officer Candidate School (Ibid. 2). His first attempt at separating from his idealized father had not stuck. A second and new form of separation was initiated when he told his mother and grandmother of his plans to enroll in the Marine Officer School while the Vietnam War was taking place. What the young Moore saw in their eyes was either their fear of his death or their disapproval of his risking his life. His mother (and grandmother) had put a wedge between the young Moore and his father by appealing to his own wish to live (Ibid. 2). The young Moore accepted their invitation to make the separation from his idealized father.

Moore himself tells us that once he had separated himself from his father's identity he felt the need "to reconnect to the energy and meaning that continued to flow from the image of [his] father" (Ibid. 5). Moore thus found himself in the contradictory situation that he wanted to be both separate from and remain connected with his father. He found a solution to this challenge in what in Lacanian terminology is called a metaphoric move.[32] Having refused to become a Marine because that might lead to death, the young Moore lost an important connection with his father. Moore recovered that connection with his father by becoming a Jesuit. Moore writes about this decision: "Being a Jesuit was like being a Marine. Sometimes the Jesuits were even referred to as the Pope's Marines. Furthermore, the idea of joining a religious order carried with it an image of dying, dying to the world, particularly the world of marital love" (Ibid. 3).[33] By the metaphorical power of the words "Marine" and "dying" the younger Moore was able to reconnect with his father after having separated himself from him.[34]

CONCLUSION

The analysis of Moore's undoing of his denial can help us clarify the concept of self-deception. One is right in saying that the younger Moore deceived himself when he was telling himself and others during his adolescence that he could not miss his father since he never had one. One is also right in saying that the younger Moore did not know that he was deceiving himself. He only knew that he had been deceiving himself after he was helped by his psychiatrist-psychoanalyst, who told him that one can also miss what one never had but knows one had every right to have.[35] At that moment the younger Moore knew that he had been deceiving himself; he knew that his claim that one cannot miss a father one never had was a denial. One can therefore claim that it is possible to deceive oneself without knowing that one is deceiving oneself. Self-deception is thus, strictly speaking, not a lie.[36] It becomes a lie only after the moment in which a denial has been intellectually undone and the person refuses to do the emotional work involved in taking the steps implied by the intellectual undoing.

Freud praised the linguistic symbol of negation as a great instrument of freedom. It would be wrong, however, to attribute the healing of Tony Moore simply to the magic power of the symbol of negation in his fundamental denial. The healing was also based on several acts of cutting himself loose from his father and on the great metaphor of being a Jesuit. I believe that I have been able to show that Freud's analysis of the function of negation is but the tip of an iceberg in the process of healing. The iceberg includes at least the idea that one has to cut oneself loose from others with all the aggression (and guilt) that this involves and the idea that the richness of language must be used in its many dimensions, including the metaphoric dimension made available by the cultural tradition in which one lives. I was able to rely on Spitz for pointing out the negative acts required for personal growth. I was able to rely on Lacan and Hegel to point to the requirement that the totality of human life needs to be elevated to the level of language. Clearly, correcting the epistemological mistake present in a denial requires addressing the great anthropological puzzle of human growth with its demand for aggressive separation from and creative (metaphorical) connection with our original caregivers. Not properly dealing with the demand for separation and connection with his father was for Moore a form of self-deception even before he formulated a denial. When Moore formulated his denial, it was possible for others to see the self-deception at work. Only when he was able to intellectually undo his denial was Moore confronted with the choice of lying to himself or being authentic. As I see it, Moore avoided lying to himself because he was willing to face the difficult emotional demands made on himself in order to deal in a different way with the need to separate himself from his father while satisfying his need to remain connected with him. Thus, although the concepts of denial, self-deception, and lying about oneself partially overlap, they are not identical and should be carefully distinguished. I will devote the next chapter to this problematic.

TWO

The Epistemological Problem of Self-description in Freudian Psychoanalysis

abstract. Freud's theory of denial (negation) implies several theses about human self-knowledge. The first thesis is that self-knowledge is not identical to self-revelation; human beings reveal more about the self than they are able to acknowledge consciously. The second thesis is that self-knowledge can be contradicted by self-revelation and can therefore be proven false. The third thesis is that unacknowledged self-revelation can be used to correct or broaden one's self-knowledge. The fourth thesis is that human beings encounter limits to self-knowledge. Therefore errors in the description of the self are not necessarily lies or expressions of bad faith. The fifth thesis is that the limits to self-knowledge are not fixed; they can be changed. These limits can be altered not only by personal effort, but also by appropriate help from others. In this chapter I concentrate on the ethical implications of Freud's theory of self-knowledge as implied by his study on denial (negation): mistakes in self-description, when put into the terms of ethical language, should not always be called lies.

INTRODUCTION

In this chapter, I will develop five points. First, I will briefly map out the Freudian concepts that point to erroneous self-expressions or self-descriptions such as: lies, hypocrisy, mistakes, illusions, and disavowals. Second, I will draw attention to the phenomena (the use of denial and negation as first revelations of painful truths) that Freud wants to explain with his theory of negation. Third, I will demonstrate that these phenomena are crucial in psychotherapy and that Freud gradually came to perceive their central function. In Freud's oeuvre, one can find vestiges of his emerging awareness of the importance of facts and events. Fourth, I will show the far-reaching epistemological implications of Freud's theory of negation for a theory of self-knowledge. Fifth, I will ponder about some apparent contradictions.

1. A MAP OF FREUD'S CONCEPTS OF ERRONEOUS FORMS OF SELF-DESCRIPTIONS

In this section, I want to prepare the analysis of Freud's approach to negation (denial)—a form of self-interpretation—by taking a look at a number of other Freudian concepts related to different forms of self-expression and self-interpretation. I propose to classify these concepts in four categories: the morally negative, the morally neutral, the morally ambivalent, and the morally positive. Candidates for the first category, the morally negative, are: *Lüge* (lies); *Heuchelei* (hypocrisy); and *Selbstverrat* (self-betrayal). Candidates for the second category, the morally neutral, are: *Fehlleistung* (parapraxis); *Irrtum* (mistake); *Illusion* (illusion); and *Täuschung* (error). Candidates for the third category, the morally ambivalent, are: *Leugnung* (disavowal); *Verleugnung* (disavowal); and *Verneinung* (denial). The candidate for the fourth category, the morally positive, is: *Glaubwürdigkeit* (credibility).

A look at the cross-references between these concepts, however, provides arguments to call into question the validity of the above classification. Thus, the morally negative concepts (lies or hypocrisy) refer respectively to a morally ambiguous concept (disavowal) and a morally neutral one (mistake). The morally neutral concept (error) refers to two other morally neutral concepts (illusion and mistake) and to two morally negative concepts (hypocrisy and self-betrayal). A closer look at the meaning that these concepts had for Freud is thus advisable. In the morally-negative concepts category, a closer examination reveals that the typical psychoanalytic use of these concepts is not clearly morally negative. Although Freud uses the "lie" concept at least once in the commonplace meaning of a morally negative act, where it is used in an enumeration with such other morally-negative concepts as "fraud" and "calumny,"[1] more often Freud uses the concept "lie" in a specifically psychoanalytic way where the concept of lie is explained as a sign of emotional impotence. This is the case when Freud talks about "the lying poetic fancies of prehistoric times," (*S.E.*, XVIII, 136) or the lies of children (*S.E.*, XII, 305ff; or *S.E.*, X, 102–103).

In his article "Two Lies Told by Children," (*S.E.*, XII, 303–309) Freud presents and analyzes the case of a girl who denied stealing fifty "pfennigs" from her father and the case of another girl who denied to her teacher using a pair of compasses for what was supposed to be a freehand drawing.

In the first case, Freud discovered that the father's anger over the theft was a turning point in the girl's life. Before the incident, she had been "wild, self-confident" (Ibid. 305). Afterwards, she was "shy and timid" (Ibid.). Freud discovered that, for the girl, taking money from her father was associated with an incident in which the nursemaid gave the girl money to remain silent about the nursemaid's erotic relations with a doctor. Through this association, taking money was unconsciously associated with an offer of tenderness, with "a declaration of love" (Ibid. 307). The anger of the father meant that her offer was rejected.

In the second case, Freud discovered that, when his patient was a young girl, she could not deal with the fact that her father was less powerful than she had thought. She adored and identified with her idealized father. One of the talents the girl admired very much in her father was his drawing talent. Her attempt to draw a perfect circle was thus an attempt to show not only how she could draw, but also how well her father could. She could therefore not acknowledge anything that would diminish the achievement.

In his introductory and concluding remarks, Freud writes that such lies should not be interpreted morally; rather, educators should become concerned about the child's unconscious problems. In the main text, Freud links children's lies to the lie's hidden meaning. About the first case, Freud writes: "She could not admit, however, that she had appropriated the money; she was obliged to disavow it, because her motive for the deed which was unconscious to herself, could not be admitted" (Ibid. 307). The reason why it could not be admitted becomes clear when Freud summarizes the two cases at the end of his paper: "an admission was impossible for the same reason that was given in the first of the observations: it would inevitably have been an admission of her hidden incestuous love" (Ibid. 308–309).

Clearly, Freud intends to argue in this article that a lie is to be interpreted in some cases as the *impossibility* of self-knowledge when self-knowledge would be incompatible with self-love based on identification with an idealized person.

Hypocrisy too is interpreted not so much as a conscious lie as it is a failure to live up to an ideal. Freud infers such a failure from mistakes that patients often unconsciously make. Thus, in his article "Thoughts for the Times on War and Death," (*S.E.*, XIV, 273–300) Freud defines hypocrisy as that attitude which tries to follow cultural prescriptions even if one's own drives are really desiring something different. Hypocrisy is then described as follows:

> Anyone . . . compelled to act continually in accordance with precepts which are not the expression of his instinctual inclinations, is living, psychologically speaking, beyond his means, and may objectively be described as a hypocrite, whether he is clearly aware of the incongruity or not. (Ibid. 284)

The sign that a person is living beyond his means is "the perpetual readiness of the inhibited instincts to break through to satisfaction at any suitable opportunity" (Ibid.). Clearly, failure to live up to an ideal is not so much an act of deceit as it is an indication of a person's inability to realize fully an ideal.

On the other side of the spectrum, a word used for a morally positive attitude, *"Glaubwürdigkeit"* (credibility), is not so unequivocally positive in the psychoanalytic vision of the person. Indeed, Freud derives his certainty about the truth or correctness of his patients' answers, not from the patients' explicit statements, but from a series of side phenomena such as the difficulty of resistance that had to be overcome or the indirectness of confirmation techniques that had to be used. Thus, credibility is not connected with the patient's moral use of freedom but with the indirectness of the revelation of truth.

Nevertheless, if lies, hypocrisy, and credibility are non-moral categories and if self-expressions or statements about the self often fail, then the habit of regularly interpreting these non-moral categories as moral categories is problematic. Freud's theory of negation is a crucial contribution for clarifying the problems encountered in this problematic confusion of moral and non-moral meanings of categories.

2. FREUD'S EMERGING AWARENESS
OF THE FUNCTION OF NEGATION

Freud's theory of negation first attempts to explain the appearance of a linguistic expression (i.e., a negation) which fallaciously changes the meaning of statements. Freud already observed this phenomenon in the treatment of Emmy v. N. (1888–89) (1893).[2] Thus, Freud suggests, in a footnote, a relationship between a negative statement and repression. (*S.E.*, II, 57, n. 2)

In his analysis of the Rat-man (1907) (1909), and again in a footnote, Freud shows that he is already familiar with the curious phenomenon of denial. Indeed, he writes: "This is a common type of reaction to repressed material which has become conscious: the 'No' with which the fact is first denied is immediately followed by a confirmation of it, though, to begin with, only an indirect one" (*S.E.*, X, 183, n. 2). This leads Freud to make, some ten pages later, a distinction between two forms of knowing:

> It must therefore be admitted that . . . there are two kinds of knowledge, and it is reasonable to hold that the patient 'knows' his traumas as that he does *not* 'know' them. For he knows them in that he has not forgotten them, and he does not know them in that he is unaware of their significance. (Ibid. 196, n. 1)

In his study of Judge Schreber (1911), Freud mentions the use of negation as one of the techniques by which the patient indirectly reveals the truth.

Finally, Freud again discusses the problem of negation twelve years after his article on "Negation," in his study "Construction in Analysis" (1937). Here Freud adds a further idea: A denial is an indication that the labor of uncovering the truth is *incomplete*; a negation is not to be interpreted as an indication that the proposed statement is false.

The idea that obfuscation is helpful for truth's emergence and the insight that obfuscation techniques and negation are related, are already expressed in Freud's case study of the Ratman (1909). There Freud mentions that the Ratman explicitly denied having had death-wishes towards his father. The patient then remembers a scene in Sudermann's novel in which one person wishes another person's death in order to be able to marry. Then, suddenly, the Ratman says: "He [the Ratman] could understand this [other person's death-wish]." The Ratman then continues, saying that: "it would be only right if his thoughts were the death of him, for he deserved nothing less" (*S.E.*, X, 183). In a footnote, Freud writes: "This sense of guilt involves the most glaring contradiction of his opening denial that he had ever entertained such an evil wish against his father. This is a common type of reaction to repressed material which has become conscious: the 'No' with which the fact is first denied is immediately followed by a confirmation of it, though, to begin with, only an indirect one" (*S.E.*, X, 183, n. 2). Freud explicitly mentions the obfuscation necessary for the emergence of unconscious truth: "I am in the habit of regarding associations such as this, which bring forward something that agrees with the content of an assertion of mine, as a confirmation from the unconscious of what I have said. *No other kind of 'Yes' can be extracted from the unconscious*" (Italics added) (*S.E.*, VII, 57).

The later Freud is so familiar with with his patients' need for obfuscation that he remarks, almost casually, in a prelude to his interpretation of the Schreber case (1911):

> . . . we have only to follow our usual psychoanalytic technique—to strip his sentence of its negative form, to take his example as being the actual thing, or his quotation or gloss as being the original source—and we find ourselves in possession of what we are looking for. . . . (*S.E.*, XII, 35)

In his 1915 publication "The Unconscious" Freud mentions this idea in a broader context:

> There are in this system no negation, no doubt, no degrees of certainty: all this is only introduced by the work of the censorship between the Ucs (unconscious) and the Pcs (preconscious). Negation is a substitute, at a higher level, for repression. In the Ucs, there are only contents, connected with greater or lesser strength. (*S.E.*, XIV, 186)

Finally, in his 1915 publication "Thoughts for the Times on War and Death," Freud writes:

> What we call our 'unconscious'—the deepest strata of our minds, made up of instinctual impulses—knows nothing that is negative, and no negation; in it, contradictions coincide. For that reason it does not know its own death, for to that we can give only a negative content. (*S.E.*, XIV, 296)

Another source of arguments in favor of the thesis that negation is not present in the unconsciousness can be built from the fact that dreams—the royal road to the unconsciousness—contain no negatives. Thus, in a somewhat guarded way, Freud writes in two places: "'No' seems not to exist so far as dreams are concerned" (S.E., IV, 318; S.E., V, 661). He will point out, however, that there are roundabout methods of expressing negatives and contradictions such as failing to achieve something notwithstanding serious attempts (S.E., IV, 337). Ten years later Freud writes about his remark concerning negations and contradictory elements in dreams:

> I did not succeed in understanding the dream-work's singular tendency to disregard negation and to employ the same means of representation for expressing contraries. . . . (S.E., XI, 155)

In 1916 Freud writes more precisely: "This connects with the further fact that a representation of 'No'—or at any rate an unambiguous one—is not to be found in dreams" (S.E., XV, 178).

3. FROM EPISTEMOLOGY TO ANTHROPOLOGY AND ONTOLOGY

Freud's theory of negation stresses the fact that negation can only be explained within a dual framework: an archeology and a teleology.

The archeological aspect comes through clearly in the following sentence:

> To negate something in a judgment is, at bottom, to say: 'This is something which I should prefer to repress.' A negative judgment is the intellectual substitute for repression; its 'no' is the hall-mark of repression, a certificate of origin—like, let us say, 'Made in Germany.' (Freud, S.E., XIX, 236)

Thus, without a prior repression, negation would be deprived of its function as a subsitute, a hallmark, and a certificate of origin. Therefore, negation cannot be fully understood without an appreciation of repression.

The teleological aspect comes through when Freud writes, "With the help of the symbol of negation, thinking frees itself from the restrictions of repression and enriches itself with material that is indispensable for its proper functioning" (Ibid. 236), and again when, later in the essay, he writes:

> But the performance of the function of judgment is not made possible until the creation of the symbol of negation has endowed thinking with a first measure of freedom from the consequences of repression and, with it, from the compulsion of the pleasure principle. (Ibid. 239)

According to this line of reasoning, negation is a creation that has the purpose of freeing thought or, alternatively, the purpose of enriching thought with previously repressed unconscious content.

SELF-DESCRIPTION IN FREUDIAN PSYCHOANALYSIS   31

The linguistic signifier "negation" is thereby interpreted as a pivotal instrument whereby a "telos" can become the partial victor over an undesirable "arche." The rest of Freud's article on negation presents the reader with several unexpected turns in the argumentation. A very abrupt turn comes when Freud attempts to demonstrate that his negation theory is valid for both attributive and existential judgments. In the course of his argument, Freud ties his epistemological argument to an anthropological one. The anthropological view, presented as a companion thesis, is that the self constitutes itself even in its epistemological capacities. Concerning the epistemological task of making attributive judgments, this anthropological thesis claims that the self successively develops three attitudes toward attributes. The key text for our interpretation of Freud's claim is: "What is bad, what is alien to the ego and what is external are, to begin with, identical" (Ibid. 237).

We interpret this text to mean that, in the historical development of the individual, there is a period in which the self creates a fictitious distinction between the outside world and the self (i.e., the inside). The self classifies something as being inside or outside by using the criterion of whether it is good or bad for the ego. It is a purely narcissistic criterion in so far as the self imaginarily identifies all bad things with the outside world and all good things with itself. One must think of this move by the self as having been preceded by a period in which the ego did not make the distinction between inside and outside on the basis of the aforementioned narcissistic criterion. (In his article on negation, Freud claims that the self bases the distinction on the pleasure principle.) When the self is not yet using a narcissistic criterion to establish a distinction between inside and outside, it lives in the feeling of oceanic *unity* with everything.

One must also conclude that, after the self makes the narcissistic distinction between inside—as all good—and outside—as all bad, the self still needs to develop the capability of recognizing good elements in the outside world and bad elements in itself. Concerning the epistemological task of making existential judgments, the anthropological thesis claims "that a precondition for the setting up of reality-testing is that objects shall have been lost which once brought real satisfaction" (Ibid. 238). Freud arrives at this anthropological thesis by way of two intermediate epistemological claims. The first claim is that the problem of existential judgments related to finding an object is a kind of dialogue between a perception and a representation. The second epistemological claim is that finding an object is thus always a matter not of *finding* the object but of *refinding* it (Ibid. 237). Given this anti-Kantian epistemology, where the constitution of an object is not explained by the use of *a priori* categories, Freud is forced to interpret finding as refinding an object. This epistemological vision therefore requires a particular anthropology: that is, that there was such a thing as a primal object which was available to the subject from the beginning. Put in a more positive way, the anthropological thesis is that the self experiences unity with the world prior to experiencing differences with the world. Within such a view, the anthropological prerequisites for the epistemological possibility of existential judgments are that "objects shall have been lost," and that the self has the strength and tools to overcome the dictates of the pleasure principle. In the second period of the self's self-constitution, the pleasure principle demands that all good objects—be they lost or not—be imaginatively classified as part of the ego. In this period—the period of the pleasure-ego's pre-dominance—the loss of an object is countered by an effort to create an illusionary presence of the object and furthermore by an effort to identify with that object. In that period, objects can not subjectively be experienced as lost.

Towards the end of his paper, Freud complements his epistemological and anthropological claims with an ontological one. He uses three parallel pairs of concepts to present his argument for an ontology of the human person. (Ibid. 239). The three pairs of concepts are: the epistemological actions of affirmation and negation; the ontological entities Eros and the instinct of destruction; and the concepts serving to relate the epistemological pair to the ontological pair.

I would like to make the tentative claim that in the asymmetry of the concepts Freud uses to relate the epistemological pair to the ontological pair, we may find a possible key to Freud's ontology. Indeed, Freud says that affirmation is a substitute for unity, whereas negation is a successor to expulsion. The word expulsion presupposes a prior unity, and an action that breaks this unity. Negation is a successor to that action. The word substitute (*Ersatz*) is more often used to point to a thing replacing another thing than to an action following another action. Therefore, affirmation is said to be a substitute for another non-action, that is, the primal situation of unity. Unity must, therefore, be thought of as ontologically primary.

This tentative claim regarding Freud's ontology is supported by its ability to explain the sentence immediately following the introduction of the parallelism of the three pairs of concepts. The sentence it helps explain is:

> The general wish to negate, the negativism which is displayed by some psychotics, is probably to be regarded as a sign of a defusion of instincts that has taken place through the withdrawal of the libidinal components. (Ibid. 239)

According to my reading, this would mean that the psychotic has become psychotic because of a fatal developmental move. The fatal move is the withdrawal of libidinal components. Within Freudian terminology, this means that, whereas the self was originally psychologically united with somebody because of the self's libidinal investment in him or her, the self now separates itself from that other by means of withdrawal. Now that the forces of Eros (libidinal investments) are neutralized, the only effective force that remains is the instinct of destruction. Freud claimed that negation is one of the products of that instinct. The psychotic's overproduction of negative sentences therefore becomes intelligible.

In order to make our understanding of Freud's theory of negation complete, we need to reflect further on two more points: the loss of the original object and the relationship between negation and repression.

Let us start with the relationship between negation and repression. According to Freud, negation in a denial is a substitute for repression. Within the Freudian oeuvre, the concept of repression has a central function. It involves a double aspect. The already repressed refuses the newly repressed material access to consciousness while at the same time attracting and connecting this newly repressed material to the already repressed. Freud argued for this view of repression because the self seemed unable to undo what it had suppressed. But this interpretation of the concept of repression required Freud to postulate some first-repressed material, which, although not attracted to prior-repressed material, nevertheless remained out of reach of the conscious self. Therefore, Freud coined the concept of primal repression. This concept was originally only a theoretical term (De Waelhens 1978, 49–56). Later, Freud linked the concept of primal repression to the idea of fixating instincts to a representation. Freud did so by connecting the concept of primal repression with the idea of the original object's loss and by his analysis of the "fort-da" game of his grandchild (*Beyond the Pleasure Principle*, S.E., XVIII, 14–17; also S.E., XIX, 239).[3]

The explanation runs as follows: The child is very much in need of the first love object—the mother. The absence of the mother creates unrest, anxiety, and tears. This was not the case, however, in one of Freud's grandchildren. This child had succeeded in substituting first a toy and then words for the real disappearing mother. The child was able to master its "instinctual need" for the mother, its first object, by libidinally investing in its toys. This libido inscription entails a libido fixation. Such a libidinal inscription means a fixation of that libido. At the same time, this inscription is a repression of the libido's immediately desired gratification and an accepted—albeit sublimated—loss of the first love object.

Clearly, this act of primal repression sets the child on its way to the constitution of itself as a self, that is, as independent of others. This act of primal repression is not conscious. It is an act that makes awareness of someone other than the self possible. As such, the self emerges out of an act of the subject which is logically prior to consciousness. All that falls under the power of primal repression shares this inaccessibility to consciousness. Consciousness can and should attempt to recover contents from repression, even from primal repression. The act of recovering such content is a challenge. Failure in the task of recovering this content, however, should be interpreted as absence of acts of recovery, or as absence of successful acts of recovery, not as a morally wrong activity. Thus, a denial is not a lie; it is a testimony to the uncompleted task of recovering contents from the repressed.[4]

4. IMPLICATIONS

a) Freud's epistemological view of negation is linked with an anthropology of the self as self-constituting. It is further linked with the idea that consciousness must labor in order to make available for itself contents which it does not possess naturally, but which the unconscious possesses.

It is worthwhile to draw attention to the fact that Freud's theory is relevant first of all to the domain of self-knowledge, even though Freud does not explicitly say so. Freud's theory of negation implies that the self does not necessarily possess true knowledge about itself. Logically wrong statements about the self, therefore, are not necessarily lies. They are only a testimony to the fact that this concrete self has not yet advanced far enough in the labor of self-possession to know its own self. A conscious lie is an act of deceit. A denial is an act of impotence.[5]

b) In the following statement Freud himself provides an argument that real self-knowledge (knowledge wrested from the unconscious) is a victorious achievement: "There is no stronger evidence that we have been successful in our effort to uncover the unconscious than when the patient reacts to it with the words: 'I didn't think that' or 'I didn't (ever) think of that.'" Thus, self-knowledge, which previously was not available to consciousness, can, with effort, be obtained.

The above interpretation of Freud's theory of knowledge faces two problems, one theoretical and one practical. Sartre most sharply formulated the theoretical problem: If a content is really unconscious, how can one's consciousness know that a particular content is precisely that one which the individual was looking to uncover? Sartre's solution is his general theory of bad faith. The unconscious is only that which one refuses to know, and is therefore not really out of consciousness's sight. A lie, in this Sartrian view, remains a lie.

The practical problem is that my interpretation of Freud's theory of negation might not square with some of Freud's other statements. Indeed, Freud also wrote: "It happens particularly often that, after we have laboriously forced some piece of knowledge on a patient, he will declare: 'I've always known that, I could have told you that before'" (S.E., II, 299). Clearly, this statement falsifies my whole interpretation of Freud's theory of negation and would allow us to come close to equating Freud's concept of repression with Sartre's concept of bad faith: The unconscious is not hidden from consciousness.

c) What are we to do with these objections to my view of Freud's theory of negation? First of all, I would like to stress that the equation of Freud's concept of repression with Sartre's concept of bad faith is unacceptable because it would make it impossible to incorporate other parts of Freud's oeuvre.

Second, I have a direct statement from Freud to help us. Indeed, Freud says that the proposition, "I've always known that. I could have told you that before" is an act of ungratefulness and is recognized as such by some patients: "Those with some degree of insight recognize afterwards that this is a piece of self-deception and blame themselves for being ungrateful" (Ibid. 299).

Interestingly enough, Freud later explores the way in which an ego, enriched by ideas that were previously unconscious, relates itself to its previous self. He notices that patients say about these new ideas: "But I can't *remember* having thought it" (*S.E.*, II, 300).

Freud continues by asking the theoretical question of how this nonavailability of thought content (ideas) must be interpreted. Freud proposes two possibilities. The first is that the patient is simply withholding recognition of his own thought. (He would then be in bad faith). The second possibility is the following: ". . . are we to suppose that we are really dealing with thoughts which never came about, which merely have a *possibility* of existing, so that the treatment would lie in the accomplishment of a psychical act which did not take place at the time?" (Ibid. 300)

In a text written prior to 1898, Freud addresses this question by writing: "It is clearly impossible to say anything about this—that is, about the state which the pathogenic material was in before the analysis—until we have arrived at a thorough clarification of our basic psychological views, especially on the nature of consciousness." (Ibid. 300)

I believe that I have succeeded in demonstrating that the later writings of Freud allow us to conclude that the repressed and consciousness are two different things. If the self succeeds in the task of conquering the contents of the unconscious, it establishes a unity which it did not have for itself before. The self then inscribes an unconscious thought in a new register, that is, in consciousness. Thus, the later Freud provides evidence that his second hypothesis is the correct one; a thought merely had the *possibility* of existing as conscious thought. Thus, the psychotherapeutic treatment lies in the accomplishment of a psychical act which did not exist before.[6]

In the same year that Freud wrote his article "Negation," he wrote another article: "A note upon the 'Mystic Writing-Pad'" (1924/1925). In that article Freud explicitly confirms my interpretation. Indeed, Freud compares the unconscious and consciousness with two methods of writing down ideas. One method achieves permanence—writing in ink on a piece of paper. Another method allows people to always write down new ideas as long as they erase the previous ones—the blackboard. At this point, Freud draws attention to a new device that achieves the two methods at once: the "Mystic Writing-Pad." This device has three layers. The lower layer is a slab of dark brown resin or wax. The middle layer is a translucent waxed paper. The upper layer is a transparent piece of celluloid. The function of the upper layer is to protect the translucent waxed paper. For purposes of clarifying methods of writing down ideas, it can be overlooked. Writing occurs when one uses a stylus to press the translucent waxed paper down on the dark brown slab. The points of contact provide the letters. This "Mystic Writing-Pad" can be used over and over again. One simply has to lift the translucent waxed paper away from the dark brown slab, in order to write down a new message. The "Mystic Writing-Pad" is thus like the blackboard. However, if we look at the dark brown slab, the first message remains inscribed in it, although we now need special light to see it.

Freud now compares the system of perception with the translucent waxed paper and the protective celluloid. He compares the unconscious with the dark brown slab. According to Freud, consciousness occurs when the translucent waxed paper and the dark brown slab touch each other.

Freud adds one further correction which addresses the Sartrean objection. The correction is that one must see the writing in the consciousness-unconciousness system as resulting, not from an external hand, but from internal energy emanating from the dark brown slab which makes the translucent waxed paper receptive to the external stimuli. Interruption of the energy emanating from the unconscious (i.e., libidinal withdrawal) is similar to separating the translucent waxed paper from the dark brown slab. This leads to the destruction of the writing in consciousness without the writing being destroyed in the unconscious. Therapeutic efforts can thus be understood as efforts to bring the two layers together. One had preserved the writing, but in an invisible way. The other is the layer by which the writing alone can become visible. Unconscious thoughts are thus only potentially available for the conscious self. Thus, labeling all mistakes about one's self-description as lies is a categorical error. To do so means that one considers these mistakes to be the result of an act, whereas they are actually the result of the lack of an act. Mistakes about one's self-description need not be the result of an act of deceit; they can also be the result of lack of self-possession.[7]

THREE

Denial and Hegel's
Philosophical Anthropology

abstract. In this chapter I demonstrate that the applicability of Freud's theory of negation (denial) is not restricted to therapeutic situations with mentally ill persons, but in fact applies generally to human beings. First, I provide descriptive proof by showing that denials occur as a crucial part of the plot in two great tragedies: Sophocles' *Oedipus, the King* and Ibsen's *The Ghosts*. Second, I construct a general proof of my claim by means of Hegel's dialectical anthropology. Here again I start by using, firstly, Hegel's concrete analyses that reveal universal structures: i.e., Hegel's analyses of self-consciousness (master-slave dialectic) and of the human will. Secondly, I use a general anthropological claim by Hegel to make my main argument, namely his claim that the road to truth is not just a path of doubt, but more accurately, a highway of despair. If the road to truth is as painful as Hegel describes it, I have discovered a philosophical reason why human beings might want to avoid the truth and fall into the trap of denial.

INTRODUCTION

Freud's theory of negation and denial implies a concept of a person in whom there are two centers of thought: the center of "conscious thought" and the center of "unconscious thought." Freud's theory further implies that in cases of denial—including boasting—the unconscious knows, whereas conscious thought misunderstands. Freud gradually came to the conviction that conscious thought uses linguistic negation as the instrument to formulate its misunderstandings and to hide emotionally difficult insights. In the following chapter I will study whether Freud's claim that denial in self-knowledge is universal is indeed true, and if it is universal, why?[1] I will rely on Hegel's anthropology to demonstrate the necessity and unavoidability of the forces of the negative implied by denial.[2]

1. DENIAL'S PERVASIVE PRESENCE IN SELF-KNOWLEDGE

Outside the psychoanalytic tradition, do we find a similar view of the person: that is, a view that holds that a human being, at some obscure level, understands, whereas, at the conscious level, he misunderstands? I believe that many literary masterpieces present such a view. Let us recall *Oedipus, the King* by Sophocles[3], and *Ghosts* by Ibsen. Both tragedies present a person forced to change his or her conscious self-understanding. In the process, the first conscious self-understanding is demonstrated to be a misunderstanding. Thus, early in the play, Oedipus angrily rejects (lines 300–461) Teiresias's accusations: "I say you are the murderer of the king whose murderer you seek" (362) and "He shall be proved father and brother both to his own children in his house; to her that gave him birth, a son and husband both; a fellow sower in his father's bed with that same father that he murdered." (457–59).[4] At the end of the play, however, Oedipus exclaims in self-accusation: "Accursed is my living with them I lived with, cursed in my killing." (1184–85).

Similarly, in *Ghosts*, Mrs. Alving completely changes her self-understanding. At the beginning of the play, she views herself as the betrayed wife who carries the burden of her female duty of staying with her husband and protecting her child from evil examples. Thus, she says:

> I had to bear it for my little boy's sake. But when the last insult was added; when my own servant maid—; then I swore to myself: this shall come to an end! And so I took the reins into my own hand—the whole control—over him and everything else. For now I had a weapon against him, you see; he dared not oppose me. It was then I sent Oswald [her child] away from home. He was nearly seven years old, and was beginning to observe and ask questions, as children do. That I could not bear. It seemed to me the child must be poisoned by merely breathing the air of this polluted house. That was why I sent him away. And now you can see, too, why he was never allowed to set foot inside his home so long as his father lived. No one knows what that cost me. (Ibsen 1908, 209–10)

When her grown-up son returns in despair from Paris and complains that "the joy of life, Mother—that's a thing you don't know much about in these parts of the world" (Ibid. 259), Mrs. Alving changes her self-understanding and says:

> A little while ago you spoke of the joy of life; and at that word a new light burst for me over my life and everything connected with it. . . . You ought to have known your father when he was a young lieutenant. He was brim-

ming over with the joy of life. . . . It was like a breezy day only to look at him. And what exuberant strength and vitality there was in him. . . . Well then, child of joy as he was—for he was like a child in those days—he had to live at home here in a half-grown town, which had no joys to offer him— only dissipations. He had no object in life—only an official position. He had no work into which he could throw himself heart and soul; he had only busi- ness. He had not a single comrade that could realize what the joy of life meant—only loungers and boon-companions. . . . Your poor father found no outlet for the overpowering joy of life that was in him. *And I brought no brightness into his home*. (Ibid.; emphasis mine)

And then Mrs. Alving continues with a remarkable self-confession:

> They had taught me a great deal about duties and so forth, which I went on obstinately believing in. Everything was marked out into duties—into my duties, and his duties, and—I am afraid I made his home intolerable for your poor father, Oswald. (Ibid. 277–78)

Both Sophocles and Ibsen present tragedies in which the main character (Oedipus/Mrs. Alving) radically change their self-conception. These charac- ters may help prove the general validity of Freud's theory; both Oedipus and Mrs. Alving knew, on some level, the truth about themselves before they came to pronounce that truth.

The novelty of Freud's thesis is that a change of self-conception is based on an unconscious and true self-understanding and that the change of con- scious self-conception begins with a denial. More precisely, Freud writes that the ego's recognition of the unconscious is expressed in a negative formula. The force of the article's argument, however, is that the ego's recognition of the unconscious *must* be expressed in a negative formula. This is evident from the following sentence in Freud's article:

> But the performance of the function of judgment is not made possible until the creation of the symbol of negation has endowed thinking with the first measure of freedom from the consequences of repression and, with it, from the compulsion of the pleasure principle. (*S.E.*, XIX, 239)

According to Freud, freedom of thought depends upon the creation of the linguistic symbol of negation. Is there any way in which we can clarify why negation must play such a crucial function in an individual's attempt to reach the truth about him or herself?

2. THE FORCES OF THE NEGATION IMPLIED BY DENIALS

It is useful to restrict the domain of the puzzle. Indeed, Freud's examples all refer to knowledge about the self. Perhaps the same thesis holds for knowledge of the external world.[5] However, here I will address only the puzzle of knowledge about the self.

At the beginning of our analysis it is useful to remember that Freud's thesis about self-knowledge is diametrically opposed to the Cartesian tradition, which stresses the theme of the self-presence of consciousness. Several 19th-century philosophers presented a view of mankind, that radically departed from this Cartesian tradition. Among them are Hegel, Marx, and Nietzsche. It might be useful to rely on Hegel to elucidate Freud's thesis.

I hope to make progress by analyzing a famous passage of Hegel's *Phenomenology*; "Lordship and Bondage" (Hegel 1977 b, 229–40). In that passage, Hegel describes the emergence of self-consciousness. Consciousness is ready to become self-consciousness when it discovers its essential contribution to perception. Perception is not just passive registration of the outside world. Perception involves activity on the subject's part. At first, however, consciousness is not aware of its active participation in perception, and therefore does not know itself. Hegel claims that it is the encounter with another consciousness that allows it to become aware of itself and to differentiate itself from the object of perception.[6] When becoming self-aware, consciousness first experiences that it is different from objectivity (self-consciousness is not one's knowledge of one's own weight, height, grades, etc.). This experience, however, is a subjective conviction, not a proven truth. The proof that a particular consciousness is not something objective lies in the fact that this consciousness is willing to risk its very objectivity, that is, its life.[7] There must be another consciousness, however, for whom one can prove one's conviction and who can then recognize the truth of this conviction. This other consciousness must have the same purpose. Jointly, these two consciousnesses can now prove to each other that they are as consciousnesses something other than objectivity because in a life and death struggle both are risking their lives.

Only if one consciousness experiences the fear of death shall this struggle end in something other than actual death. Actual death must be avoided because the death of either consciousness prevents the other consciousness from recognizing the truth of what consciousness is. Fear of death, however, implies that one consciousness is changing its self-conception. Fear of death entails emotionally accepting that life, the body, food, shelter, and so on, are all essential for consciousness. The life and death struggle, however, does not allow for one consciousness to affirm the two characteristics that consciousness discovered to be essential for consciousness: that is, on the one hand, that consciousness is not objectivity and thus that objectivity is worthless to it while, on the other hand, that objectivity (life, the body, etc.) is essential for consciousness.

The two characteristics cannot be affirmed simultaneously, because in a life and death struggle, one either continues the struggle—thereby demon-

strating that life is a secondary value—or gives up the struggle—thus indicating that life is crucial to consciousness. One cannot do both at the same
time. We thus discover that consciousness cannot make the transition to self-
consciousness alone.[8] It needs another consciousness. Two consciousnesses
can make that transition because each can prove one of the two necessary but
contradictory or mutually exclusive features of consciousness. The consciousness that is willing to continue to fight proves that objectivity is secondary
for consciousness. The consciousness that fears death proves that objectivity
is essential for consciousness. The first is called the master. The second is
called the slave.

Both the master and the slave have opted for a specific self-conception.
Both hope to realize a self by means of a self-image. In his analysis, Hegel
explains the disappointment of the master by showing how his self-image
cannot possibly be a reliable guide towards self-fulfillment. Hegel offers two
arguments as to why the master's self-image is or will be a disappointment.
The first argument is a general, and thus an abstract, argument: the master's
ultimate desire, Hegel reminds us, was the will to be recognized as a consciousness that is beyond objectivity and is thus unique. The master must
receive that recognition from the slave. The master, however, is not able to
value the slave because the slave has opted to identify himself with life and
objectivity—the very things that the master considered secondary. Thus, by
looking down on the slave, the master has deprived himself of the possibility
of receiving worthwhile recognition, even though the slave may hasten to
give the master recognition.

The second argument that Hegel gives is based on the master's description of the actual experience of pursuing the realization of his self-conception. The master in effect acts according to his self-conception and lets the
slave fulfill his objective needs. He also reserves for himself the right to think
when he and the slave are together. Thus, he can give orders[9] while the slave
is supposed to execute them. In both cases, though, the slave is forced to work
and to transform the external world; he thus develops skills[10] that the master
does not possess. The master, however, needs the slave's skills to pursue the
actualization of his self-conception. The master therefore becomes dependent
on the slave. This part of Hegel's dialectic shows that the master actualizes
the opposite of his self-conception in the process of pursuing his self-conception. Indeed, the master's self-conception denied the validity of one of the
two basic principles of consciousness: that is, the fact that life and objectivity are essential for consciousness. The realization of the master's self-conception is therefore possible only if someone else (the slave) takes care of this
neglected (or repressed) principle. Thus, the master must become the slave of
the slave. This outcome is not at all what the master had intended.

The analysis of "Lordship and Bondage" teaches us a crucial lesson about
the becoming of self-consciousness. An individual must discover who he or

she is and then try to become that person. In "Lordship and Bondage," however, Hegel demonstrated that human consciousness possesses contradictory characteristics. Only one of them can be affirmed at any one time by consciousness. The other aspect must then be affirmed by another consciousness.[11] Hegel writes in his *Philosophy of Right* (#7):

> It [the will] is the *self*-determination of the ego, which means that at one and the same time the ego posits itself as its own negative, i.e., as restricted and determinate, and yet remains by itself, i.e., in its self-identity and universality. It determines itself and yet at the same time binds itself together with itself. The ego determines itself in so far as it is the relating of negativity to itself.

This text summarizes Hegel's view on the problem of the will.[12] Hegel sees an individual's will as caught between two imperatives. The first imperative of the will is to be directed towards the universal. That is to say that no particular object of the will is capable of satisfying the will directly. The second imperative of an individual's will is that, in order for the will to function, it must will something determinate and particular. The experience of the will is therefore that, in willing anything, it posits itself as something it is not. A concrete example helps illustrate Hegel's general thesis. A student who earns his college tuition by washing dishes in a restaurant is not willing to be identified as a kitchen-helper. At the same time, this student actually does wash dishes. Hegel's theory further suggests that human beings have a method of overcoming this impossible situation. They can relate negatively to what they are willing while at the same time willing it. In our example, the student can deny that he is a kitchen-helper, while at the same time, he continues to clean dishes in a restaurant. He can say that he is not a kitchen-helper but that he is earning tuition by cleaning dishes. The statement: "I am earning tuition" allows the student to relate negatively to what he is doing while also allowing him to continue to do what he is doing. The linguistic expression "I am earning tuition" thus relocates cleaning dishes into another space—the motivational space of preparing for a career in a society where social mobility depends on individualistic, marketable skills. A particular activity (washing dishes) is thereby given a more universal meaning. It allows the student to relate negatively to his activity of washing dishes, for he is not washing dishes; he is earning tuition.

Let us remember that Hegel's general thesis can be understood as a lesson learned from the master-slave dialectic. One consciousness chose the role of master for itself. That consciousness, however, experienced the master's role as different—and practically opposite—from what it had imagined the role to be. Being a master does not entail becoming independent as was hoped, but rather involves becoming dependent on the slave, who had accepted the role of dependency. Consciousness is therefore not what it chose to be.[13] Consciousness will therefore have to relate negatively to what it decided to be.

It might be useful to draw attention to the fact that this process is closely related to Freud's description of what happens in the process of denial. Freud writes about denial: "With the help of negation only one consequence of the process of repression is undone. . . . The outcome of this is a kind of intellectual acceptance of the repressed, while at the same time what is essential to the repression persists" (S.E., XIX, 236). Relating negatively to the repressed through denial allows an unacceptable state of affairs to continue, similar to the case of the student who continues to do what he does not want to be identified with (i.e. dishwashing), or to the case of emperor Marcus Aurelius who continued to reign even though being on the throne had become unessential for him as a stoic.

There is, however, a crucial difference between the master-slave situation analyzed by Hegel and the process of denial described by Freud. In the case of the situation analyzed by Hegel, one has a desirable and constructive outcome. In the process described by Freud, one has an undesirable and regressive outcome. We do not yet have the conceptual framework to understand the difference.

Hegel's second general statement applicable to our problem can be found in the introduction to the *Phenomenology*:

> Because of that, the road can be looked on as a path of doubt, or more properly a highway of despair. For what happens there is not what is usually understood by doubting, a jostling against this or that supposed truth, the outcome of which is again a disappearance in due course of the doubt and a return to the former truth, so that at the end the matter is taken as it was before. On the contrary, the pathway is the conscious insight in the untruth of the phenomenal knowledge. (1977 b, 135–36)

This text is a comment upon Hegel's analysis of phenomenal knowledge and the ego's conception of its own function within phenomenal knowledge. The comment is applicable though to many dialectical turns in the *Phenomenology*. It states that the road to truth will involve a change in self-conception. It further claims that such a change requires more than doubting; it involves despair. Doubt is questioning a particular truth, whereas despair is experiencing the untruth of one's self-conception. One could ask, however, why doubt about one's self-conception is not simply doubt, but despair.[14] Hegel does not elaborate upon this question. A dictionary definition, however, might offer some possible clues to an answer. The *Standard College Dictionary* defines doubt as "to hold the truth, validity, or reliability of as uncertain; hesitate to believe or accept." The same dictionary defines despair as "to lose or abandon hope; be or become hopeless" (Funk and Wagnalls, *Standard College Dictionary*). Thus, a crucial definitional difference between doubt and despair is that despair involves a loss of hope. Hope is defined in the same dictionary as "to desire with expectation of fulfillment."[15]

The dictionary definition allows us to point to some precise differences between doubt and despair. Although both states question a previously held truth, despair also involves eliminating the possibility of desire, for despair is losing the expectation of desire's fulfillment.

When we now returns to the master-slave dialectic, we must remember that in that passage, Hegel describes a moment in the self-constitution of consciousness. This moment requires that desire find an ego-model (ego-ideal) by which it hopes to be recognized. The first consciousness's hope was to find self-fulfillment and recognition in the role of master. The second consciousness's hope was to retain its essence in the role of the slave. An important step in consciousness's development is thus the moment of choosing the ego-model (ego-ideal) by which consciousness hopes to realize itself. That choice indeed determines what consciousness will take as a valid object of desire. That choice determines to what consciousness, as desire, will attach itself in order to find itself back in that object or that ego-model.

Hegel, however, stresses the fact that consciousness is not guiding the choice of ego-model (ego-ideal). The choice is determined by the state of desire. That state is radically different for the two consciousnesses. Indeed, the desire of the consciousness that will accept the role of the slave is a desire that has been radically transformed. The desire of the consciousness that will choose the role of master is non-transformed desire. The transformation of the desire of the future slave is the result of a fear of death. Hegel describes that transformation as follows: "It (consciousness) has been in that experience (fear of death) melted to its inmost soul, has trembled throughout its every fiber, and all that was fixed and steadfast has quaked within it" (Ibid. 237). Given that the desire of the consciousness that will choose the role of the master has not been transformed because that consciousness does not know the fear of death, one must therefore conclude that the master cannot find a true object for its desire in the slave's role.

We are now ready to discover the full consequence of the master's experience and life project. Hegel makes it clear that it will not be the master's consciousness that discovers the falsehood of its own ego-model. If that were the case, the master would have knowledge of his falsehood. The falsehood of the master's role will be demonstrated for the reader who is willing to follow Hegel's description and reasoning. Through Hegel, the falsehood of the master's ego-model becomes evident for the outsider.

Informed by Hegel, we know that it is logically impossible for desire to find recognition by means of the master's ego-model. Like all desires, the master's desire is intentional. It must have an object. Furthermore, that object must be found to be a valid or true object for desire. Given, however, that the desire of the master is not a transformed desire, the master cannot accept an ego-model other than its own as a true or valid object of its desire. If the master recognizes his ego-model's falsehood, he will be without an object of desire. Hegel calls this state despair. If the state of being without an object of desire must be avoided, the figure of the master has no other choice but to try to justify the truth and validity of the only object his desire can choose. The master must therefore try to defend the validity of the role of master, even though Hegel has taught us the falsity of that role.[16] Clearly, this is a defensive and incorrect strategy. Freud's case studies reveal similar faulty strategies. These strategies lead to Freud's examples of denials. Remember Freud saying that the statement: "It is not my mother," means "It is my mother." Freud gave us empirical examples of denials.[17] A close reading of Hegel gives us an insight into the inevitability of such denials.

The constructive solution for the master is to become a stoic. A stoic integrates the truth of the role of both the master and the slave by modifying or negating some aspect of each role. This is precisely what Hegel says when he writes:

> This consciousness in consequence takes a negative attitude towards the relation of lordship and bondage. Its action in the case of the master results in his not simply having his truth in and through the bondsman; and, in that of the bondsman, in not finding his truth in the will of his master and in service. The essence of this consciousness is to be free, on the throne as well as in fetters, throughout all the dependence that attaches to its individual existence, and to maintain that stolid lifeless unconcern which persistently withdraws from the movement of existence, from effective activity as well as from passive endurance, into the simple essentiality of thought. (Ibid. 244)

A constructive approach for the master would be to accept work (the contribution of the slave) as essential for the self-realization of consciousness. Let us, however, not forget that the ability to recognize the value of the slave's contribution requires, as we saw, a radical transformation of the desire of the master. If that radical transformation is present, then the master can relate positively to the contribution of the slave and negatively to his own role. In relating negatively to his role of master, the master has become truthful to himself. Indeed, earlier in this chapter, we learned that the will is negativity relating to itself. The master as stoic relates negatively to his role as master. This is the true solution for the master because—as we saw—the role of the master could not possibly realize what the desire of the master hoped to realize. In order for the master to be able to reach a true relationship within himself, he needs to undergo a radical transformation of his desire.

From an analysis of the role of the master the following conclusions can be drawn:

1. Consciousness as desire to be a master will be unsatisfied with its own self, because that ego-model cannot provide the recognition hoped for by desire.
2. Consciousness as non-transformed desire (as master) cannot see another ego-model as a valid object of desire.
3. Such a consciousness (the master) can thus only *act out* these two moments. It can act out its despair and thereby demonstrate that, in fact, it has no valid object of its desire. It also can refuse to accept that another ego-model is a valid object of its desire. It thereby demonstrates that the required transformation of its desire has not yet taken place.

These moments, outlined in Hegel's philosophy, are essentially present in the case studies of Freud. For a patient to come to psychotherapy is to confess, at least implicitly, the despair of a consciousness without true object. In denials, the patient refuses to acknowledge meaningful relations presented by unconscious material. Acknowledging such relations would amount to accepting a new ego-model (ego-ideal) as valid. Freud teaches us that patients can do so only after the labor of the transference has radically changed the structure of their desire. In Freudian terminology, the repressed must have been undone.

CONCLUSION

1. We started with a problem in Freud: Is negation or denial necessary for consciousness?
2. From Hegel we learn that the constitution of self-consciousness requires a transformation of desire and that the will must relate negatively to itself because no object or ego-model is the realization of the universal longed for by the will. This shows that negation is, in fact, necessary to consciousness. This negation can take place, however, in two manners, a constructive one and a defensive one.
3. A constructive solution occurs when consciousness, having been radically transformed in its desire, relates negatively to its own ego-model by situating it verbally or in thought as a contributing factor (i.e., as a particular) to a higher synthesis (i.e., a more universal mode of existence).
4. A defensive solution acts out the negativity without synthesis. It expresses the despair of a consciousness without a true object of desire. It expresses in negative sentences the refusal or the inability to see the truth in alternative ego-models. It is this latter phenomenon that we witness in denials.

FOUR

Denial and Hegel's
Theory of the Will

abstract. In his analysis of the will, Hegel teaches us that human beings can solve the paradox of the human will in different ways. A will that is true to its essential form must negate the objectively given. Instead, the will informed by consciousness must take responsibility for its decisions. This is Hegel's arbitrary will. However, in order to be true to its content, the will cannot simply disregard the objectively given, it must evaluate the given and submit it to its own chosen norm. This is Hegel's eudemonic will. Clearly, the eudemonic will is a more subtle form of negating the authority of the objectively given than the one used in arbitrary will. I will argue that a denial can be understood as a misapplication of the forces of the negative necessary for freedom—a misapplication borrowed from the arbitrary will. Therapeutic intervention, I will argue, seems to aim to bring the patient to a position in which the strategy of the eudemonic will can be used. The objective connections cannot be denied by the patient. Instead, these connections need to be intellectually recognized. The force of the negative must then be introduced as the power to evaluate the objectively recognized facts and connections in light of a freely chosen norm of consciousness.

INTRODUCTION

For Hegel, freedom is connected with negativity. Thus, in his *Philosophy of Right*[1] Hegel describes the solution to the paradox of the will as "relating negativity to itself" (#7) and he describes freedom as a will that is free "not only in itself but for itself also, i.e. it determines itself as self-related negativity" (#104). The study of Hegel's concept of free will therefore provides valuable insights for understanding the puzzling phenomenon of denial.[2] In his *Philosophy of Right*, Hegel provides the key to understanding his theory of freedom by analyzing the concept of the will. The kernel of that analysis is to be found in ##5, 6, and 7 of that book.[3] Pedagogically, the best approach to explain these difficult and poorly written paragraphs is to start with three examples from everyday life. The first two examples allow us to see that the will is caught in a paradox. Typical of Hegel, the paradox is formulated in dialectical form. The will is said to aim at one thing (thesis, #5). The will must, however, also aim at the opposite (antithesis, #6). The third example attempts to illustrate the way out of the paradox. It tries to illustrate the path of synthesis (#7).[4] These examples and their explanations will take up the first part of this chapter. In the second part, I will show how Hegel uses his idea of the will as free will to classify and to criticize conceptions of the will offered by the philosophical tradition. As these conceptions of the will imply necessarily specific views of morality, Hegel's criticism can also be read as a criticism of alternative views of morality. In the conclusion I will clarify the phenomenon of denial by means of insights derived from Hegel's study of freedom and the will.

1. THE PARADOX OF THE WILL

As our first example let us imagine a person who is in personal difficulties and who wants to talk. Suppose I have ample time and I start the conversation by asking my visitor how old he is, how tall, and how much he weighs. After listening to the answers I say, "Now I understand you" (in the sense of: I am able to grasp your essential identity). My visitor would be accurate in saying, "No you do not." Suppose I continue my quest for objective information about my visitor by asking him how many brothers and sisters he has, whether he is married, if he has children, and how many he has. After hearing the answers, I restate my conviction, "But surely I now understand you." My visitor would be right in again saying, "No you do not." Suppose that I once again continue my inquiry and ask my visitor whether he went to college and if he did, where and what grades he obtained. Would my visitor not be right every time he rejected my claim that I understood him based on objective information? Could we then not say that my visitor declines to be identified with an objective content? This is precisely Hegel's statement about the will: "The will . . . involves the dissipation of every restriction and every content . . ." (#5).[5] One can call this dissipation the first moment in the drama of the will. It is the thesis.[6]

Let us now turn to a second example. Consider the situation of late adolescents and early adults. Students at that age face a difficulty inherent in the act of willing. Students at that age have to make many choices. They have to make decisions about careers and relationships, among other things.

Let us concentrate on the choice of a future job. Clearly, there are many things one desires from a job. One expects a job to be interesting and fulfilling. One expects a job to be socially useful, so that one can contribute to society. One expects the job to pay well, so that one can provide for oneself and for one's family. After one is clear about all the desirable characteristics of a potential job, it is necessary to take a look at the available jobs. Some jobs pay well but are boring or morally compromising, other jobs are interesting (for example, artistic careers) but are low-paying. So, late adolescents or young adults sometimes adopt the attitude that there is no job good enough for them. Such an attitude lacks an essential moment of willing according to Hegel. The lacking moment in such an attitude is that such persons are unable to decide. To will, however, is to be able to decide. To decide is to become something specific, something determinate. In Hegel's words: "the ego is also the transition from undifferentiated indeterminacy to the differentiation, determination, and positing of a determinacy as a content and object" (#6).[7] One can call this the second moment in the drama of the will. It is the antithesis, because it requires the will to do the opposite of the first requirement (which required the will to refuse to identify itself with anything objective.)[8] The will is thus caught in a paradox because it has to satisfy two opposite demands.

Let us now turn to our third example in which I will illustrate how Hegel tries to solve the paradox of the will. During the summer, one can meet students who are working in hotels, in offices, on construction jobs, and in many other places. Suppose one talks to a student who does typing work in an office and asks, "are you a secretary?" It is very likely one will hear the following answer, "No, I am earning money to pay for college." This student has been able to decide. He has accepted a position as an office secretary. His reply that he is not an office secretary, however, means that he relates negatively to his own choice.

The above negation could be thought of as a denial. It is not a denial, however, because the negation, unlike a denial, does not prevent action. Rather, the student's negation promotes action, that is, commitment to a task. The negation promotes action because it is a negation of an unacceptable aspect of a situation, which would have undermined the student's commitment to his task. This negation transforms a humble task into a promising endeavor. Hegel calls this negation a "negation of a negation" (#104).

In Hegelian language, the student who denies being an office secretary has become other than he wishes to be by accepting to become an office secretary. The solution to this predicament is not for the student to give up his job. If the student were to do so, he would end up without a job and he would not be a will because to be a will means to settle upon some content. The real solution is for the student to find a motivation for performing his job that transcends the particularity of the job itself. Such a solution could be the claim that the student is earning tuition money by means of his summer job. Clearly such a motivation does not specify that the student must take an office job; such a motivation only says that the student has to take some job.

Let us now reflect upon the consequences of sticking it out with the summer job and justifying it with the motivation of earning tuition money. The first consequence is that the student denies that he is stuck with the secretarial job. Indeed, he does not take the job because of the job itself but because of some other goal. The student can claim that performing secretarial tasks is incidental, while earning tuition is essential. The student can say that while performing secretarial services, he is not really performing secretarial services but earning tuition. He can thus deny that he is doing secretarial work. Instead, he is really earning tuition (in the sense of existentially intending that aspect of his act to be the essential aspect of the act). The second consequence is that the student can continue to do his job, because it earns money for tuition. The third consequence is that the student can simultaneously deny that he is doing a secretarial job and continue to work at the job in actuality. He distances himself from the particular job, while accepting the job as a particular instance to reach a (more) general goal.

Denying that he is doing the particular job is holding on to the moment described in #5. Continuing to do the job is obeying the imperative of #6. Using the motivation to do the job while at the same time claiming that performing the job is not what one is doing is achieving the synthesis described in #7. In that synthesis the student accepts doing something which is determinate (being an office secretary) and does something that the will as such cannot will, because it does not fulfill the will. Thus, the will of the student accepts becoming other than itself; it accepts externalizing itself. I take this to be an illustration of the will as negativity, as a force compelled and capable of transcending itself, of going outside itself. The student does not, however, surrender to this alienating situation.

The student, as it were, recaptures his own loss. He takes back his decision, but he does so in an ideal way, not in a material way. Thus, while materially continuing to perform the office secretary job, he says that he does not perform this job, but rather, that he earns tuition. Clearly, this move involves a negation (not a denial). It is by this negation that the student undoes that alienating aspect of accepting and performing a particular job. Hegel calls that undoing, that act of negation, an act of negativity. We are now ready to understand the crucial part of #7: "it [the will] is the relating of negativity to itself."[9] One can call this the synthesis. Indeed, in negating the particular that the will has accepted, the will preserves the demand of #5. However, the demand of #5 is not preserved in its unmediated form. It is preserved in a transformed way in the synthesis. Hegel specifies this act of transformation as "idealizing" the determination demanded in #6 (remark to #7).

I take Hegel's use of the word "idealization" to be a confirmation of my interpretation of #7 as illustrated by my example. Indeed, the student's ability to give meaning to his summer job through the motive of earning tuition can be called an act of idealizing his job. I wish to stress that this is a successful idealization because holding a summer job as an office secretary is a generally accepted motivation in an American student. Holding that job for more than a summer or beyond one's early twenties requires a different idealization and another kind of motivation, such as: it provides for a living, it is a job, it gives me great opportunities to meet people. Rather than providing a sociological study of the idealization involved in creatively solving the paradox of the will, Hegel gives us a dialectical analysis of progressively more "true" idealizations.

The three movements of the will, described in ##5, 6, and 7 as pure negation, acceptance of determination, and negative relation to an accepted determination (negation of negation or self-related negativity) are also present in the three moments of self-consciousness described in the *Phenomenology* as the master who relates negatively to all objectivity, including life (Hegel 1966, 231); as the slave who in his fear of death identifies with his body and his life (Ibid. 234); and as the stoic who relates negatively to his acceptance of objectivity by thinking and working (Ibid. 242–43). Hegel gives these three moments ontological status in his *Logic* when he describes them as three moments of the notion: the notion as universality (self-identity is achieved by exclusion of all differentiation), as particularity (the notion accepts content and becomes a particular notion), and as individuality (the notion as self-relating despite being a particular notion).[10]

2. CLASSIFICATION OF DIFFERENT CONCEPTIONS OF THE WILL

In his Introduction to the *Philosophy of Right*, Hegel further analyzes four general strategies that mankind has developed to deal with the paradox of the will. Hegel labels the four strategies: the natural will, the arbitrary will, the search for happiness (the eudemonic will), and the free will. Let us analyze each of these strategies in turn. I will try to reconstruct these four strategies in a dialectic fashion.

The first strategy is the one referred to as the strategy of "the natural will" (##11–14). This will needs to be determined. It allows itself to be determined by inclination—by whatever it happens to feel an impulse or a passion for doing. It thus abandons the need to decide by allowing itself to be determined by what nature happens to make attractive to it. Thus, when such a will feels an impulse to drink, it is bound to look for a drink. One can call this the thesis in the drama of the experience of the natural will (#11).

The difficulty with such a will is that there could be many impulses which emerge at the same time. The will could simultaneously feel inclined to drink, eat, read Kant, and listen to Chopin. In such a situation the natural will does not know what to do. In addition, when one is thirsty, one can drink coffee, tea, coke, or milk, among other beverages. The principle adopted by the natural will does not provide a guideline to solve this second impasse either. This failure is the antithesis in the drama of the natural will (#12).

More abstractly, Hegel summarizes the impasse of the natural will as follows: the natural will acts as if it has rules for deciding and thus has the formal characteristic of being a free will. However, the natural will allows the content of its decisions to be determined by something other than its own will. The content of the will's decision will be decided by the emerging inclinations or impulses. The form and content of the natural will are therefore not identical (#13). A person accepting the strategy of the natural will can say, "I decided" or, "It is my decision." The "mineness" of the decision is rather superficial; it does not reach into the decision's content. Rather, it resembles the act of someone who receives a gift and stamps his name on the gift. It is his gift, but someone else selected it.

One may say that the natural will does not possess enough negativity. It is not able or not willing to deny natural desires the right to automatically decide the will's actions. The natural will is not free because it does not exercise the power to negate the right of natural desires to automatically determine the will.

The second strategy is the one of the "arbitrary will" (##15–19). This will appears as the synthesis that solves the problem of the natural will. Indeed, the natural will's impasse occurs because it does not possess a rule on how to decide when faced with the presence of multiple impulses or with the multiplicity of objects that could satisfy one impulse. Another way of formulating a criticism of the natural will is to recall that this will does not itself decide the content of its decisions. It does not have the capability to negate natural desires' automatic push to determine the outcome of the will's decision. The arbitrary will's strategy is to accept the duty of having to decide, as well as to decide the specific content of available choices. The arbitrary will accepts as rule for its decisions: I have to decide and I have to decide in all matters. I do not surrender the right and the duty to decide to my natural inclinations. Furthermore, it has a second rule: one does not need to follow rules when deciding; one simply has to decide. This form of the will is the arbitrary will (#15). Confronted by two or three impulses, or two or more possibilities to satisfy an impulse, the arbitrary will is not immobilized. It will decide this way one time and that way another time. When asked why, the arbitrary will can answer, "because I will it so."[11] The arbitrary will is not required under its own strategy to give a reason. This is the moment of the thesis.

The antithesis emerges when one realizes that decisions have consequences. If a student decides in the beginning of the year to use his pocket money to visit France, he might not have future opportunities to make financial decisions (##16–17). Thus, the strategy of the arbitrary will finds its limits in the restrictions that reality imposes on the acting will.

Philosophically, Hegel puts his criticism as follows: the arbitrary will decides without binding itself to its decisions. Because they are arbitrary they could have been replaced by other decisions. Thus, the content of the arbitrary will's decisions is not worth defending because it could have been different (#16). The content of the arbitrary will's decisions is thus always contingent; it is never necessary.

The third strategy is the one used by the "eudemonic will," or the will in search of happiness (#20). This strategy emerges as a solution to the difficulties of the arbitrary will. The eudemonic will has accepted that the will needs to coordinate its decisions. For that purpose it needs a norm. Particular decisions of the will which are made in accordance with a norm cease to be contingent. They receive the form of necessity and are coordinated with other particular decisions.

Happiness is a norm which has often been proposed in the history of mankind. The strategy of the eudemonic will is that it sees the need to evaluate all possible decisions in light of one norm: what decisions will bring the most happiness? The great contribution of this strategy is that it accepts the interconnection of thought and will in order to bring about freedom of the will.[12] A further contribution of this strategy is that it introduces the need to coordinate and thus the need to to refine, to transform, and to educate the different human impulses.

Freud points to two important achievements in the therapeutic work with someone who has uttered a denial (Ver Eecke 1984, 14). Both seem related to the positive contribution made by the eudemonic will.

The first achievement is that the person uttering a denial becomes able to undo the intellectual negation embedded in a denial. The symbolic connections are intellectually acknowledged and respected. This first achievement parallels the achievement of the eudemonic will which, in its decision procedure, respects connections between, for example, decisions and expected results. This is progress compared to the arbitrary will, which decided on its own authority without necessarily having recourse to objectively observed (or expected) connections.

The second achievement in the work with a person uttering a denial is that such a person also accepts the implications for action demanded by the intellectual acknowledgment. Accepting implications for action often requires dealing with emotional wishes and fears. It requires that the patient be capable of becoming master of his or her emotions. This is a demand similar to the one faced by the eudemonic will, which, for its exercise, requires the refinement and education (i.e., rational control) of wishes, impulses, and emotions.

The fatal flaw in the eudemonic strateg, which will allow the emergence of its antithesis, is the fact that the eudemonic will pursues a strategy it cannot guarantee. Indeed, a person can do many things in order to make happiness possible. He cannot, however, guarantee his own happiness by what he does. Suppose, for example, that one has worked one's whole life for good grades, in order to go to a good school, in order to have a good job, in order to have a good income, in order to be able to provide for one's family. Suppose one has succeeded in accomplishing all of the above but then discovers that one has cancer. This would undoubtedly make one very unhappy. The purpose of one's whole life would thus be lost. A strategy which leaves open the possibility that the meaning of one's life project could be destroyed is a strategy that is rationally defective.

The fourth strategy, the one used by the free will, is a successful and open-ended strategy (##21–28). This fourth strategy is the solution to the previous strategy's problem. The problem was that the eudemonic will was pursuing a goal it could not guarantee. The strategy of the free will is to will its own freedom (#21). The free will has to involve thinking to a higher degree than even the eudemonic will is prepared to do.[13] The free will has to ask from thought what is required to be and to remain free. Suppose that an adolescent plans to have a family, but decides that he does not like school. If he drops out of school, he will not acquire the skills necessary to earn a decent salary in today's society. When he later starts a family, he might realize that he cannot afford what he wanted to provide for his family. He becomes disillusioned and thus, in some sense, unfree. To aim at freedom means one is required to think what one has to do in order to be, as well as to remain, free. In addition, one must accept what one has thought.

Thinking has a crucial function for the free will. It tells a person what choices to make. Philosophy, in particular Hegel's *The Philosophy of Right*, presents us with a rough sketch of what is required to maintain freedom. Hegel writes that what thinking discovers as freedom's requirements are: "the principle of right, morality, and all ethical life" (#21). Now these three principles are the three parts of *The Philosophy of Right*. Ethical life itself contains three substrata: the family, civil society, and the state. I understand Hegel to be saying that in order to be and to remain free one needs property rights, morality, and the ethical institutions of the family, the free market, and the state. These different domains are not just preconditions for freedom; they are embodiments of freedom as well. By willing all the embodiments of freedom, the will makes its existence correspond to its concept (#23). In other words, for Hegel, to be free means that two totally different requirements need to be fulfilled. First, "freedom shall be the rational system of mind" (#27). Second, "the rational system of mind . . . shall be the world of immediate actuality" (#27).

These two requirements amount to saying that there must be a certain mentality and a number of objective conditions that are fulfilled. We can understand this double requirement if we reflect on some other traditions and thinkers. The Christian tradition is a good place to look for an illustration of the first requirement because Christianity has always stressed that the inclination of the heart (the presence of a mentality) is crucial. For an illustration of the importance of objective conditions, one can go to the Greek philosophers, who affirmed that the good human life is only possible in a good society. Hegel approvingly quotes the following story: "When a father inquired about the best method of educating his son in ethical conduct, a Pythagorean replied: 'Make him a citizen of a state with good laws'" (#153).

The logic of these four forms of solving the paradox of the will is similar to the logic of judgments (Hegel 1989, 622–63). The natural will corresponds to the judgment of existence (also called judgment of inherence). Hegel gives as examples: "Gaius is learned, or the rose is red" (Ibid. 632). In such a judgment, the predicate affirms something that happens to be immediately visible. It describes this rose here and now as red. Another rose could be yellow or orange. Tomorrow the original red rose could become orange. The predicate attributed in a judgment of existence depends upon what one happens to see (Léonard 1974, 355). The natural will also lacks a necessary connection between itself and what it wills. The natural will wills that which happens to present itself to the will as an inclination at that particular moment.

The arbitrary will corresponds to the judgment of reflection. Hegel gives as examples: "man is mortal, things are perishable, this thing is useful, harmful" (Hegel 1989, 643). In this judgment the predicate captures an essential relationship between the subject and its environment. The subject is no longer a 'determinate being' but rather an 'existence.' The subject is no longer part of the logic of being but is now part of the logic of essence. In so far as the judgment of reflection captures something essential, one is able to affirm that the predicate belongs to the subject in some necessary way. Contrary to the rose which could be red or not, it is not permissible to claim that a man is not mortal. The comparison of the arbitrary will with the judgment of reflection thus invites us to look for the essential dimension that the will reached in becoming arbitrary. That essential dimension consists of the fact that the will as arbitrary accepts as its duty the fact that it has to decide. The will as natural will avoided that task by allowing natural inclination to have a decisive influence on what the will decided. Whereas the natural will avoids the task of deciding in its own right, the arbitrary will accepts such a task and thus becomes phenomenologically that which it essentially has to become.

If we are now more accurately aware of an aspect of the arbitrary will, this is due to comparing the arbitrary will to the judgment of reflection, rather than considering the arbitrary will alone. Hegel teaches us that, with the arbitrary will, human beings have reached a development in which some essential characteristic of the will is realized. That characteristic is the fact that the will has the power to refuse any objective datum the capability to determine its decision.

A denial has a progressive and a regressive aspect. It is progressive in that it reveals a content. It is regressive in that the revealed content is not acknowledged. Remember Freud's example of a patient's reply to his question as to the identity of a woman in her dream: "That (domineering) woman in my dream is not my mother." Understanding the nature of the arbitrary will gives us an additional way of presenting the progressive aspect of a denial. It looks as if, in the negation of a denial, the will tries to realize the essential achievement of the arbitrary will: I do not grant anything the power to decide for me; I decide and in this case I decide that I am not a person who would present such a negative picture of my mother. Unfortunately, as I argue later, this is a misapplication of the progressive dimension of the arbitrary will.

The eudemonic will corresponds to the judgment of necessity. Hegel gives as examples: "the rose is a plant," (Hegel 1989, 651) "If A is, then B is; or the being of A is not its own being, but the being of another, B" (Ibid. 652) or "Colour is either violet, indigo, blue, green, yellow, orange or red" (Ibid. 656). In a judgment of necessity the subject and the predicate are connected by means of a thoughtful understanding of a conceptual connection. The eudemonic will too is characterized by the use of thoughtful understanding of conceptual connections. The eudemonic will must relate a concrete option with the conceptual norm it has chosen for judging the desirability of alternatives. Utility or happiness are such norms. The eudemonic will does not deny the given; it does subject it, though, to a norm. This is a more constructive use of the negative than the method used by the arbitrary will.

I will argue that therapeutic intervention with a person uttering a denial can be understood as aiming at the constructive usage of the negative's force as it is present in the eudemonic will. Real freedom is not the intellectual negation of what is given; it is the submission of the given to a reasonable norm.

The fourth form of the will, the free will, corresponds to the judgment of the notion. Hegel gives the following examples: "This house is bad, this action is good" (Hegel 1989, 659). He stresses that the essential characteristic of a predicate in a judgment of the notion is that it includes an "ought-to-be," that is, how the house ought to be (Ibid.657). The will which corresponds to the judgment of the notion therefore must include an "ought-to-be," that is, the idea of having to be free and to be able to remain free. As this interpretation of the will includes an "ought-to-be," there is room for philosophy to try to determine what the will "ought-to-be" in order to be a free will. Hegel schematically announces what this "ought-to-be" needs to include: "the principle of right, of morality, and of all ethical life" (Hegel 1967b, #21). Hegel then uses these three principles to structure his *The Philosophy of Right* into three parts. These three principles correspond logically to the three forms of syllogism discussed in the *Logic*.[14]

CONCLUSION

I now want to use Hegel's analyses of the will, in particular his analyses of the arbitrary will and the eudemonic will, to better understand both the progressive and the regressive aspects of a denial.

1. In order to proceed, we first need to understand the difference and similarity between an act of the will and a denial. The difference between the two is that the will relates to deciding whereas denial relates to acknowledging or, more precisely, refusing to acknowledge symbolic connections as they are presented to consciousness (e.g., in dreams or slips of the tongue). Thus, the will operates in the domain of doing whereas a denial takes place in the domain of knowledge. Therefore we can conclude that the performance of an act of the will and a denial take place in two different ontological domains.

The similarity between an act of the will and the performance of a denial consists in the fact that they both ultimately aim to be operative in the same ontological domain. As already stated, the will explicitly relates to deciding. I will now demonstrate that a denial is implicitly about deciding as well. Take our classic example of the statement: "This (domineering) woman in my dream is not my mother." That statement does not just intend to deny a symbolic connection. It is also about avoiding having to make certain decisions. Indeed, the semiotic statement that the person in the dream is domineering demands certain actions, for example: avoiding such a person or standing up to him or her. Having denied the connection, the reason for such action is nullified. A denial can thus be understood as grounds for avoiding certain actions.

2. We are now in a position to use Hegel's analysis of the will for the purpose of clarifying the process of denial. My thesis will be that, in a denial, a human being tries to exercise freedom by incorrectly applying something to the domain of knowledge that can be applied legitimately only to the domain of action. If my thesis is accurate then correction of the mistake will have to address errors in the two domains. Thus changes will have to occur in both the domain of symbolic connections (epistemology) and the domain of action.

A DENIAL AS A CATEGORY MISTAKE OF THE URGE TO FREEDOM

A denial typically concerns symbolic connections presented by the unconscious. With reference to such unconscious symbolic connections, a person is not normally in a position to formulate a conscious decision to act. Nevertheless, notwithstanding such unconscious connections, a human being still remains at least partially free. The first form of the will which is phenomenologically true to its essence is the arbitrary will. We can therefore assume that human beings subject to unconscious symbolic connections might affirm their freedom by relying on that first form of the will which expresses its true essence: the arbitrary will. The freedom of a human being exercising his will as arbitrary will consist in refusing to grant any objective datum the power to decide upon a course of action. In a denial, a human being exercises his or her freedom by wrongly applying to the domain of knowledge what can be applied legitimately to the domain of action.

Essential for human freedom is the ability and the willingness to deny any objective datum the right or the authority to decide a course of action. That right belongs to the individual. That right is affirmed by the strategy of the arbitrary will. Prior to denial, however, a person is burdened with a given unconscious symbolic connection. It is as if, in a denial, the person makes the move typical of the arbitrary will: The subject denies being tied to an unconscious symbolic connection. However, in doing so, the person uttering a denial misapplies the principle of the arbitrary will. The arbitrary will has the right to appropriate to itself the right to authorize an action. The arbitrary will, however, does not have the right to appropriate to itself the authority to accept or refuse as true a given unconscious symbolic connection. Rather, the challenging task for consciousness is to recognize and accept the given as it reveals itself. It is as if a human being, in producing a denial, makes a category mistake. He does not use the negative force of freedom to deny something objective as the automatic motive or reason for an action—which is legitimate. Instead, the subject uses the negative force to deny the truth of an objective datum. In a denial, one mistakenly uses the negative force of freedom.

A denial can thus be understood as an illusionary affirmation of the will as arbitrary will: an unconscious connection is gratuitously denied.

CORRECTING THE CATEGORY MISTAKE IN DENIAL

According to Freud, the therapeutic process dealing with denials consists of two steps. It consists of both an intellectual and an emotional move (Ver Eecke 1984, 14, 25–27, 144–45). The intellectual move consists in helping the patient undo the intellectual negation of a denial. That process requires many subsidiary moves. In his example of the woman dreaming about a lady, not acknowledged as her mother, Freud perhaps elicited a description of the lady. Perhaps he then pointed out the similarities between the female figure in the dream and the patient's mother. The patient might then come to the conclusion: the woman in the dream wears a dress, shoes, and a watch similar to those of my mother; she has the hair and the eyes of my mother. Thus, it must be my mother. Freud states that such a recognition on the patient's part does not mean that the unconscious connection has been emotionally accepted. If that is the case then therapy needs to promote a second move: the emotional acceptance of the unconscious connection.

The first task of the therapist dealing with a denial is to correct the illegitimate move at the epistemological level using the force for freedom in the subject. The second task is to search for a correct expression of freedom.

I now wish to describe that double therapeutic task, described by Freud, as helping the patient to move from an arbitrary form of the will to a eudemonic form of the will.

The great difference between the arbitrary and the eudemonic forms of the will is the fact that the eudemonic will gives great weight to thought whereas the arbitrary will does not. Indeed, the arbitrary will affirmed its freedom without paying attention to intellectual arguments. Objective givens did not matter. The eudemonic will, on the other hand, pays attention to the objectively given without allowing the given to become authoritative for decisions of the will. Instead, the eudemonic will acknowledges the objectively given and submits it to a calculation aimed at achieving a freely chosen goal (happiness). As the essential move of the eudemonic will is submission of the objectively given to a calculation, the eudemonic will can use the force of the negative, not to deny the objective data, but to submit them to a goal. The eudemonic will thus gives the forces of the negative, inherent in freedom, a new object. Instead of falsely denying objective connections, the goal is now to evaluate truthfully those connections (weigh their relative importance; put them in a hierarchical order; etc.) in order to justify concrete actions.

Hegel hints at the great efforts required to succeed in submitting objective givens to a goal. He points out that this requires education in the double sense of having formal education (promoting the exercise of thought) and in the sense of personality formation (reaching the maturity to be able to submit impulses to thought) (Hegel 1967b, ##20, 187). No wonder Freud laments the difficulty of the therapeutic process dealing with a person uttering a denial. He writes: "We succeed . . . in bringing about the full intellectual acceptance of the repressed; but the repressive process itself is not yet removed by this" (Freud, S.E., XIX, 236). Indeed, the therapeutic process must both enlighten the patient about true objective givens and educate her towards emotional maturity. This is a tall order.

3. After comparing the process of denial with Hegel's analysis of the will and its freedom we can now formulate the progressive and regressive moments in the act of denial.[15] The progressive dimension in a denial is the negation, a sign of the presence of the force of the negative required in the exercise of freedom. The regressive dimension in a denial is the misapplication of the force of

the negative. Instead of being properly used in the domain of action, it is improperly used in the epistemological domain. We can therefore first expect therapeutic work to make a correction in the epistemological attitude of the patient. Second, we can expect the work to lead the patient towards the emotional maturity required to take the reasonable action that was avoided, by defective means, in the denial. That is exactly what Freud describes the therapeutic work as consisting of in the case of a denial.

FIVE

A Child's No-Saying

A Step toward Independence

abstract. Spitz uses the two concepts of indicator and organizer to point to a new behavior in the child's development. I distinguish between a weak and a strong sense of organizer. The weak sense of organizer means that the indicator of a new behavior is not a necessary condition for the new and higher level of activity reached by the child. The new and higher level of activity can be assumed to be present even if the specifically studied indicator does not appear. The strong sense of organizer means that the indicator of the new behavior creates the new and higher level of activity reached by the child. I argue that stranger anxiety at eight months is a weak organizer for a deeper form of the child's attachment to familiar persons. Absence of manifest signs of that anxiety does not mean that this deeper form of attachment is not taking place. I argue that the no-saying, which occurs around 15 months of age, is a strong organizer. By its mere presence, it creates a higher level of activity in the child. Spitz argues that it creates the first unequivocal concept. I argue that it creates a new degree of emotional independence for the child. My thesis can thus be taken as a confirmation of the Freudian claim that the acquisition (and effective usage) of the linguistic form of negation is a precondition for freedom.

INTRODUCTION

According to Spitz, it is incorrect to look upon the first few years of the child's development as a simple linear development. Instead, Spitz believes that there are multiple lines of development which come together to make a new form of behavior possible for the child. This new behavior is so different from the child's previous behavior that Spitz claims the new behavior indicates a higher

61

level of psychic structure. He calls the moment when such new behavior appears a critical period. Since these critical periods function to synthesize several developments into a new form of behavior that is in turn the beginning of a new psychological development, Spitz also calls these indicators organizers of psychic structures (Spitz 1965, 177).

Spitz lists three such critical periods during the first twenty months of the child's life. The indicators of these critical periods are: the smile at about three months of age; stranger anxiety at about eight months; and the no-saying after about fifteen months (Ibid. VI, VIII, XI).

The first two critical periods are related in a special way to the function of seeing. The child smiles at about three months of age in response to seeing the human face. Anxiety at eight months is a reaction triggered by seeing a stranger—or, correcting Spitz, I will argue that anxiety at eight months is a reaction to being seen by a stranger.[1] The third critical period concerns the child's no-saying. It is this latter phenomenon that interests us, but its subtle meaning can only be understood after understanding the two chronologically prior phenomena.

In this chapter, I will present Spitz's theory of these three critical periods and demonstrate that, in several crucial areas, Spitz's description of these periods is richer than his theory. I will complement or correct Spitz's theory with my own theory, often relying on a Lacanian framework. I will distinguish between weak and strong organizers. This will help to prevent inaccurate predictions about the future mental health of a child in whom an organizer is absent.[2] In my conclusion, finally, I will appeal to Hegel in order to demonstrate that my strategy of giving no-saying and negativity such a central role in philosophical anthropology falls well in line with what we know about human beings from speculative philosophy.

1. THE FIRST ORGANIZER: THE SMILE

A new behavior can be observed in children at about three months of age. The child smiles when she sees a human face.[3] Three months is only a statistical average, but the smiling response is definitively tied to a specific age period. Thus, according to Spitz, only two percent of children under two months of age smile at the sight of a face and only five percent of children continue to smile indiscriminately, including at strangers, after six months of age (Ibid. 88). Spitz's empirical results are still valid, as can be confirmed by the survey article by Melvin Konner for the now classic volume on *The Development of Attachment and Affiliative Systems*. Summarizing the work of Ambrose; Emde, Gaensbauer, and Harmon; Emde and Harmon; Spitz and Wolf; Sroufe and Waters; and Gewirth; Konner writes:

> For practical purposes this behavior [the social smile] is absent at birth and emerges during the first few months of postnatal life. Incidence of smiling

in naturalistic social contexts (Figure 2A) or in experimental settings in which the infant is presented with a face (Figure 2B) is two orders of magnitude higher at four months of age than at term, and the response cannot be indisputably identified until some time in the second month. . . . Considerable quantitative variation attributable to learning occurs after four months of age, but variation in early incidence and in rate of emergence among samples in different environments, although statistically significant, is quantitatively minor.[4] (1982, 145)

Typically, between the ages of two and six months, the child smiles even at strangers. Aptly, Spitz calls it "indiscriminate smiling" (Ibid. 88), implying that the smiling response cannot be interpreted as a sign that the child has already established emotional ties with a particular person. In psychoanalytic language, this means that the smiling response is not a sign that true object relations have been established. Again, Spitz's view is generally confirmed by Konner's survey article on the mother-infant bonds. Thus Konner, summarizing the existing research, writes:

social smiling is well established but *relatively undiscriminating*. It appears to the observer to be associated with positive emotion, but the emotion seems *impersonal*; almost anyone can elicit it and, despite subtle signs of discrimination of primary caretakers, *strong emotional bonds do not appear to exist* [emphasis mine]. (149)

Spitz's claim about the absence of true object relations or of the absence of emotional ties to a particular person runs counter to the view of a group of authors (e.g., the Hungarian school of psychoanalysis; the attachment theorists)[5] who argue that the child is attached to a specific person from very early on. Even Konner, in the text just quoted, writes that there are, "subtle signs of discrimination of primary caretakers." To add support to Spitz's detractors, let us present a case from a psychoanalyst's consultation. This psychoanalyst was consulted because an infant refused the bottle after her mother had died. The psychoanalyst asked if any of the deceased mother's unwashed undergarments remained. She further advised winding this underwear around the bottle before giving the bottle to the infant. When this method was followed, the infant accepted the bottle. Such a case does indeed confirm the attachment theorists' theoretical claim and seems to invalidate Spitz's conclusion that the infant cannot be said to have true object relations.

My position is that the attachment theorists are correct and that Spitz overstated his conclusion. I believe, however, that there is a truth to Spitz's claim. The challenge is to acknowledge Spitz's observation about indiscriminate smiling without overstating the conclusion drawn from the observation. The fact that, at first, the child smiles at everybody—and even smiles at masks—whereas, at eight months of age, the child starts to show anxiety towards strangers, must have significance. The significance cannot be, as Spitz claims, that the infant does not develop attachments to particular persons prior to showing anxiety toward strangers. Rather, it means, according to my understanding, that the particular person to whom the child is attached gains a new significance, meaning, and function at around the age of eight months.[6]

Psychoanalytic authors might be right in claiming that only the acquisition of that new function allows one to call the relations between child and mother true object relations. Konner writes that attachment theorists agree with the view that a fear of strangers is a sign of deepening emotional relationships. Bowlby gives a nice overview of the new emotional relations that develop during the period of the child's life when the eight-month-anxiety emerges (Bowlby 1982, 670–71). We will therefore use the expression "true object relations" in the sense that a deepening of emotional relations occurs with particular persons (the primary caretaker[s]), while refusing to go as far as Spitz does when he claims that, before this phase, the infant does not attach herself to a particular person. This is the correction that attachment research requires us to make.

Returning to Spitz, we notice that he clarifies the indiscriminate smiling response by arguing that it is a behavioral act triggered by a Gestalt. The crucial elements of the Gestalt are the forehead, eyes, nose, and movement of the whole head—for example, nodding (Spitz 1965, 89). The child does not respond if one or two eyes are covered, if the face is not moving, or if the face is presented in profile (Ibid. 94).

Spitz maintains that the child's failure to smile at a face in profile is proof that the child's smile is not a smile in recognition of a human partner. Spitz replaces the human face with a mask in order to enable him to study the essential elements of the Gestalt which provide stimuli for the child's response. Spitz found that a mask was as effective in triggering the smiling response as the human face, provided that it consisted of a forehead, eyes, nose, and movement of the whole head. Given that the smile of a three-month-old child can be triggered as easily by a mask as by a human face, Spitz draws his conclusion: The child smiles, not at the Gestalt of a face, but at a sign Gestalt of it (the mask being the symbol of a face) (Ibid. 91). Spitz calls this new relation of which the three-month-old child is capable a pre-object relation. He considers it a transition from the perception of "things" to the establishment of the libidinal object (Ibid. 91). In somewhat behavioristic language, Spitz then claims that seeing a "sign Gestalt"—forehead-eyes-nose-head in motion—is "the key stimulus of an IRM (innate releasing mechanism)" (Ibid. 94). In less reductionist terms, we can say that the human face is a privileged visual object for the infant.

It might be useful here to introduce Lacan's unique perspective on this phenomenon. I will use Spitz's own terminology to specify the difference between their respective theories. Spitz talks about indicators and organizers (Ibid. 117). He explicitly calls the smiling response an indicator, and, in order not to be misunderstood, he writes:

> I repeat: the smiling response as such is merely the visible symptom of the convergence of several different developmental currents within the psychic apparatus. The establishment of the smiling response signals that these trends have now been integrated, organized, and will thenceforward operate as a discrete unit within the psychic system. The emergence of the smiling response marks a new era in the child's way of life; a new way of being has begun, basically different from the previous one. (Ibid. 119)

Lacan concentrates on seeing and talks about the recognition that occurs in the mirror image. He too points to the joy and the smile that is produced in the child when recognizing her image, her Gestalt, in the mirror or in the figure of a real person, mostly the mother. In contrast to Spitz, Lacan does not describe the child's smiling response to seeing her Gestalt as an indicator for marking the child's new level of psychic organization. Rather, Lacan will intepret seeing as a psychological faculty which must be called an organizer of the child's psychic life.[7] For Lacan, seeing at this age will be understood as producing an effect rather than merely indicating an effect's presence. Lacan will go so far as to claim that seeing is a faculty that bridges the physiological and the psychological dimensions in human beings, so that he will be able to claim that there may even be physiological effects produced by the psychological act of seeing. (Ver Eecke 198 a, 115–16) Spitz, on the other hand, only claims that seeing a specific sign Gestalt triggers an innate mechanism.

Interestingly enough, in Spitz one can find a number of remarks which show that the smiling response of the three-month-old baby has more mysterious aspects to it than Spitz's theory explains. We can use these remarks to justify the Lacanian radicalization of the interpretation of the baby's seeing and smiling.

Indeed, Spitz reports that the child does not only smile, but also becomes active and starts wriggling when she sees a human face (Spitz 1965, 89). The smile is thus but one of the reactions a child has to seeing a human face. The full reaction spreads over the whole body.

Spitz cautions the reader against misunderstanding his theory of "sign Gestalten, releaser mechanism triggering innate responses," warning us not to conclude from the theory that "a mechanical doll, fitted with the sign Gestalt can rear our children . . ." (Ibid. 95).

Spitz further explains this warning by elaborating on his theoretical interpretation of the infant's smile. He argues that "although the innate equipment is available to the baby from the first minute of life, it (the innate equipment) has to be quickened" (Ibid. 95). This could mean that a certain time is required for the innate mechanism to become operative. Such an

interpretation would remain consonant with the theory of innate mechanisms. However, Spitz interprets the need to quicken the innate equipment
by saying:

> The vital spark has to be conferred on the equipment through exchanges
> with another human being, with a partner, with the mother. Nothing less
> than a reciprocal relation will do so. Only a reciprocal relation can provide
> the experiential factor in the infant's development, consisting as it does of
> an ongoing circular exchange, in which affects play a major role. (Ibid. 95)

My reaction to Spitz's warning is rather complex. My sense is that Spitz
is an astute observer and I am therefore prepared to accept his insight as true.
However, there is a large discrepancy between the theory Spitz uses to
explain the smiling response as an innate mechanism and the theory one
would need to construct in order to understand Spitz's warning that seeing is
not sufficient and that a "vital spark has to be conferred on the equipment
through exchanges with another human being." Indeed, a theory that can
explain such a warning would have to explain how intersubjective relations
are a necessary factor for the smiling response. The theory that Spitz actually
uses to explain the smiling response is a theory of innate mechanisms. Such
a theory is not rich enough to justify the crucial "spark" that Spitz warns us is
necessary.

Nevertheless, Spitz's warning will be very useful in helping to build my
own theory about both the fear of strangers and the child's no-saying. Let us
therefore make full use of Spitz's warning and quote his explanation of why a
"relation between a mechanical, automatic doll and the baby would be one-
sided" (Ibid. 96). Spitz writes:

> It is the mutual give and take, its single elements constantly changing and
> shifting (though its sum total remains the dyadic relation), which represents
> the essence of what we are trying to describe and to convey to the reader.
> The reciprocal feedback within the dyad between mother and baby, and
> baby and mother, is in continuous flux. The dyad, however, is basically
> asymmetric. What the mother contributes to the relation is completely dif-
> ferent from what the baby contributes. Each of them is the complement of
> the other, and while the mother provides what the baby needs, in h[er] turn
> (though this is less generally acknowledged) the baby provides what the
> mother needs. (Ibid. 96)

A full understanding of the three-month-old's smiling response when
seeing the sign Gestalt of the human face therefore requires an understanding of the role of the mother-child relationship. Spitz himself made a crucial
contribution to this problem through his study of hospitalism.

Thus, the proper reaction to Spitz's warning is to not ignore the need for
a mutual relation between mother and child as a necessary condition for the

smiling response. I take this to be a warning about the broad context necessary for the smiling response to take place. In order to explain the smiling response, Spitz uses a theory where a sign Gestalt functions as a releaser mechanism triggering an innate response (Ibid. 95). My difficulty with Spitz's theory is that he, in effect, uses a two-part theory to explain the smiling response. He has a theory proper: releaser mechanism triggering an innate response. He also has a requirement about the context necessary for the smiling response. In Spitz's writings, the connection between the explanation of the event and the requirement about context is only an observed connection. Spitz in no way presents a theoretical frame that would make the connection between his theory of innate mechanism and his requirement about the general context a necessary connection. One purpose I have will be to work towards a theoretical framework that will make it possible to see the above connection as a necessary connection. I will work out this claim for the two other indicators.

2. THE SECOND ORGANIZER: EIGHT-MONTH-ANXIETY

Another remarkable change in behavior takes place in children between the ages of six and eight months. Before that age, the child smiles any time she sees someone approaching and shows signs of displeasure any time an adult leaves (Ibid. 150, 155). Between six and eight months, the child begins to differentiate between a familiar figure, in particular the mother, and a stranger. The child continues to smile at familiar figures but manifests apprehension or anxiety when a stranger approaches. The child expresses her apprehension or anxiety in a variety of ways. She might lower her eyes shyly, cover her eyes with her hands, lift her clothes to cover her face, throw herself down on her bed, hide her face with her blanket, or even weep or scream. Spitz interprets this behavior as "a refusal of contact, a turning away, with a shading of anxiety" (Ibid. 150).

In general, Konner confirms Spitz's empirical claims. Konner reviews the major publications on social fears in the previously mentioned survey article about the mother-infant bond. Thus, referring to the research of Morgan and Ricciuti; Tennes and Lampl; Lewis and Rosenblum; Ainsworth, Blehar, Waters, and Wall; Bretherton and Ainsworth; Bowlby; and Ainsworth, et al.; Konner writes:

> Strangers begin to be discriminated in social responding, often negatively, and increasingly so through the course of the second six months; . . . crying when left by the mother in a strange situation, with or without a strange person, becomes common, although it is certainly not universal; . . . vulnerability to the adverse effects of separations of substantial duration from primary caretakers become demonstrably more marked . . . and "attachment

> behaviors" such as following, clinging, and cuddling become frequent in dis-
> tinctive relation to the primary caretaker(s), especially in strange situations
> or in the presence of strange persons. . . . (149)

Konner continues by referring to Kagan's and Super's research:

> All the above measures have been made in at least some non-Western cul-
> tures, with the result that the underlying concepts now have considerable
> cross-cultural validity. . . . The growth of the social fears and the concom-
> mittant growth of attachment, as defined by these and related measures, is
> a putative universal of the second half-year of human life (with much indi-
> vidual variation in the degree of overt expression). (149)

Konner reports that children are not only showing anxiety with
strangers, but are "crying when left by the mother in a strange situation, with
or without a strange person." Second, Konner reports that "'attachment
behaviors' such as following, clinging, and cuddling become frequent in dis-
tinctive relation to the primary caretaker(s), especially . . . in the presence of
strange persons" (Ibid. 149). Third, there is great variability in the age of
onset of the fear of strangers, but most researchers put the onset after the first
six months. However, in a graph Konner borrowed from Kagan, it looks as if
fear of strangers—the so-called eight-month-anxiety—could start as early as
the age of five months in some children.

My theoretical explanation of the eight-month-anxiety will not explain a
child's fear of strange situations. Neither will it try to explain a fear of strangers
in general. My explanation will apply only to a child's fear of a stranger who
looks at the child. As I now see it, my theory would be falsified if the child's
fear of a stranger's look were to occur prior to the child's jubilation before the
mirror. However, I was unable to find any empirical studies about the relative
timing of these two phenomena. My theory would not be falsified if a child
feared strangers who did not look at the child or if a child feared strange situations. The child's fear in these two situations involves matters beyond the
scope of my theory. In particular, it is possible to argue that seeing is a privileged sense in humans even though other senses can at least partially replace
some of seeing's functions. This line of reasoning might find support in
Fraiberg's and Freedman's research as reported by Konner: "blind infants
develop social smiling . . . a month or two later than sighted infants." Konner
may overstate his interpretation of this research when he writes: "a crucial role
for visual perception in the growth of the behavior can be ruled out" (Ibid.
146). If the social smile, on average, starts between two and three months of
age and blind children need one or two months more to begin smiling socially,
then blind children need between thirty percent and fifty percent more time
to achieve the social smile. I consider that a significant difference. Still, it does
mean that, at least for some functions, seeing can be replaced by other senses.

Returning to Spitz, I agree that the eight-month-anxiety is an indicator of the child's new psychic achievement. The child is now able to distinguish between friend and stranger. Moreover, the child's attachment to the familiar figure and his anxiety in the presence of strangers demonstrates that the child has developed special or deeper bonds with the familiar figure (usually the mother). Based on these observations, Spitz concludes that this new behavior, which occurs at about eight months of age, indicates that the child has succeeded in creating true object relations. Her mother has become her libidinal object, her love object (Spitz 1965, 146).

Because the eight-month-anxiety indicates that the child succeeded in achieving true—or deeper—object relations, I prefer to call the eight-month-anxiety an indicator of a new achievement. I would hesitate to call it an organizer of new behavior except in a weak sense. By the weak sense of organizer, I mean that the behavior indicates that the child has reached a new level of development and can therefore be expected to be able to perform several new tasks which it was unable to perform before. By the strong sense of organizer, I mean that, not only is the child's new behavior an indicator of a new level of psychic development, it (the behavior labeled as an indicator) is also the cause of the child's reaching a higher level of psychic development. This difference between a weak and a strong organizer becomes important in interpreting a case in which a behavior deemed an indicator of a higher level of psychic activity is absent in a particular child. If the absent indicator is only an organizer in the weak sense, one would not rule out the presence of a higher level of psychic organization and would look for other indicators of the presence of this higher level of psychic development.[8] If the absent indicator is an organizer in the strong sense, then one must accept that its absence means that the child has not reached the higher level of psychic development. I take the eight-month-anxiety to be an indicator that is an organizer in the weak sense. I will interpret no-saying as an indicator which is an organizer in the strong sense. Publications and research centered around the hypothesis that the absence of eight-month-anxiety is indicative of defective object relations all make the mistake of interpreting the eight-month-anxiety as an organizer in the strong sense.[9]

Spitz also interprets the new behavior that occurs at about eight months of age as a sign that the child can experience a new affect: anxiety. Spitz differentiates anxiety from fear. Fear occurs because there are "memory traces related to certain recurrent and to the child particularly unpleasant situations." The reactivation of these memory traces "elicits a specific unpleasure affect" (Ibid. 154). Fear, for example, is experienced by children who are repeatedly innoculated. Anxiety differs in that it is a reaction "to something or somebody with whom [s]he [the child] never had an unpleasure experience before" (Ibid. 155). Indeed, she likely has never met the strangers whose looks trigger such anxiety.

Clearly, Spitz has good arguments to back his claim that the child's eight-month-anxiety reaction is an indicator of a higher level of psychic structure, but this new affect still remains to be explained. Spitz explicitly rejects the hypothesis of Szekely, which supposes that the Gestalt "eyes-forehead" acts as an innate "releaser stimulus" representing the phylogenetic survivor of the enemy in the animal world. The infant's smile at three months would be, according to that theory, an indication of an early attempt at mastering this archaic anxiety (Ibid. 157). The eight-month-anxiety would be an indication that the child has regressed and that the "eyes-forehead" Gestalt again functions as a stimulus for the archaic fear.

Spitz rejects Szekely's hypothesis because the eye configuration does not function as an innate releaser. Some maturation of the child's nervous system is required. Furthermore, the eyes do not provoke fear but rather a smile, as we saw in the analysis of the three-month-old infant's smile. Finally, if eyes actually provoke fear, the child should be relieved when the observer's face is changed to a profile. On the contrary, however, in such circumstances the infant shows bewilderment and it becomes quite difficult to reestablish emotional contact with the child so as to calm him down (Ibid. 159).

Spitz's own explanation is based upon the following interpretation of anxiety: "What he reacts to when confronted with a stranger is that this is not his mother; his mother 'has left' him" (Ibid. 155). When formulating his explanation, though, Spitz can only explain the affect disappointment:

> However, when a stranger approaches the eight-month-old, [s]he is *disappointed* in h[er] wish to have h[er] mother. The anxiety [s]he displays is not in response to the memory of a disagreeable experience with a stranger; it is a response to h[er] perception that the stranger's face is not identical with the memory traces of the mother's face. (Ibid. 155, emphasis mine)

Spitz later puts this explanation in psychoanalytic terms: The eight-month-anxiety is a "response to the intrapsychic perception of the reactivated wishful tension and the ensuing disappointment" (Ibid. 156). Spitz interprets the disappointment as the cause of separation anxiety.

My summary objection to Spitz's theory is that it explains disappointment; it does not explain anxiety. A closer look at Spitz's writings, however, invites a more sympathetic presentation of his theory and thus also a more detailed criticism.

A careful reading of Spitz shows that Spitz argues for disappointment as a *cause* of anxiety. Still, the concept of disappointment remains crucial for Spitz's explanation. Indeed, in each of his three major publications on a child's first year of life, Spitz explicitly uses the word 'disappointment' or its French equivalent: "l'enfant se trouve *deçu* dans son désir de revoir la mère."[10] In order to explain his argument that disappointment leads to anxiety, Spitz refers to a passage from Freud in his article "Negation":

The child produces first a scanning behavior, namely the seeking for the lost love object, the mother. A decision is now made by the function of judgment "whether something which is present in the ego as an image, can also be re-discovered in perception." (Freud 1925 [Negation]) (Spitz 1957, 54)

The connection between the postulated disappointment of the child and anxiety is made again by Spitz on the basis of a reference to Freud (1926, "Inhibitions, Symptoms and Anxiety"). Of particular interest is what Freud writes in part C of the Addenda: "Anxiety, Pain and Mourning":

. . . the situation of the infant when it is presented with a stranger instead of its mother. It will exhibit the anxiety which we have attributed to the danger of loss of object. (Freud., S.E., XX, 169)

And one page later:

In consequence of the infant's misunderstanding of the facts, the situation of missing its mother is not a danger-situation but a traumatic one. Or, to put it more correctly, it is a traumatic situation if the infant happens at the time to be feeling a need which the mother should be the one to satisfy. It turns into a danger-situation if this need is not present at the moment. Thus, the first determinant of anxiety, which the ego itself introduces, is loss of perception of the object (which is equated with loss of the object itself). (Ibid. 170)

Thus, Spitz's argument amounts to claiming that the child at eight months is unable to see the face of a stranger without feeling a strong longing for the mother. Furthermore, the stranger not only provokes that longing (because the child might have been happily playing before), but she also fails to fulfill the longing that she provoked in the child. The resulting disappointment, finally, is said to produce the so-called eight-month-anxiety.

I have two main objections to this more detailed reading of Spitz's text. First, Spitz's theory is incomplete inasmuch as he does not talk about the danger that appears to be present at eight months but not at six months, when most babies smile at any human person approaching them. My theory could then be seen as complementary to Spitz's, in that it demonstrates the specific danger with which an eight-month-old has to deal, which has not yet presented itself to the typical six-month-old child.

Second, Spitz's theory can be said to be wrong in that his theory would have to predict a behavior different from what is actually observed. Spitz observes: ". . . the child looks back at the stranger again and again. [S]he peeks between h[er] fingers, [s]he lifts h[er] face from the blanket-and hides it again" (Spitz 1957, 55). Now, even if the child is in the arms of her mother, the child continues to look, from time to time, at the stranger. It is this last behavior which I believe Spitz's theory cannot explain and would probably predict differently. If the face of the stranger provokes a longing for the mother and disappoints that longing, why would the child continue to peek at the stranger while she is still in the arms of her mother? Spitz suggests that the actions of the baby (covering eyes, hiding his head in the pillow, pulling his shirt over his eyes, etc.) are actions intended to make the stranger disappear. He writes: "[the child] tries in a wishful way to make the stranger disappear" (Ibid. 55). But if the child's wish for the mother is satisfied because the child is in the arms of the mother, why would the child still want to peek at the stranger? My theory will suggest that the stranger's look is a major cause of the child's anxiety.[11] That cause remains even if the mother is present. However, the presence of the mother helps the child to deal with the look of the stranger. My objection to Spitz's disappointment theory thus stands even after a close reading of Spitz's argument.

With the help of Lacan's theory of "the mirror stage" and Sartre's theory of "the look," the eight-month-anxiety shall be explained without recourse to the concept of disappointment. The explanation will, however, claim that being seen, rather than seeing, is the cause of the anxiety of the eight-month-old baby.[12] Furthermore, the explanation will specify the new danger that the child faces at about eight months of age.

Sartre's analysis of the look can be found in *Being and Nothingness*. In the French edition it covers 58 pages out of a total of 722. The passage on the look is, therefore, not unimportant, and its importance increases once one understands its crucial function within Sartre's philosophical anthropology. By analyzing the function of the look, Sartre wants to clarify two problems at the same time: the existence of others and one's own bodily existence. (This purpose is reinforced by the titles of the three chapters of Part Three). In Sartre's theory, the close relationship between the existence of others and one's own bodily existence culminates in his concept of the body as being-for-others. It is that concept that Sartre has chosen as the title of Part Three which contains the section on the look.

Crucial to an understanding of Sartre's insights about the look is his description of a person who hears footsteps as he is looking through a keyhole in a hall (Sartre 1966, 317). If I were in such circumstances I can easily imagine, so Sartre argues, that I would become ashamed. I become ashamed about myself for another when I think that another might be looking at me. The thought that another might be looking at me is the occasion for my shame. In that shame I become aware of a dimension of myself of which, without shame, I am not aware. For Sartre, the shame I experience at the imagined look of the other "reveals to me that I am this being . . . [that] I have an outside, [that] I have a nature" (Ibid. 321–22). He goes on to claim that "Shame . . . is the apprehension of myself as a nature although that very nature escapes me and is unknowable as such" (Ibid. 322). Or further, "Thus in the shock which seizes me when I apprehend the Other's look, this happens—that suddenly I experience a subtle alienation of all my possibilities . . ." (Ibid. 324). Or "The appearance of the Other, on the contrary, causes the appearance in the situation of an aspect which I did not wish, of which I am not master, and which on principle escapes me since it is for the Other" (Ibid. 325). Or "For in shame . . . I do not cease to assume myself as such. Yet I assume myself in blindness since I do not know what I assume. I simply am it" (Ibid. 325). In his rhetorical style Sartre calls this assumption of one's determinate character, of one's bodily being, "my original fall" (Ibid. 322).

Interpreting Sartre, one can say that, for Sartre, consciousness becomes aware of its bodily dimension by imagining the look of the other. Consciousness thus becomes aware that as body it is determinate and for-others. The fact that I am determinate accounts for the possibility that I might be something I do not wish to be. I take this to be the source of what Sartre calls the "alienation of myself, which is the act of being-looked-at" (Ibid. 323). The fact that I am this determinate being for-others before I am aware of it makes me vulnerable to the look of the other. For Sartre, this is an ontological alienation and an ontological vulnerability. I believe that Sartre has discovered an important aspect of the human condition and of the look of others. Indeed, people report that they feel very uncomfortable when, for instance, while sitting in a train, they sense that they are being looked at.

That which is an ontological alienation or an ontological vulnerability is of course a permanent problem for a human being. It is my general hypothesis that there is a moment in the child's development when the child is explicitly confronting each of the ontological problems of the human condition. Freud's theory of the Oedipus complex illustrates my general hypothesis insofar as, during the Oedipus complex, according to Freud, the child confronts the problem of sexual differentiation in an acute way.

My claim then is that, at around eight months of age, the child confronts the ontological problems Sartre described as being connected with the body. My claim has the advantage of supplying the specific problem that is addressed in the eight-month-anxiety.

My specific hypothesis is thus both consistent with and complementary to the genetic view typical for psychoanalysis. It is consistent with the framework Freud assumed in presenting his theory of the Oedipus complex (a permanent problem in human psychology, such as sexual difference, is specifically confronted at a definite point in a child's development). My specific hypothesis is complementary to the existing body of psychoanalytic literature in that I claim that there is an additional problem that human beings must face. That additional problem is the assumption, the appropriation, of the body. Logically, I need to then also postulate that every child explicitly faces that problem at some point in her development. Also, I logically must accept that the problem of appropriating the body should be prior to the problem of facing sexual difference, because sexual difference is, among other things, a matter of bodily differentiation. These two logical requirements are satisfied in my specific hypothesis that the child faces the problem of appropriating, of assuming, his body at about eight months of age. My hypothesis therefore locates the problem of appropriating the body prior to the problem of facing sexual difference.

In applying Sartre's insights to the interpretation of children's behavior, I will criticize his interpretation of the look. I will argue that the look can be supportive (the mother's look) as well as alienating (the look of the stranger). The look has either one of these roles, depending upon the emotional context (Ver Eecke 1975, 241–43). The supportive look requires a maternal emotional context, as Spitz's study on hospitalism demonstrated.

3. LACAN'S THEORY OF THE MIRROR STAGE

Lacan first presented his theory of the mirror stage in 1936 and published a revised version of it in 1949 (Lacan 1977, 7ff.). In that paper, Lacan makes seeing, not just an indicator of a higher psychic structure, but the organizer and creator of that higher structure. Lacan depends on Hegel and two empirical studies to support his basic claim about the function of seeing.

From Kojève's interpretation of Hegel (1969), Lacan borrows the idea that an ego needs another ego in order to exist as an ego. Kojève puts it roughly this way: an ego is what it desires. An ego who desires only food is not really an ego but a stomach. Only an ego who desires another ego is an ego in the full sense of the word. Of course, desiring another ego involves the risk of conflict, even deadly conflict. This Hegelian conclusion gave Lacan the opportunity to see the close connection between the mirror stage and narcissism on the one hand and aggressivity on the other hand.

Later in his career, Lacan argued that such a deadly conflict—which is present in Hegel's text of the master-slave dialectic (Hegel 1977 b, 111–19)—can be avoided if the symbolic order mediates the relation between the egos. The power and efficacy of the symbolic order, in particular of words, was brought home to Lacan by Lévi-Strauss's text on the efficacy of rituals, words, and symbols for difficult childbirths in primitive cultures (Lévi-Strauss 1949). Lacan then turned to de Saussure (1959) and Jakobson (Jakobson and Halle, 1956) in order to discover what mechanisms language makes available for mediating interpersonal relations and for structuring our desires. From de Saussure Lacan borrowed the idea of the opposition between signifier and signified. From Jakobson Lacan learned that language's two crucial mechanisms are metonymy and metaphor. Jakobson himself documented that deficiencies in each of these two functions lead to different deficits in the linguistic ability of the speaker. At the time that Lacan first presented his theory of the mirror stage he had not yet created his linguistic theory of the unconscious nor had he introduced the concept of the symbolic.[13]

From L.H. Matthews's empirical study of pigeons and Chauvin's study of locusts, Lacan learned that the visual faculty performs a pivotal function in connecting the psychological and physiological dimensions (Ver Eecke 1983a, 113–26).

Matthews concludes: "the stimulus which causes ovulation in the pigeon is a *visual* one" (1938–39, 558, my emphasis). For ovulation to take place, the presence of a male pigeon is not necessary; the female pigeon need only see herself in a mirror. The sexual activity of ovulation thus requires a psychic act which is not obviously sexual: seeing one's own body. From this study of certain physiological functions activated only through seeing, Lacan derives the insight that seeing one's own body transforms the body.

The crucial result of Chauvin's study of locusts is that transition from a solitary to a gregarious form is possible if nymphs of the solitary locust have contact with members of their own species during early phases of their development. The gregarious and the solitary form of locust differ in behavior, color, metabolic activity (oxygen and food intake), and physiology (Chauvin 258). Thus, again, contact—be it visual or tactile—has physiological consequences.

Lacan uses the ontological function of the other ego, learned from Hegel, and the pivotal function of seeing, learned from the experimental research of Matthews and Chauvin, to correlate two totally different phenomena. The first phenomenon deals with a human being's imagination and fantasy life, in particular a fascination with dismemberment as evidenced in such cultural habits as "tattooing, incision, and circumcision" or dreams about "castration, mutilation, dismemberment, dislocation, evisceration, devouring and bursting open of the body," or in the historically documented preoccupation "with the cruel refinement of weapons" and torture-tools, or finally, the imagination of an individual as it is objectified in the painting of dismembered bodies, particularly those of Hieronymus Bosch (Lacan 1977, 11, 12, 4; Ver Eecke 1983a, 117). The second phenomenon is what embryologists have called the foetalization of a human being at birth. This refers to the anatomical incompleteness of the human brain and neurological system that results in "signs of uneasiness and motor uncoordination of the neo-natal months" (Lacan 1977, 4; Ver Eecke 1983a, 117).

Lacan's mirror stage theory claims that in seeing himself in the mirror or in recognizing his own Gestalt in the Gestalt of another person at about six months of age the child discovers a (bodily) unity and a completeness he did not experience before. Prior to the mirror stage, Lacan postulates that the child's image of himself is one of separate body parts: a hand, an arm, a foot, a leg, a thumb. If for any reason the child or, for that matter, an adult, must give up his attachment to that image, Lacan claims that fear of dismemberment and/or body disintegration will be experienced. Thus, one's own image discovered in another is the protection against the hallucinatory experience of dismemberment and/or bodily disintegration.

As proof of his mirror stage theory, which is uniquely applicable to humans, Lacan points to the difference in the behaviors of a human baby and a baby chimpanzee at about six to eight months of age. On the one hand, the chimpanzee has a greater problem-solving ability than the human baby. On the other hand, the chimpanzee does not grasp the meaning of the mirror image, while the human baby can. When the chimpanzee sees himself in the mirror, he tries to look behind it in order to locate the "other chimp." When he realizes that there is nothing behind the image, he loses interest in it. Either the chimpanzee does not recognize himself in the mirror or he has no interest in a mere reflection. The human baby's reaction is totally different. He responds with great interest, even excitement, to seeing his own image. In Lacan's words, the excitement is so intense that it manifests itself in: "a flutter of jubilant activity" (Lacan 1977, 1; Ver Eecke 1983a, 115).

There is a second advantage that the child gains from the mirror stage. In the mirror stage, the baby discovers himself as a possible object of his own libido. Therefore, in Lacan's theory, the mirror stage is the beginning of narcissism (Lacan 1984, 44). Lacan summarizes the gains that the baby experiences in the mirror stage as follows:

> What the subject welcomes in it is its inherent mental unity. What he recognizes in it is the ideal of the imago of the double. What he acclaims in it is the triumph of a tendency towards salvation. (Lacan 1984, 44) [translation mine]

There is, however, a negative aspect to Lacan's mirror stage theory. The human baby finds satisfaction in being or wanting to be a whole, a completeness, an image that he is not. Lacan calls this the ontological origin of human alienation (Lacan 1977, 4; Ver Eecke 1983a, 119–20).

Clearly, seeing makes a more radical contribution in Lacan's theory than in Spitz's. In Lacan's theory, it transforms the psychic structure. For Lacan, seeing, at about six months of age, is an organizer in the strongest sense of the word. For Spitz, the different behavioral reactions of the child when he sees a human being are interpreted as indicators of his new psychic structure, or as organizers in the weak sense of the word.

Reading Spitz, however, can help us better understand Lacan. Indeed, in his book Les Complexes Familiaux, Lacan analyzes the mirror stage theory in a subsection of his chapter on "The Intrusion Complex."[14] This suggests that the mirror stage must be understood as a moment in the baby's struggle to maintain his exclusive relationship with his mother. Lacan stresses this struggle by emphasizing jealousy of siblings as the crucial feeling of that period. Lacan's analysis, however, lacks any description of the mother's positive contribution as it relates to the intrusion complex or the mirror stage. Spitz writes:

[I]t [the innate equipment] has to be quickened; the vital spark has to be conferred on the equipment through exchanges with another human being, with a partner, with the mother. Nothing less than a reciprocal relation will do. Only a reciprocal relation can provide the experiential factor in the infant's development, consisting as it does of an ongoing circular exchange, in which affects play a major role. (Spitz 1965, 95)

It is the mutual give and take, its single elements constantly changing and shifting (though its sum total remains the dyadic relation), which represents the essence of what we are trying to describe and to convey to the reader. (Ibid. 96)

What the mother contributes to the relation is completely different from what the baby contributes. Each of them is the complement of the other, and while the mother provides what the baby needs, in his turn (though this is less generally acknowledged) the baby provides what the mother needs. (Ibid.)

What exactly does the child get from this mutual, dyadic relation? Again, Spitz's study of hospitalism is helpful in providing an answer (Ibid. 277). Briefly, hospitalism is a symptom present in young children who are brought to a hospital and given hygienic and physical care that is better than the care they received at home. Spitz's amazing discovery was that these children—separated for three months or more from their mothers at the age of three months—did not develop as well as children who stayed home with their mothers. In some cases, their development regressed or even stopped. Symptoms of increasingly serious deterioration appeared and were at least partially irreversible (Ibid. 277). Some of the results observed were retardation in motor development and progressive passivity. These children would lie supine in their beds and would not achieve the motor control necessary to turn into the prone position. Their faces would become vacuous, their eye coordination defective, and their expressions often imbecilic. Some would show bizarre finger movements reminiscent of decerebrate or athetotic movements (Ibid. 278). Finally, these children had a shockingly high mortality rate. By the end of the second year, thirty-four of the ninety-one children observed had died. Spitz summarizes:

Absence of mothering equals emotional starvation. We have seen that this leads to a progressive deterioration engulfing the child's whole person. Such deterioration is manifested first in an arrest of the child's psychological development, then psychological dysfunctions set in, paralleled by somatic changes. In the next stage this leads to increased infection liability and eventually, when the emotional deprivation continues into the second year of life, to a spectacularly increased rate of mortality. (Ibid. 281)

The question arises as to why the absence of mothering or maternal emotional deprivation leads to such negative developmental consequences for the infant. Many psychoanalysts (Erikson, Sullivan, Klein, Winnicot, Bowlby, Mahler, Kohut, and M. Mannoni, to name only a few) have made extensive comments on the importance of the mother in a child's development. While there is no one theoretical explanation of why mothering is important or which aspects of mothering matter most, there is no disagreement about the importance of the maternal role. Depending on whether the author accepts a drive model or an object-relations model, the argument is either that the mother satisfies a need or that the mother allows the child to experience trust in others.[15]

Lacan's student, M. Mannoni, indicates that, even though Lacan did not explicitly analyze the mother's role, his theory still points to that role's centrality (Mannoni 1972). Furthermore, my reading of Spitz's work convinced me of the importance of the mother's role in the development of the child. Lacan's theory of the mirror stage, as I make use of it, will be a theory that stresses the mother's emotional role. I prefer Lacan's theory because he emphasizes the crucial role of seeing in child development and because of his explanation of the origin of primary narcissism.[16]

Lacan's use of his theory of the mirror stage to explain the origin of narcissism of course raises the question as to how his view of narcissim compares to those of two important American psychoanalysts who have also written on this subject: Kernberg and Kohut. A study of their views on narcissism and their respective relations to Freud's changing views on this matter deserves a separate article.

Returning to Lacan's theory of the mirror stage, let us recall that Lacan makes this stage responsible for the emergence of primary narcissism or self-love. Informed by Spitz, I put forward the claim that the quality of the child's self-love depends on the emotional quality of the mother-child relationship. One can therefore say that the child takes possession of and appropriates itself in the mirror stage as a bodily unity by means of the maternal emotions invested in it.[17]

The ideal-ego or the image of bodily unity incorporated in the mirror stage at about six months of age is not identical with the infant's subjectivity or his "inner self." The child thus becomes, in some sense, alienated from itself. Therefore, according to this theory, the way the child experiences itself prior to the mirror stage is entirely different from the way he experiences himself after the mirror stage. Prior to and even during the process of bodily appropriation, as it takes place in the mirror stage, the child continues to produce a "social smile," defined as the child smiling to anybody approaching him, because he has no reason to be apprehensive of other people. However, after the process of bodily appropriation that occurs in the mirror stage, the baby is an alienated subject. Hence, the mother and the stranger will from now on have a different effect upon the child because the child experiences the mother and the stranger in relation to himself—now split between an interiority and an appropriated exteriority—in a different way. The baby experiences the mother or the familiar person as relating to it as subject, as "inner self," and not as relating exclusively to its exterior, bodily appearance. Therefore, the mother or the familiar figure do not assume the role of alienating onlooker as described by Sartre. The mother remains reassuring.

The baby experiences the stranger, however, as relating not to his subjectivity, but to his alienating imaginary bodily unity. Lacan granted seeing the power to achieve this imaginary bodily unity in the mirror stage. Could it be that the baby experiences the look of the other as focusing on and thus as a reminder of its alienating imaginary bodily unity?

I, therefore, prefer to explain the child's anxiety at eight months by saying that the look of the stranger reminds the baby of the split in his own personality as he created it in the mirror stage. Sartre called the look alienating because it makes consciousness aware of its determinate character as bodily being and because of the fact that as bodily being consciousness is for-the-other before it is for-itself. I believe that Lacan's theory allows us to better specify the cause of the anxiety produced in the child by the look of the stranger. At eight months (roughly two months after the mirror stage), the look of a stranger reminds the child, not just of its bodily dimension, but of the split in his personality that resulted from the mirror stage. Or, to put it another way, the look reminds the child of the alienating aspect resulting from the imaginary bodily unity achieved in the mirror stage. Alienation, for Sartre, is the mere fact of embodiment, which makes us beings-for-others. Alienation, for Lacan, is that the child assumes and appropriates his body imaginarily—in the mode of an image that is more perfect than the existentially experienced body. The difference between the image and the existential experience is the split in the personality of the eight-month-old, which I consider to be a potential cause of the eight-month-anxiety. The look of a stranger, which reminds the child of this split, is then the occasion or the proximate cause for the eight-month-anxiety.

This explanation has the advantage of accounting for anxiety, whereas Spitz's theory explains only disappointment. Even the young child's extreme joy at the game of peek-a-boo can hereby be explained as an attempt to actively master the anxiety-producing look of another person.

In his Presidential Address of 4 April 1975, later reworked as an article entitled "Emergent Themes in Human Development," Jerome Kagan presented what appears to be a competing theory of separation anxiety (this is the new name for Spitz's eight-month-anxiety). I will first present Kagan's theory and then argue that his theory does not necessarily compete with mine. Rather, my theory is complementary to Kagan's, which in fact requires such a complementary specification.

Kagan's theory is based upon a general view of child development in which the author argues that the nine-to twelve-month-old child has the competence to activate relational structures. By that competence Kagan means that the roughly one-year-old is "capable of actively generating representations of previously experienced absent events . . . and comparing these representations with the perceptions generated by the situation he is in at the moment" (Kagan 1976, 188). Kagan further states that: "The one-year-old shows prolonged attention to events that are discrepant transformations of his knowledge, compared with the minimal attentiveness at seven months" (Ibid.)

Kagan's explanation of separation anxiety then takes the following form: "distress to [sic] separation is the result of the new ability to generate a question or representation concerning the discrepant quality of the separation experience coupled with the temporary inability to resolve it" (Ibid. 189). As empirical confirmation for his theory, Kagan reports several cross-sectional and cross-cultural experiments that drew the following conclusions:

> The main result was that there was no significant decrease in play, a sensitive sign of apprehension, or occurrence of crying following the departure of either parent until the child was about nine to twelve months old. These two signs of apprehension or distress increased linearly until eighteen months and then declined at twenty-one months. (Ibid. 188)

It is worth noting that the variations in empirical results related to the anxiety's peak and decline. For example, in one experiment, the result is: "occurrence of crying following maternal departure when left with a stranger . . . increased to a peak value between twelve and fifteen months, and then declined" (Ibid. 189–90). In another study one finds: "separation fear . . . peaked during the second year" (Ibid.). Kagan reports the separation anxiety data that supports his theory: "the latency to distress was greater than five seconds for about one-third of those who cried, which suggests that the child was thinking about the separation event before he began to fret" (Ibid. 190).

I now want to turn to my claim that Kagan's theory complements my own. First, there is Kagan's attempt to buttress his theory with results from studies of children whose mothers had unobtrusively rubbed a little rouge on their child's nose and who were then brought before a mirror. Kagan writes:

> The probability that the child would touch his nose was very low at 9 months but increased linearly through the second year—paralleling the

growth curve for separation protest. . . . We believe that the older but not the younger children were relating the discrepant information in the mirror to their *schema of selfhood*. (Ibid. 190, emphasis mine)

Second, Kagan claims that maturational factors play a role in separation anxiety:

> The complete corpus of data suggests that 'separation anxiety' is being monitored closely by maturational factors, for it does not emerge until the last third of the first year, peaks during the middle of the second, and then declines in samples differing widely in rearing conditions. (Ibid.)

Third, in his explanation of separation anxiety, Kagan overemphasizes, in my opinion, the cognitive factor in the maturation process. He writes: "We suggest that the maturation event that mediates the separation response is primarily but not solely cognitive in nature" (Ibid. 190).

For Kagan, the cause of anxiety is not so much a new danger experienced by the child as it is the child's ability to ask questions about his situation. In my view, the cause of the child's anxiety is a change in his own situation: the child has become a split person because of the mirror stage. Kagan does not feel that there is an important change in the child's situation. Only, the child is now able to evaluate his situation because he can ask questions. The one-sidedness of Kagan's viewpoint is obvious when he writes:

> Separation distress occurs when the child is mature enough to ask questions about the parental departure and his response to it—Where is mother? Will she return? What should I do? What will the stranger do?—but not mature enough to answer those queries. . . . When he is mature enough to resolve those questions, his distress disappears. (Ibid. 190)

Could it be instead that the child has failed to mature in noncognitive areas so that the child needs the mother now—around nine months of age—more than before, but will not need her as much later on—around fifteen months of age, when he has matured in those noncognitive areas? My theory finds support in the fact that the separation anxiety peaks in the middle of the second year and then declines, because that is also the precise time during which the child's no-saying to the mother emerges, accompanied by a feeling of autonomy. Furthermore, Kagan's explanation does not address the fact that seeing and being seen by a stranger play an important role in the kind of reaction the child displays. Spitz writes:

> He [the child] may lower his eyes "shyly," he may cover them with his hands, lift his dress to cover his face, throw himself prone on his cot and hide his face in the blankets, he may weep or scream. The common denominator is a refusal of contact, a turning away, with a shading, more or less pronounced, of anxiety. (Spitz 1965, 150)

Kagan is right in claiming that there is a specific maturational factor play-ing a role in separation anxiety. Separation anxiety requires what Kagan calls the capability of activating relational structures. But the capability is not exclusively used to create comparisons about others; it can also be used to cre-ate, in Kagan's words, "a schema of selfhood." Even if Kagan does not inter-pret "schema of selfhood" the same way I do, I believe that nothing in Kagan's theory prevents me from claiming that the child's maturation includes the use of his "capability of activating relational structures" for the creation of a body image that allows him to actively inhabit his body. This is what I claim hap-pens in the mirror stage, creating an unforeseen vulnerability for the child that becomes manifest as separation anxiety. My claim gains plausibility when one considers the crucial results reported by Selma Fraiberg and Edna Adelson (1973). These authors claim that: "Among children blind from birth there is typically a delay in the acquisition of 'I' as a stable pronoun" (Fraiberg et al. 1973, 539). They further claim "that the acquisition of personal pronouns goes beyond practice with grammatical tools" and that "The blind child's delay in the acquisition of 'I' as a concept and a stable form appears to be related to the extraordinary problems of constructing a self-image in the absence of vision" (Ibid. 559). Or: "It is vision that gives unity to the disparate forms and aspects of hands and brings about an elementary sense of 'me-ness' for hands. Body image is constructed by means of the discovery of parts, and a progressive orga-nization of these parts into coherent pictures" (Ibid.). And finally: "Kathie's [the blind child] achievement of a stable 'I' at the age of four years, ten months corresponds exactly with her capacity to represent herself in doll play and to invent an imaginary companion" (Ibid. 561). Thus, seeing can be said to be crucial for the construction of a self-image, which in turn is required for being able to consistently use the pronoun 'I.' Seeing can thus be credited with a spe-cial function in the achievement of what one could vaguely call 'selfhood.'

4. THIRD ORGANIZER: SAYING "NO"

In his analyses of "saying "no"" Spitz gives equal consideration to shaking the head in a refusal gesture and using a verbal "no." His thesis is that, from the point of view of the adult communicating with the child, no-saying is the first semantic sign or gesture (Spitz 1965, 182). Saying "no," according to Spitz, implies that the child possesses a concept of refusal; saying "no" is not just a signal, it is a sign. This distinguishes "no" from other words already used at that age, such as "mama" and "dada." Children use these words to represent different wishes at different times. They could mean "mother," "father," " food," "I am bored," or "I am happy" (Ibid. 183). Therefore, the child uses these words more as a signal than as a linguistic sign. Spitz clearly expresses this theory in the title of one of his books: *No and Yes. On the Genesis of Human Communication.*

Spitz proves his thesis by showing how the child uses no-saying to extricate himself from situations that pose a dilemma. On the one hand, the child has created a libidinal bond with his mother. Spitz demonstrates this through his analysis of the second organizer: the eight-month-anxiety at seeing strangers. I believe that his study of hospitalism shows the child's dependence on its mother in even greater depth. Lacan's mirror stage theory can be used to explain the specific problem for which maternal support is helpful for the child.

On the other hand, the child is pushed towards aggressivity, provoked by the many frustrations imposed upon him. These include, among others, those the child's mother imposes when the child's surges of activity start to replace the passivity of the previous stage.

Since the reader is already familiar with Spitz's theory of the child's libidinal bond to his mother, I will now concentrate on the frustration in the mother-child relationship. As the child starts to walk, the relationship between mother and child changes drastically. Prior to that event, "infantile passivity and maternal endearment and supportive action constituted the major part of" (Ibid. 181) their relationship. Now, "the exchanges between mother and child will . . . center around bursts of infantile activity and maternal commands and prohibition" (Ibid.). The child, however, does not realize that his activity often damages things or that he is doing something dangerous. Therefore, mother is "forced to curb and to prevent the child's initiatives" (Ibid. 181). Furthermore, the child's locomotion puts distance between the mother and the child. The mother, therefore, must increasingly rely on "gesture and word" (Ibid.).

In explaining why the mother does this, Spitz advances the proposition:

that the mother is the child's *external ego*. Until an organized structural ego is developed by the child the mother takes over the function of the child's ego. She controls the child's access to directed motility. She cares for the child and protects him, she provides food, hygiene, entertainment, the satisfaction of the child's curiosity; she determines the choice of avenues leading into the various sectors of development; . . . the mother must act as the representative of the child both in respect to the outer world and to the child's inner world. (Ibid. 181–82)

The child, according to Spitz, does not understand all that is involved in maternal prohibitions. At about fifteen months of age, the child is able to perceive the gestures or the words used to impose prohibition. He does not understand the conscious motivation behind the prohibitions. He also only vaguely understands the affective relation of the mother towards the child. He does not understand the difference between a prohibition issued out of anger and one issued out of fear. The mother's gestures and words used to impose prohibitions are experienced as negative feelings. According to Spitz, this negative affective cathexis ensures the permanence of the memory trace of both the gesture and of the word "no" (Ibid. 185).

Furthermore, the frustration imposed by the maternal prohibitions forces the child back towards passivity. According to Spitz, this provokes, "an aggressive thrust from the id" (Ibid. 183).

Thus, the child's dilemma is that he experiences aggressive impulses toward his mother to whom he also has libidinal ties. Spitz suggests that the child solves this dilemma by a well-known defense mechanism discussed by Anna Freud: identification with the aggressor. Aggressivity thus becomes the emotional force which makes the refusal gesture available to the child.

According to Spitz, his explanation of the mechanism by which the refusal gesture (or the word "no") becomes available to the child proves that the child has access to the abstract concept of refusal. The child is not just imitating the mother. Indeed, the mother's "no" is mostly, if not always, a prohibition of an action the child initiated on his own. The child, however, uses his newly acquired "no," not only to impose a prohibition upon his mother, but also, to refuse demands or even to refuse offers made by the mother. "Johnny, do you want a piece of cake; do you want candy?"—"No" is often the reply.

Spitz believes that the child has acquired the capacity to communicate because he can now, by means of a linguistic sign, convey an unequivocal meaning: the meaning defined by the concept of refusal.[18] Let me quote Spitz's comments regarding his own explanation:

> With the acquisition of the gesture of negation, action is replaced by messages, and distance communication is inaugurated. This is perhaps the most important turning point in evolution, both of the individual and of the species. Here begins the humanization of the species; here begins the *Zoon Politikon*; here begins society. For this is the inception of reciprocal exchanges of messages, intentional, directed; with the advent of semantic symbols, it becomes the origin of verbal communication. (Ibid. 189)

A careful reading of Spitz's explanation of the acquisition of no-saying suggests that there is more to this achievement than the beginning of language as communication. Indeed, Spitz argues that the child acquires no-saying by means of an identification with the aggressor (the mother) (Ibid. 187). But, following Anna Freud, he adds that this identification "will be followed . . . by an attack against the external world" (Ibid.). Spitz then writes the following remarkable passage:

> In the fifteen-month-old infant, this attack takes the form of the "no" (gesture first, and word later), which the child has taken over from the libidinal object. Because of numerous unpleasurable experiences, the "no" is invested with aggressive cathexis. This makes the "no" suitable for expressing aggres-

sion, and this is the reason why the "no" is used in the defense mechanism of identification with the aggressor and turned against the libidinal object. Once this step has been accomplished, the phase of stubbornness (with which we are so familiar in the second year of life) can begin. (Ibid. 187)

But what is the aggressivity and the stubbornness supposed to achieve? Psychologists have reported that the child says "no" more often to the mother than to any other person. This evidence is sufficient to suggest a second function of no-saying that takes this aggressive component into account. One can explain that function either in terms of Spitz's or Lacan's theory.

In a text that I have already quoted, Spitz described the dyadic relation between mother and child, from the point of view of the mother, as follows:

the mother is the child's *external ego*. Until an organized structural ego is developed by the child the mother takes over the functions of the child's ego . . . the mother must act as the representative of the child both in respect to the outer world and to the child's inner world. (Ibid. 181–82)

The child's no-saying, particularly irrational no-saying, therefore becomes the means by which the child affirms his will and right to a point of view within the dyad.[19] It is the beginning of autonomy.[20]

Lacan taught that in the mirror stage the child appropriates his body. One could emend this Lacanian insight by claiming that the child appropriates his body by, among other means, using the maternal emotions invested in him. Spitz's study of hospitalism clearly demonstrated the importance of maternal affections. Anxiety at eight months can be interpreted as a child's confession that he needs a maternal figure to be able to live with his appropriated body.[21] The aggressive and irrational no-saying after about fifteen months of age can therefore be interpreted as the child's way of demonstrating to his mother that he has learned to live with his appropriated body and does not need his mother's support any more.

This second function is different from but not contrary to the first function. Spitz stresses the first function. It is possible to argue that Spitz, in describing the significance of the first function of saying "no," includes elements that remind us of the second function. Thus, in explaining the great achievement of the acquisition of saying 'no,' Spitz writes: "*distance communication* is inaugurated . . . here begins the "zoon politikon" (Spitz 1965, 189; emphasis mine). Indeed, one could argue that where there is distance communication or political life there must be separation between participants. My point, however, is that saying "no" created that distance and brings about a rupture from the mother. Saying "no" as a means of separating from the mother is an act of aggression. It makes sense then that one sees signs of guilt in the child after such no-saying.[22] Furthermore, if the primary purpose of no-saying is communication, then it is not clear why the child would use no-saying in an irrational way, such as saying no to a mother's offer which the child obviously wants to accept. If one of the purposes of no-saying is to separate from the mother, then aggression and irrationality make sense.

In order for the child to be able to learn to say "no," someone must first say "no" to the child; someone must be able to impose prohibitions and refusals. Given the closeness of the mother-child relationship, that task must first be the mother's. The symbiotic relationship between mother and child makes it difficult for the mother to perform that task. That task is easier for the mother if, besides the relationship she has with her child, she also has an emotionally significant relationship with some third person, say, her husband. In Lacanian terms, the mother's respect for the word or the name-of-the-Father allows her to transcend the symbiotic mother-child relationship. Her saying "no" to the child places the child within the triadic structure of child-mother-father. The child's "no" can then be interpreted as the child's acceptance of his introduction into that triadic structure, or saying "yes" to that triadic structure (Ver Eecke 1984, 78–84). Such yes-saying is what Lacan interprets Freud to mean by "Bejahung" (affirmation) in his article "Negation." An absence of this process would mean "retranchment" (later relabelled "forclusion"), that is, foreclosure of the Name of the Father. No-saying therefore also means that the symbolic order and its triadic structure gets hold of the child. In other words, one could say that the third function of no-saying is allowing language to get hold of the child.[23]

Two examples illustrate my thesis. Some years ago, as a foreign student, I was invited to an American home. At the dinner table the following occurred: The dinner was coming to an end. The mother was cutting the cake and, before serving anybody else, she addressed her two-year-old child sitting next to her and asked if he wanted a piece of cake. The child said "no." I could see the amazement on the mother's face. She repeated the question a second time. The child again said "no." The mother, still incredulous, repeated her question a third time. The child again said "no," took his mother's hand and kissed it. This elegant solution allowed the mother to serve the cake. After everybody had finished their cake, the hostess asked, addressing my side of the table, as I was the guest, who wanted another piece of cake. I did not have a quick command of English at that time. The cake had been delicious. I was trying to find a way to express in polite terms that I would like another piece. But, before I could speak, I heard the child say, "I want one." Clearly, the child understood the intellectual meaning of the word "no." The child, however, sensed that the refusal of the cake was not the only thing at stake. If the refusal of the cake had been the only thing at stake why would he have asked for a piece the next chance he had? And, above all, why would he have kissed his mother's hand after the third refusal? The no-saying was a necessary act of aggression against the mother, in which the child affirmed his sense of autonomy and his will to differentiate himself from her by essentially telling her: If you think you know what I want, you are wrong; I want what I want, even if that means that I need to forego the cake I want.[24]

The second example concerns a three-year-old who had fully mastered the use of "no" as the victorious battle cry Spitz described. In the late afternoon the child saw that his siblings had eaten several bags of Doritos. He asked one of his parents if he could have some Doritos. The parent first said "no," but, after the child repeatedly requested chips, the parent acceded to the request and said, "If your brothers have eaten some, we cannot refuse your request." The child went to the cabinet where the chips were and commented to himself in a self-satisfied manner, "I asked and they said yes." About two hours later, five minutes before dinner was to start, the same child took two more bags of chips out of the kitchen cabinet. The father asked the child to put them back and explained that he had to eat dinner. The child said "no" he would not put them back and "no" he would not eat dinner. The mother reinforced the prohibition and added that the chips were needed the next day as snacks for lunch and that he could put one in his lunchbox. At first, the child said "no" and commented that he was not going to put one in his lunchbox. Suddenly, the child put one bag of chips back in the kitchen cabinet and said that only one bag of chips was needed for his snack the next day and asked if he could eat the one remaining bag. The mother and father repeated their prohibition and their various arguments, to which the child replied each time with a forceful "no." After some mild coaching, the child took his seat . . . and suddenly produced a contented face, put the one remaining bag of chips next to his soup plate and said, more to himself than to anybody else, "I did not open the bag." (When he finished his soup, the child asked if he could now eat his chips. After a second's hesitation the parents let him have them.)

Again, it was clear that the child understood the intellectual context of no-saying. It was also clear that there was an aggressive component to the child's "nos." But twice the child's own comments illustrated that no-saying was a process by which he resisted but also slowly and partially allowed language to interfere with his demand for immediate gratification.

CONCLUSION

1. I agree with Spitz's method of using the concept of indicator, critical time, or organizer of the development of the child. I like the three indicators used by Spitz: the smile at two to three months, the eight-month-anxiety and no-saying after fifteen months. However, in contrast to Spitz's, my interpretation of the eight-month-anxiety relates it to the appropriation of the body and not so exclusively to the establishment of a love object. Lacan's theory of the mirror stage can be used to explain appropriation of the body, provided

that one supplements his theory with the insight that the mother's emotional relation to the child is crucial for that appropriation. Thus, the eight-month-anxiety, as I understand it, includes the mirror stage as one of its moments.

2. In interpreting the three indicators, Spitz has a reductionist tendency which he corrects by including a richer contextual description of the three indicators than his own explanation and theory incorporate. Each time, his corrections concern the emotional significance of the mother figure for the child. This leads me to argue that Spitz's explanation of the function of seeing in the period of the eight-month-anxiety is unsatisfactory because it can only explain disappointment and not anxiety. Lacan's mirror stage theory leads me to argue that the eight-month-anxiety is caused by the look of a stranger who reminds the child of the alienating aspect of his appropriated body.

When it comes to no-saying, I disagree with Spitz's interpretation of this achievement as being, at most, the acquisition of language as a method of intellectual communication. Again, I find in Spitz's own descriptions elements which go beyond the explanatory power of Spitz's theory. I argue instead that saying "no" is a victorious slogan for the child because it establishes the child's will for his own point of view, even if that point of view is irrational. It is this irrational aspect of the child's no-saying which is the decisive element in my argument that no-saying is more than a beginning of communication, as Spitz claims. Furthermore, I argue that no-saying also functions as a tool through which the child uses language to control his needs for immediate gratification. While these two interpretations are not to be found in Lacan, I am indebted to the Lacanian framework in formulating them.

3. Spitz makes no clear differentiation between the concepts of indicator and organizer. By calling the social smile, the eight-month-anxiety, and no-saying indicators and organizers, Spitz stresses that those three phenomena organize past achievements and prepare the child for a higher level of future psychic activity. I argued that these are organizers in the weak form. The strong form of organizer would be one in which a behavior is not just an indicator of a higher psychic activity but one in which it is, by itself, the cause of that higher activity. It is, in my opinion, wrong to argue that a child who does not show eight-month-anxiety has not established true object relations and is thus emotionally deficient. Eight-month-anxiety is but an indicator of true object relations. It is not that alone by which object relations are established. The real organizer behind the eight-month-anxiety is, according to my theory, the creation of the body image (in the mirror stage) by which the child appropriates its body. Of Spitz's three indicators, only no-saying would qualify as an organizer in the strong sense. Among other things, the no-saying by itself creates the separation of mother and child. Without the aggressive act of no-saying the separation of mother and child is not achieved. This conclusion clarifies and justifies the Freudian claim in

"Negation," to which this study is devoted: the creation of the symbol of negation creates a measure of freedom that will make the function of judgment possible (Freud, S.E., XIX, L.39).

4. Clearly, I have not fully explained the relationship between negation and freedom, but I hope I have made a contribution.[25] In order to put this problem within a philosophical perspective, I wish to end with a quote from Hegel about free will: "it determines itself as self-related negativity" (Hegel 1952, #104). This occurs within the moral point of view. The no-saying child is not yet there, but Hegel's speculative formulation allows us to glimpse the child on its way.[26]

SIX

Oedipus, the King

How and How Not to Undo a Denial

abstract: In this chapter I make use of Sophocles' piece *Oedipus, the King* in order to answer a number of questions about denials such as: can undoing a denial avoid the tragedy experienced by Oedipus? Why was Teiresias' intervention unhelpful? Why was Oedipus able to make use of the information given by Jocasta, the messenger, and the shepherd? I will further argue that Sophocles' *Oedipus, the King* invites us to make a distinction between truth and meaning. For truth to become meaningful, a person must integrate actively the forgotten and repressed events. It is no help for others to tell someone the truth about himself. Truth about oneself thus possesses a characteristic which is different from truth about the objective world, where telling the truth and presenting arguments for it are effective ways to promote the truth.

INTRODUCTION

Psychotherapy teaches us that the emergence of true self-knowledge meets with resistance. It is futile for somebody (e.g., the therapist) to tell the patient what she thinks about the patient. Such an approach leads only to the rejection or the denial of the truth. Only a search conducted by the person her or himself can lead to the discovery of the truth about the self. Sophocles' drama *Oedipus, the King* can serve as a valid example of the psychotherapeutic experience of looking for true self-knowledge. Generations of people have seen in that drama a true expression of many aspects of the human condition.

Sophocles starts the drama at a point in time when Oedipus adheres to a self-image that is incomplete, if not wrong. Then Sophocles lets Teiresias reveal the truth to Oedipus. Oedipus, however, cannot accept this truth.

Sophocles ends the drama when Oedipus has accepted the truth and thus sees his life in a totally new light. The whole drama is nothing but the description of the path leading to Oedipus's discovery and acceptance of the truth. I will pursue two questions: Why does Oedipus deny the truth about himself when Teiresias presents it? And how is he ultimately able to overcome his denial of the truth? The answers to these two questions will first necessitate an analysis of Oedipus's self-image at the beginning of the drama.

1. OEDIPUS' SELF-IMAGE AT THE
BEGINNING OF THE TRAGEDY

In the prologue, Oedipus appears as a magnanimous king and a concerned monarch who cares for a city afflicted by the plague (verses 63–64).[1] Once already he had saved the city from misfortune when he solved the riddle of the sphinx (35–37). Now, possibly suffering from hubris, he promises, almost recklessly, to find and to avenge the injustice (105–108) that caused the plague (137). He promises to do everything that is necessary and to spare no one. Oedipus's confident self-image is based upon and justified by one important past event: solving the sphinx's riddle.

Oedipus and the Thebans considered the events before Oedipus solved the sphinx's riddle to be prehistory. It could be and was, in fact, forgotten. Nevertheless, events took place in that prehistory. These events are not integrated into Oedipus's current self-image; therefore, one cannot call the king's self-image complete. If these events are also denied, one would have to say that the king holds a false self-image. As the drama progresses, it reveals the forgotten or repressed events. They include: Oedipus's killing of a group of people (810–13) and his marriage to Jocasta, notwithstanding the warning from Delphi that he would kill his father and marry his mother (791–94). There is also the reproach from a Corinthian that Polybus and Merope are not his real parents (779–81). Finally, there is the fact of Oedipus's scarred ankles, testifying to their having been pierced when Oedipus was still an infant (1033).

The relation between all these facts or events is not clear to Oedipus. This, however, does not put Oedipus in an exceptional situation. Indeed, it is typical of the human situation that one has to reckon with unclear and incomprehensible facts. It is true that Oedipus encounters facts that have profound significance, but this is only a difference in degree, not in substance.

Faced with these threatening facts, particularly the frightening warning of the oracle of Delphi, Oedipus runs away from Polybus and Merope. This act of running away does not solve at all the problems or mysteries raised by events or facts in Oedipus's past. Indeed, the scars on Oedipus's ankles remain and the warning of the oracle that Oedipus will kill his father and marry his mother has not been invalidated.

One could object to the value of using this tragedy for making general conclusions about people, by pointing out that the tragedy is based on an oracle, and the oracle almost seems to be a contingent event, a kind of *deus ex machina*, which dominates the life of Oedipus, not from the inside, but from the outside. For the Greeks, however, an oracle was no more contingent and no more external than, for example, the sudden death of a child in our civilization. Indeed, the sudden death of a child from an incurable disease is, in our civilization, an event that often promotes soul searching and self-accusations. The mourning parents almost naturally look for events in the past which could have been warnings about the illness. In both Greece and our own civilization an event that is external to a person—an oracle in Greece, the biologically caused death of a child—can set in motion a process of self-interrogation. Thus, even from this angle, the case of Oedipus is not exceptional.

Oedipus's attitude towards the prehistorical events is one of flight. He runs away from Corinth. These prehistorical events are left out or repressed in Oedipus's self-image as king. They have no meaning for the present.

2. DENIAL AND REJECTION OF THE EMERGING TRUTH

In order to fulfill his royal promise of purifying the city of injustice, Oedipus calls upon the divinely-endowed prophet Teiresias. After much prevaricating, Oedipus forces Teiresias to tell him what caused the plague and who the murderer of Laius is. In verse 353, the prophet answers: "You are the land's pollution." In verse 362, Teiresias explains himself by bluntly affirming: "I say you are the murderer of the king whose murderer you seek." And in verses 366–67 Teiresias adds: "I say that with those you love best you live in foulest shame unconsciously and do not see where you are in calamity." Shortly before he leaves, the prophet speaks without hesitation in clear and non-metaphorical terms:

> He shall be proved a father and a brother both to his own children and in his house; to her that gave him birth, a son and husband both; a fellow sower in his father's bed with that same father that he murdered. (457–59)

Teiresias presents an interpretation of the plague which implicates Oedipus. The interpretation is put forward categorically. Oedipus, the accused, regards Teiresias's statement as an untruth. He must therefore reject it.[2] In order to augment the plausibility of Oedipus's rejection of and his resistance to Teiresias's interpretation, Sophocles precedes Teiresias's intervention with a quarrel between Oedipus and Teiresias, but this is only a theatrical artifice to prepare the audience. Oedipus cannot accept any interpretation of events which categorically contradicts his self-image. The truth of this self-image depends on Oedipus's forgetting a number of events, or at least on his denying their relevance. By giving an ominous and crucial importance to these past events, Teiresias undermines and attacks Oedipus's self-image. Oedipus interprets Teiresias's intervention as a personal attack and begins to look upon Teiresias as a waylayer.

Viewing Teiresias as a liar is a logical position for Oedipus to take, because it is the easiest solution to the challenge. Indeed, if Teiresias's accusation is an invention and not founded on truth, then Oedipus can retain his peace of mind. He does not have to change his self-image, his view of the world, or his way of life. Teiresias started a difficult and dangerous task: that is, making a person aware of the precariousness of his self-image and of his way of life. Furthermore, he did it unskillfully. He presented his view as a truth which contradicted Oedipus's view. Sophocles presents the two views as radical alternatives without indicating any possible transition for Oedipus from the incomplete view he is holding to the more complete view that Teiresias is presenting.

3. FROM DENIAL TO ACCEPTANCE OF THE TRUTH

Although he furiously rejected Teiresias's opinion (445–47), and, in addition, accused his brother-in-law of plotting against him (378–79; 534–35; 618–19), at the end of the play Oedipus exclaims in self-accusation: "Accursed in my living with them I lived with, cursed in my killing" (1184–85). How is this change possible? What are the forces propelling this change?

The event at the origin of the change in Oedipus's views is the plague in Thebes. In the play, the plague represents the return of the forgotten or repressed events. For these forgotten events to return, however, they must emerge in a form or domain in which they are significant for Oedipus's self-consciousness. When the forgotten events become events that must be punished because he thinks, by doing so, the plague will end, Oedipus can no longer deny their relevance. Faced with a plague, Oedipus, as king of Thebes, cannot but investigate its causes. He therefore unknowingly puts in motion the effort which will lead to the rediscovery of the forgotten events. At this point in Sophocles' tragedy it is not clear what will result from Oedipus's effort, but there is a premonition of something ominous.

The event that turns Oedipus's search definitively in the direction of rediscovering the forgotten events is a conversation between Oedipus and Jocasta. In an attempt to save Oedipus by giving him a scrap of information that could be used to discard the validity of oracles and prophesies, Jocasta recalls a painful detail about King Laius's death:[3]

> There was an oracle that once came to Laius, . . . and it told him that it was
> fate that he should die a victim at the hands of his own son, a son to be born
> of Laius and me. But, see now, he the king, was killed by foreign highway

robbers at a place where three roads meet—so goes the story: and for the son—before three days were out after his birth King Laius pierced his ankles. . . . (711ff.)

This information about King Laius's death reminds Oedipus of the murder he committed. It too occurred at the crossing of three roads. Oedipus's questioning reveals that the two murderers—first thought of as different people—are in fact one and the same murderer. Verses 821–22 formulate this insight dramatically: "And I pollute the bed of him I killed by the hands that killed him . . ."

These verses indicate that Oedipus's former self-image has eroded. It will be further eroded as a consequence of a second attempt to free Oedipus from his anxieties. The oracle not only predicted that Oedipus would kill his father, but also that he would marry his mother. As long as Oedipus believes that his parents are the King and Queen of Corinth, he is protected against this prediction of the oracle. A messenger from Corinth, however, shatters this belief when he announces the death of Polybus, asks Oedipus to return to Corinth as king, and in an attempt to brush aside an objection, tells Oedipus that Polybus and Merope are not his parents (1016). This radically changes Oedipus's horizon. What Oedipus formerly feared as only a distant possibility, he must now consider as highly probable. The truth of his self-image is severely shaken once more.

The definitive turning point comes with the revelations of the shepherd of Thebes. Oedipus has questions about his pierced ankles and about being rejected at birth. Having been told by the messenger from Corinth that he received the young Oedipus from a Theban shepherd, Oedipus orders to bring him that shepherd and he forces the shepherd to reveal who his parents were. The element that links all of the information into a coherent whole are the wounds on Oedipus's ankles. Thus, Oedipus comes to recognize himself as responsible for the plague in the city.

In the three steps that brought about the total decomposition of his self-image, Oedipus played an active role. In each case, it is Oedipus who puts his self-image to a test. The circumstances in which the facts and events emerged prevent Oedipus from denying them, as he had with Teiresias's assertions. Oedipus was able to deny Teiresias's interpretation of the events by accusing him of inventing the interpretation for the purpose of plotting against him. This form of self-defense—aggressive accusation of the opponent—is made extremely plausible in the play because a dispute between Oedipus and Teiresias precedes Teiresias's devastating interpretation. Such an aggressive self-defense, however, prevented Oedipus from facing the issue on its own merit and honestly asking the question of whether he could be responsible for the plague in Thebes. Oedipus cannot use the same technique of aggressive accusation to falsify the information uncovered in the dialogues with Jocasta or the messenger or the shepherd, since they give their information in order to help him. Oedipus does not reject the questions about his past that emerge from the information they give him. Instead, he transforms these questions into self-interrogation. In his encounter with the messenger, Oedipus is so possessed by the process of self-interrogation that he forces the messenger to speak.

When the self-interrogation leads to insight, Oedipus turns his aggressiveness against himself. In an act of self-condemnation Oedipus pokes his eyes out. Instead of a regal Oedipus, there is a broken man (1360ff.). The forgotten and neglected events have done their job. They have forced their way into Oedipus's field of consciousness. Oedipus accepts them painfully, but actively, as part of his new self-image.

4. COULD THE UNDOING OF THE DENIAL HAVE UNFOLDED DIFFERENTLY?

I want to address two questions. The first is: Could Oedipus have done anything to avoid the tragedy that forced the change in his self-image? The second is: Why did Oedipus refuse to believe Teiresias? Put more positively: Could Teiresias have told the truth in a way that would have warded off Oedipus's angry rejection? Both questions intend to clarify one concern: How can denial be more effectively overcome?

As to the first question, Oedipus's original self-image did not integrate certain facts or events. Such non-integration is typical in cases of denial.

Reality, however, is harsh and demanding. Unrecognized events do eventually avenge themselves. King Oedipus finds his city afflicted by the plague. In Sophocles' drama, the unrecognized events are not yet powerful enough to avenge themselves. The consequences of the prehistoric events do not emerge automatically or independently; they get the support of angry gods. However, I wish to stress that in Greek culture, as in many ancient cultures, people saw a close connection between affliction (e.g., the plague) and moral evil. Having committed evil—even if unconsciously—Oedipus had to be punished according to the Greek vision of the world. One can translate this Greek moralistic view into the secular vision of contemporary psychoanalytic theory which asserts that "the repressed necessarily returns."[4]

This secular interpretation of the king's fall gives us a clue as to how Oedipus could have diminished the tragic results of the reemergence of the repressed events. Indeed, psychoanalysis sees the restoration of a healthy personality in the undoing of amnesia. Thus, the only creative solution available for Oedipus would have been to actively search for the significance of the prehistoric events in an effort to give them a place in his conscious self-image, instead of trying to forget them.[5] Had he then found the penitence necessary to expiate his personal guilt, he could have accepted it. Such a course of action would have given the drama a totally different turn. The city would have been spared the plague and Oedipus would not have been forced to publicize his crime. The tragedy thus illustrates one of life's demands: A human being must broaden his self-image so that as few events as possible are repressed, forgotten, or considered unimportant. An individual must regularly recreate his or her self-image and integrate the past with the present instead of forgetting the past and allowing it to become a permanent part of prehistory. In Oedipus's refusal to comply with this human "duty" lies the origin of the tragedy accompanying his change of self-image.

The second point concerns Teiresias's role. It contains something of a general application. Many people—similar to Teiresias—have little difficulty in perceiving the one-sidedness and narrowness of others' self-images. The temptation, then, to present this insight as a logical and thus a necessary conclusion is great. Such a move represents an aggressive intervention in the life of another, who in turn must experience it as an untruth. Teiresias followed this course exactly. Oedipus's response was, understandably, an explosion of rage. Was another outcome possible, given the imperious intervention of Teiresias?

The role of king was a crucial part of Oedipus's self-image. The awareness of his royalty was the pillar of his life.[6] It determined his attitudes and his efforts towards other people. One could therefore say that Oedipus's identification with the role of king was a primary way by which he supported and directed his existence. Oedipus dedicated all of his energy to this role. How could Oedipus have tolerated the undermining of his identification with this regal role? It would have meant the annihilation of the meaning he pursued in his life. No one can tolerate such annihilation.

Nevertheless, Oedipus had to change his self-image. Teiresias did not bring this change about, whereas Jocasta, the messenger, and the shepherd, unwittingly but effectively, contributed to Oedipus's transformation. They did it unknowingly because their primary purpose was to reassure Oedipus and thus to prevent him from looking further. In contrast, Teiresias, by trying to broaden the king's self-image, forced Oedipus to reaffirm his narrow self-image. This ironic relationship between intentions and results brought about by the execution of those intentions requires further analysis.

Can we find in the attitudes of Jocasta, the messenger, and the shepherd something positive that we do not find in that of Teiresias? The crucial difference seems to be that Jocasta, the messenger, and the shepherd accepted and supported Oedipus's initial self-image, whereas Teiresias the prophet was concerned primarily with the truth, without considering whether this truth would be psychologically destructive.[7] Indeed, Jocasta, the messenger, and the shepherd present Oedipus with facts unknown to him in the hope that these will confirm his self-image. Oedipus begins to broaden his views. This expansion becomes tragic for him only because the new awareness progressively confronts him with his massive guilt.

Accordingly, a change in self-image cannot be forced upon another person; the individual has to discover it for himself. Genuine reorientation cannot be arbitrarily imposed *ab extra*. Fortunately, a person searching for a new self-image usually has vague presentiments, which naturally have to be clarified. Such clarification calls for the techniques of listening and interrogation on the part of a sympathetic outsider. In this respect, Sophocles' drama foreshadows a basic principle of contemporary psychoanalysis: An outsider does not have the right to intervene imperiously in the life of another. The therapist must listen and support the search for a new self-image. Truthfulness is of only secondary importance. Of primary importance is the creation of a self-image that can be appropriated by the patient and that can give meaning to his life.

One can compare this interpretation of Sophocles' drama with an aspect of Hegelianism as well. At any moment, the conscious self-image of Oedipus appeared partial, just as the Weltanschauung of any particular figure or culture is shown to be partial in Hegel's *Phenomenology*. When unrecognized events succeed in requiring attention, then the self-image or the Weltanschauung has to change. People and cultures must continuously search for a broader view. Absolute and fixed truths are useless. Only historically-anchored truths are relevant: that is, truths in which history and individuals believe.

Freud and Hegel, each in his own way, reacted against absolute and fixed truths. The basic principles justifying such a position were presumably already intuitively understood in Greek culture. This insight, implicit in Sophocles' *Oedipus*, was developed into a philosophical system by Hegel, and into a therapeutic technique by Freud.

CONCLUSION

Sophocles' drama makes use of mythical material. The insights that I have underlined in this drama are the aggressive resistance against true self-knowledge and the peculiar position required for an interlocutor to be helpful in a human dialogue. The aggressive resistance to true self-knowledge is most clearly visible in Oedipus's reaction to Teiresias's prophetic revelation of the truth. In his search for truth, Oedipus is not willing to consider all possible leads with equal zeal. He is particularly inhibited in following a lead to truth that would destroy his self-image. I explained this by showing how one's self-image is the primary instrument for giving meaning to one's life. Thus, the Oedipus tragedy illustrates the fundamental distinction between truth and meaning. This distinction alone can explain the aggressive resistance to entertaining negative information related to one's self-image.

However, meaning derived from one's self-image is not independent from the truth of one's self-image. Therefore, meaning and truth, even though they are distinct, cannot be opposites. The distinction between truth and meaning and their relationship to one another is what creates the space for subjectivity. Indeed, to be a subject, that is, to be a conscious ego, means that one has the reflective capability to affirm the position one takes. In turn, this means one has the capability of reflectively questioning and/or confirming the truth or falsity of one's self-image. A human being cannot escape such a confirmation nor can he let somebody else make this confirmation for him. The former condition takes away the possibility of living happily and undisturbed by a discrepancy between truth and significance; the latter condition eliminates everything but the ego as the potential realizer of this confirmation. It is this last condition which explains why Teireisias's direct presentation of the truth fails and why the indirect approaches of Jocasta, the messenger, and the shepherd succeed.[8] Teireisias's approach—presenting a truth contrary to the one held by Oedipus—allows Oedipus only one way to create distance between himself and Teiresias with respect to his own self-image: rejection of Teiresias's interpretation. The intentions of Jocasta, the messenger, and the shepherd are different from Oedipus's intention. None of these three presents Oedipus with a truth about Oedipus's life that contradicts Oedipus's self-image. Rather, Jocasta wants to alleviate Oedipus's worries; the messenger wants Oedipus to accept becoming King of Corinth; and the shepherd wants to avoid a calamity he sees coming. This difference in intention by itself creates the distance between Oedipus and his interlocutors needed to allow Oedipus the personal involvement in the search and discovery of the truth about his life. This allows the objective truth to become meaningful.[9]

The myth of Oedipus as used in Sophocles' drama thus makes us intuitively aware of aspects of human subjectivity for which we only recently have developed a theory. Indeed, psychoanalytic theory argues for a number of therapeutic directives which maintain the distance between patient and therapist: for example, the analyst's first task is to listen;[10] the analytic situation is not a method for making important decisions;[11] and the influence of the countertransference must be neutralized as much as possible (Laplanche and Pontalis 93).

Myths and dramas based on myths can provide intuitive insights which are theoretically explicated only centuries later. We have not argued in this paper the more radical claim: that is, that myths give us access to insights that are theoretically unattainable.[12]

SEVEN

Denial, Metaphor, the Symbolic, and Freedom

The Ontological Dimensions of Denial

---

abstract. In the previous chapter, I analyzed the case of Oedipus. Oedipus, until forced to do so by circumstances, did not actively seek to broaden his view of himself to include such denied facts as his pierced ankles. Oedipus' failure to actively search out his truth led to tragic consequences. In this chapter, I will analyze the autobiographical account of Anthony Moore, who describes one profound denial and the many steps, he undertook voluntarily, to undo such a denial and its consequences.[1] I will first present a careful phenomenological description of that profound denial. I will then draw a number of philosophical (ontological) conclusions that I intend as correctives to the claim that human beings are autonomous creatures. The conclusions include the thesis that denial is an unconscious form of self-deception, that the achievement of personal freedom depends upon the creation of metaphors, the usage of metonymic similarities, the availability of a cultural system rich in symbols, and the ability of emotionally important persons to say "no" to deep forms of identification.

1. PHENOMENOLOGICAL DESCRIPTION OF A DENIAL AND ITS UNDOING

An Overview

In *Father, Son, and Healing Ghosts*, the author, Anthony Moore, provides us with an autobiographical account of dealing with his father's death, which occurred during the author's infancy and his fatherless childhood.[1] The book is the story of undoing a fundamental denial. It is much more detailed than Freud's examples of denial. In particular, Freud does not tell us how denials are undone. What he does tell us is that merely acknowledging the truth behind a denial—the intellectual undoing of a denial—is but a meager beginning to the work of a complete undoing.[2] The major work involves emotionally incorporating the denied truth and the world hidden behind that denial into one's daily life. The book by Moore fills this gap in the Freudian literature. Moore describes the many steps he took to undo the fundamental denial of his formative years, which had consisted in denying that he missed his father while at the same time deeply identifying with him.

In chapter 1 of this book I argued that Freud helps us to distinguish four steps in the history of denial and its undoing. Denial—so Freud reasons—is a partial lifting of the repression.[3] Hence, I postulated a first moment in which repression was not lifted but was, on the contrary, successful. In that stage a patient typically answers her therapist's question by saying that she does not know. The patient's consciousness is confronted by a blank. A second step announces itself when the patient answers the therapist's question with a negative sentence. Freud claims that such negative answers include the pertinent information in the form of a denial. The truth thus appears but as denied. In a third step, the therapist can help the patient see that her denial contains the truth. The recognition of the truth is done reluctantly or purely intellectually, as in the statement: "I guess that figure in my dream must be my mother." In the fourth step, the therapist helps the patient accept emotionally the implications of the denied truth, for instance: "If that bossy figure in my dream is my mother, then I have to learn to stand up to her or to avoid meeting her."

In my presentation of Moore's autobiographical description of his denial and its undoing I will follow the four steps discovered in Freud's analysis. Moore's first step was the moment of repressing his painful experience, a process Freud postulated. In Moore's case we see an unusually deep attachment to his dead father. There are indications of deep pain and evidence of semi or unconscious motives influencing his life decisions. Moore's second step was to deal with the pain of losing his father with a well-crafted denial. That denial was operative in spite of his deep attachment to his father. He needed the help of a psychiatrist to move to the next phase. Through his psychiatrist's effective response to his well-formulated denial, Moore took the third step, making the intellectual move of undoing the denial. Moore's fourth step, dealing emotionally with the truth hidden in the denial, had two stages. The first stage can be described as a gift to the young Moore for his willingness to acknowledge the truth. Indeed, the acknowledged truth allowed Moore to recognize important dimensions of life that his original denial prevented him from appreciating. The second stage consisted of the work that Moore performed to undo several unconscious interpretations of his father's death: his unconscious over-idealization of his father and his unconscious belief that his birth was the cause of his father's death. The first step in all denial is, according to Freud, a deep pain that the subject deals with by repressing and not accepting it. Because of the repression, the pain that will be the cause of the denial is not visible. All we can expect from the reports of a subject performing a repression are indications of a paradox and a form of self-deception used to deal with that paradox. In Moore's case we have reports that indicate his deep attachment to his father. The attachment to his dead father seems to have been deeply established in his unconscious from early infancy and leads Moore, as an adolescent, to claim that "Some separation from my father's identity was necessary . . . to be free to lead my own life" (Moore 5). The paradox in Moore's life thus seems to be connected with the young Moore's will to over-identify with his dead father to the point where he is unable to live his own life. I thus take the over-identification to be the young Moore's method of covering over an unacceptable pain. I will describe that over-identification in its unconscious depths and its overarching effects.

Let us first take a look at the depth of unconscious motives present in Moore's over-identification with his father. Moore knows the story his mother told him about how he threw up the first time she breastfed him after she received the telegram announcing her husband's death (Ibid. 1). He also remembers, as a young child, the sad whispers of grown-up voices creeping into his safe haven under the table and the deep sense of sadness that would come over him (Ibid.). Furthermore, he writes that sharing his father's first name and his middle initial increased his identification with him (Ibid. 3)

Reverence for his dead father was silently reinforced by his mother not remarrying. When Moore read with his mother, fifty years or so after the death of the husband/father, the love letters to his mother, both were surprised at the intensity of the feelings expressed. Through her tears, Moore's mother said, "Now you know why I never remarried" (Ibid. 104). In addition, Moore's mother had placed a portrait of the dead father in a Marine's green uniform on her dresser; this must have nourished Moore's attachment to his absent father. Moore stresses that his father's portrait was on his mother's dresser throughout his childhood. He even calls the portrait "a sacred icon watching over [his] childhood" (Ibid. 1). Furthermore, his mother encouraged his "wearing tie clasps and carrying handkerchiefs that bore his [father's and his own] initials" (Ibid. 4), increasing his identification with his father to the point that Anthony felt he had to live his life "in a way that was worthy of being the continuation of his" (Ibid. 4).

Second, let us look at Moore's behaviors in which we can see the far-reaching effects of his identification with his father. As a child, he was fascinated with Marines: uniforms, movies, even the Marine Corps Hymn. When he had nothing else to do, the young Moore dressed up "wearing [the] green garrison cap with a bronze 2nd lieutenant's bar on it" (Ibid. 1). Later, Anthony Moore describes himself at that time in his life as being fascinated by "anything that reminded [him] of [his] father" (Ibid. 1). The young Moore "went to military high school in part to imitate [his] father's life in uniform" (Ibid.2). Introspectively, Moore writes, "I wanted to do it as well as my father, so of course I had to be an officer" (Ibid.). Moore lets us glimpse the degree of enthusiasm required to maintain the denial (or repression) when he describes that, "I completely immersed myself in the spit and polish of a cadet's life" (Ibid.). As a senior in college he took the entrance exam for the Marine Corps Officer Candidate School, just as his father had. Commenting further on his decision to take the entrance exam, Moore writes: "Joining the Marines was also one more way to imitate my father who had enlisted in the spring of his senior year in college, 1942" (Ibid.).

We can also see how images of his father influenced important decisions. Let me elaborate on the brief analysis I made in chapter one. After giving up his dream of becoming a Marine, Moore decided to enter the Novitiate of the Society of Jesus. Moore explains the decision to become a Jesuit on multiple levels. He recounts that his decision to become a Jesuit was connected with the image of his dying father. The young Moore "wanted to be worthy of the sacrifice [his] father had made" (Ibid. 3). He felt that joining the Jesuits was "dying to the world, particularly the world of marital love" (Ibid.). Moore summarizes his motives to become a Jesuit priest as follows: "I believed that becoming a priest was a debt I owed my father for the sacrifice he made in giving up his life for me" (Ibid. 3).

With the images of becoming a Jesuit and thus "dying to the world of marital love" and of "sacrifice," we enter the domain of the unconscious processes that tie Moore's conscious decision to become a Jesuit priest to his father's death. Moore informs us of two more unconscious motives connected with his father's death. Moore's awareness that his father's death closely followed his own birth led him to the unconscious belief that the world had no place for both of them and that, in some way, he was responsible for his father's death. This irrational belief led to another irrational belief: that, just as his father induced his death by fathering a child, so the young Moore would induce his death by fathering a child (Ibid. 3). Moore developed a further unconscious fantasy when relating to his maternal grandfather, who de facto played the role of a substitute father. Affection for this substitute father was tempered by negative feelings because his grandfather was not an intellectual and was temperamentally unpredictable. Furthermore, the young Moore's whole affective relationship with his maternal grandfather was infected by denial of the pain connected with his father's death. If Moore did not miss his father, how could he feel that he had a substitute father in his grandfather? Instead, Moore writes that "he preferred to pretend that [he] did not need a father, that he had learned to be his own father" (Ibid. 4).

Moore's decision to become a Jesuit priest allowed him to begin to realize the paradox in which he found himself. Moore felt that his father had not
had the opportunity to live his life fully. Therefore, the young Moore had to
live for both himself and his father. Wasting his own life on something meaningless would mean wasting his father's life and sacrifice (Ibid. 3). However,
such an over-identification with his father made it impossible for the young
Moore to carve out his own identity (Ibid. 4). Clearly, we are here in the presence of a puzzling situation in the life of the young Moore.

Evidence that Moore had taken the second step in the process of denial
appears in a train of thoughts that are totally different from those expressing
his over-identification with his father. Moore reports responding to any
inquiry about his dead and missing father by saying, "You can't miss what you
never had" (Ibid. 1). He also reports thinking that he "did not really need a
father [because he] had learned to be his own father" (Ibid. 4). Clearly, these
thoughts form the young Moore's basic denial of the pain connected with
missing a father, who had died in battle for his country. For a long time, the
deep identification with his father and the denial of emotional pain about his
loss co-existed. Nevertheless, the turmoil of the inner conflicts led Anthony
Moore to seek the help of a psychiatrist.

The third step in the process of denial occurred when Moore's psychiatrist said the words that would enable Moore to undo his denial of missing his
father. Moore's denial took the form: "You can't miss what you never had," to
which his psychiatrist answered: "You can also miss what you never had but
know you had every right to have" (Ibid. 4).

The third step almost automatically resulted in the start of the fourth
step in the process of denial. In a first stage, Moore was, as it were, the recip-
ient of a gift of life because he had acknowledged the truth. Indeed, as a result
of truthfully acknowledging, after his psychiatrist's intervention, his feeling of
loss over his dead father, Moore "began to realize how much the presence of
[his] Italian grandfather had managed to fill the vacuum" (Ibid. 4). It is true
that his grandfather's character made the young Moore ambivalent towards
him. His grandfather was not an intellectual, having completed only two
years of school in Italy (Ibid. 4). He also had an unpredictable temper. But
these two characteristics of his grandfather did not prevent Anthony Moore
from eventually accepting that his grandfather had played a "powerful role . . .
in [his] development as a man" (Ibid. 4). Three years after his grandfather's
death, Anthony Moore allowed "him [to] be the father he had always been"
(Ibid. 4). In turn, this acknowledgment of his grandfather's paternal role
"loosened the paralyzing grip of [Moore's] over-identification with [his]
father" (Ibid. 4). Allowing his grandfather "a role within [his] conscious identity" (Ibid. 4) resulted in Anthony Moore being "able to establish some sense
of identity distinct from [his] father" (Ibid. 5). Moore's intellectual undoing
of his own denial of pain over the loss of his father thus resulted in his quick

recognition of another denied truth: his grandfather's paternal function. The undoing of this secondary denial gave Moore the possibility to experience an identity distinct from his father which, he felt, gave him the freedom "to lead his own life" (Ibid. 5). Still, intellectually undoing the denial of the pain is not the same as undoing fantasies that were unconsciously created to deal with the pain.

Thus, for Moore there was a second stage of dealing with the emotional consequences of the truth behind the denial. In this stage, Moore did the psychic work to make undoing his denial more than just an intellectual act. In particular, Moore had to deal with the illusionary fantasies that had formed in his unconscious in connection with the denied importance of his father's death and his absence in the young Moore's life. That work gave Moore a greater degree of freedom. However, in conformity with a basic psychoanalytic insight, work towards freedom takes place on different levels of personality and over different periods of one's life. In my opinion, it also takes place unconsciously and thus need not wait until the moment of intellectual undoing of a denial.[4] I interpret the psychic work Moore did in his relationship with his father as steps he took towards greater freedom. Some of these steps took place before Moore himself became aware of his denial.[5] I will therefore now describe the work Moore did in advance of unmasking his denial that helped him free himself from his defective relationship with his father.

WORK TOWARDS INCREASING FREEDOM
BEFORE THE UNMASKING OF DENIAL

A first indication of the young Moore's limited freedom from complete identification with his father was his decision to avoid ROTC in college. Moore describes the motivation for this decision in the following simple terms: "At the end of four years [of military high school], I felt I had had enough of the military" (Ibid. 2). This decision to avoid the military in college had been preceded and followed by intense emotional commitment to the military. About his decision to go to military high school, Moore writes: "I went to a military high school in part to imitate my father's life in uniform. . . . I wanted to do it as well as my father, so of course I had to be an officer" (Ibid. 2). And at the end of his senior year in college, Moore again became interested in the military. He writes: "I took the entrance exam for the Marine Corps Officer Candidate School, just as my father had. . . . Joining the Marines was also one more way to imitate my father who had enlisted in the spring of his senior year in college, 1942" (Ibid. 2). What motivated Moore to interrupt his love of the Marines and the military for three years in college? Moore gives us the laconic answer: "I felt I had had enough of the military" (Ibid. 2). This is a reasonable enough motivation when we remember that just prior he had completely immersed himself "in the spit and polish of a cadet's life" (Ibid. 2).

But the motivation to say "no" to the military had no depth. For, at that time, Moore had not yet created a positive alternative, such as dreaming of becoming a teacher, a lawyer, or a doctor. Still, we do see that the young Moore is more than the ego created by a deep identification and attachment to his father. Moore is also a subject, who can allow himself to feel that he has had enough of trying to be an ideal ego.

A second indication that Moore was not totally imprisoned in his attachment to his father was his decision not to become a Marine after college. Moore describes the context of his decision this way: "But when I told my mother and grandmother what I was contemplating [becoming a Marine], I realized that the similarities to my father's situation, which inspired me, were more than they could handle. As I looked into their eyes, I realized that I could also be killed just as my father had been" (Ibid. 2). Moore transformed his mother's and grandmother's wishes into his own by the following consideration: "I wanted to do something significant with my life, dedicate myself completely to a worthy cause [like his father], but I also wanted to live" (Ibid. 2). This second "no" to the military and the Marines stuck. This "no" originated in his mother's "no." Unlike the case of his first "no," Moore went in search of an alternative course of action. He transformed his mother's motivation into one of his own by the statement: "but I also wanted to live" (Ibid. 2). However, that "no" required further work.

In 1966, during the Vietnam War, becoming a Marine carried the risk of death. Moore made his mother's fear his own motivation by realizing that he wanted to live. Not becoming a Marine and being unwilling to die entailed that the young Moore cut two important ties with his father. The young Moore's psychic work consisted of finding a way to cut yet preserve these two important ties. A realistic solution seemed impossible given his decision not to become a Marine and thereby avoid the risk of death. Nevertheless, what cannot be done realistically can be done in imagination or, better, in the technical language of Lacanian psychoanalysis, via metaphorical moves.

The young Moore re-established psychic contact with his father, the Marine who died for his country, through a metaphorical move in two steps. First, Moore reports his fascination with the priesthood. One point stands out for the young Moore: the prayer for the dead. The rubrics request the faithful to mention the name of any dead person they want to be remembered. When he whispered "my father," Moore reports that he was with his father and his father with him (Ibid. 3). The young Moore reports "that in the liturgy of the Mass I experienced a unique moment of contact with my father. At Mass I discovered a mystery that transcended the power of death. Being a priest was a way to enter more fully into the power of that mystery" (Ibid. 3).

Second, Moore enriched his admiration for the priesthood, developed in his childhood, by a number of metaphors. We already saw that becoming a Jesuit was, for the young Moore, becoming like his father because it entailed a deadly sacrifice in the form of "dying to the world of marital love" (Ibid. 3) and because Jesuits were sometimes called "the Pope's Marines" (Ibid. 3). That the metaphorical work done by the young Moore was not purely rational is evident in the information Moore provided, information which Moore discovered only years after his decision to become a Jesuit. "When I entered the Jesuits, I was twenty-three years old . . . the same age my father was when he died" (Ibid, 3). At age twenty-three, Moore's father died physically; Moore "died" metaphorically.

The young Moore, in refusing to be a Marine who would be in danger of being killed in Vietnam, cut two important ties with his father. In becoming a Jesuit he metaphorically reconnected with these two eminent characteristics of his father: he became a Marine of the Pope and he was prepared to die to the world of marital love.

As Moore reports it, the metaphorical move of becoming a Jesuit, not a Marine, was helpful, but ultimately deficient. It was helpful insofar as the *Spiritual Exercises* of Saint Ignatius teach a method of reflection and prayer that engages the imagination in an inner dialogue with the characters of one's own life and the life of Christ (Ibid. 3). Moore reports that this form of prayer and reflection initiated a healing process which stalled, however, around issues related to his father (Ibid. 3). As Moore describes it: "A key meditation involves an intimate dialogue with God the Father. Surprisingly, I was unable to develop any real feeling around this conversation except one of frustration. For all my fascination with things pertaining to my father, he remained somehow affectively unreal and emotionally unavailable to me. These spiritual exercises clarified areas of my inner life in which I needed healing" (Ibid. 3).

Moore provides a description of the difficulty in his life that needed healing. He writes that psychoanalysis, in particular analysis of his dreams, clarified "many of the psychological distortions that inhibited my freedom. I realized that I identified with my father so completely that I was unable to be myself" (Ibid. 4). This self-description accords with Lacan's and De Waelhens's theoretical claim that distance in an identificatory relation is required in order to have the feeling of being a self. These two authors make their claim with reference to the identification with the mother (De Waelhens 1978, 81, 90,126; Lacan 1984, 57). But their claim, I wish to argue, is made with reference to identification in general, so that it can clarify the vicissitudes of the identification with either the mother or the father.

WORK TOWARDS INCREASING FREEDOM AFTER UNMASKING DENIAL

As described before, the young Moore was given the opportunity to psychologically separate himself from his father after his psychoanalyst helped him to acknowledge the pain of not having a father. Indeed, acknowledging the pain of being fatherless allowed Anthony Moore to accept that his grandfather had been an unacknowledged substitute father. Then, acknowledging the role his grandfather had played in the formation of his identity gave young Moore the ability to create "some sense of identity distinct from [his] father" (Moore 5). Moore thereby felt free enough to proceed to ordination as deacon in 1979 and priest in 1980.

Moore describes his ordination and the celebration of his first Mass as marked by a pull to the death of his father. He writes: "Lying prostate in prayer on the sanctuary floor, I could vividly sense my father's presence in the ordination ritual. . . . In my imagination, I saw him at the moment of death consoled by a vision of his son's ordination. . . . The next day, I celebrated my First Mass. On June 15, the 36th anniversary of my father's death, I led my family in prayer: 'Remember, Lord, those who have died and have gone before us marked with the sign of faith, especially those for whom we now pray.' As I voiced the words of this prayer, I again felt my father's presence. . . . By being ordained a priest I was completing a mission entrusted to me at my father's death" (Ibid. 5).

For Anthony Moore, becoming a priest had not been guided by a future mission, for example, helping the poor, teaching in the inner city, or ministering in far away places. Instead, his ordination was overwhelmingly tied to the past: the death of his father. Anthony Moore created a future for himself as a priest by seeing himself as "completing a mission entrusted to [him] at his father's death" (Ibid. 5). "The coincidence of the anniversary of his [father's] death with [his] first ritual action as a priest intensified [his] feeling of destiny . . . [he] believed [he] was doing what [he] was destined to do" (Ibid. 5). The metaphor of destiny or mission to be completed turned out not to be powerful enough to carry the weight of the decision to remain a priest. Indeed, Anthony Moore writes that as priest he was "aware of a longing deep in [his] soul that remained unfulfilled. . . . [He] felt a hole inside of [himself] which, no matter how hard [he] tried [he] could not fill. . . . It was . . . as though something were missing at the core of [his] being and needed to be found" (Ibid. 5).

IMPORTANCE OF HELP FROM OTHERS IN MOORE'S PSYCHIC WORK

Moore's further work towards freedom required the help of others. First, four women played an important role in the steps that Anthony Moore took towards freedom. They were: his mother and grandmother, who helped him break away from his complete and unconscious identification with his father; his female psychiatrist, who helped him acknowledge the pain of missing a father; and finally Michelle, who became his wife and who made it possible for him to emotionally break down at his father's grave (Moore 6–7).

The Jungian-inspired movie *Field of Dreams* also had a role in helping Anthony Moore. It provided the conviction that recovering a lost father is possible. It also provided him with guideposts for such a recovery. It taught Anthony Moore that one needs to listen to calls from within; that one needs to respond to those calls with symbolic action; that one needs to wait attentively; that one needs to make an inward journey; and that, at the appropriate time, a connection with ancestors is possible. In accepting the need to listen to an inner voice, Moore was aware that his personal identity was broader than his current conscious ego or the "I" that is "presently organizing and directing [his] life" (Ibid. 40). He now conceived of his personal identity as involving an inner dialogue with an "I" other than his current conscious ego. He accepted that his current conscious ego is not "the center of all experience and the source of all knowledge" (Ibid. 40). Something in him transcended his conscious ego. Moore called it a mystery. He personally believed it to be an encounter with God, but made it clear that this was his subjective interpretation of the experienced transcendence of the inner voice (Ibid. 40).

To connect emotionally with the journey prescribed for him by his trust in the story of *Field of Dreams*, Moore, at several turns, used metonymic moves supported by others' words. Thus, whereas the protagonist of *Field of Dreams* heard the call to make a baseball field, Anthony Moore heard the call to write a book about his search for his father. However, he entertained two other possibilities: visiting the Marine Corps Archives in Suitland, Maryland to study his father's military career or traveling to Saipan where his father died. Moore wondered whether writing a book would require sufficient physical activity to satisfy his conscious wish to take the call seriously. Recalling Seamus Heaney's poem comparing "the symbolic action of writing with the physical labor of digging" (Ibid. 41), Moore was able to accept the call to write a book about his search for his father. Still, the work of writing was slow. It is true that *Field of Dreams* recommended patience and attentive waiting; but doubts arose in Moore. He repeatedly dealt with these doubts by remembering a letter Teilhard de Chardin wrote to his impatient niece Marguerite when he was a stretcher-bearer in the French army during World War I. Moore felt that his father was using a condensed form of de Chardin's letter to admonish his son: "Trust in the slow work of God. Your ideas mature gradually. Let them grow. Let them shape themselves. Don't try to force them on" (Ibid. 43). The metonymic connection between the message of *Field of Dreams*, the words of Theilhard de Chardin, and his own father made Moore feel that the "unconscious would not fail to do its part" (Ibid. 44) in the healing work of writing his book.

Moore's inner journey took a step forward when he and Michelle visited a replica of the labyrinth in the Cathedral at Chartres. Both, but Anthony in particular, took several meditative walks through the labyrinth. During the third day's meditative walk, Moore "found [himself] thinking about [his] mother and her difficulties with the early stages of Alzheimer's disease" (Ibid. 46). Moore felt "a deep sense of sadness well up inside [himself]" (Ibid. 46).

Moore was puzzled because he had always felt happy when thinking about his mother. She "symbolizes all the security and love I knew as a child" and "provided the safe container within which I was able to weather the loss of my father" (Ibid. 46). The feelings of sadness he now felt were normally associated with "those rare moments when [he] allowed [himself] to feel the sorrow of [his] father's absence" (Ibid. 46). Moore discerned sadness for "the suffering [his] mother would encounter as she moved through the various stages of this cruel disease" (Ibid. 46), but also his "father's sadness as he experienced [his] mother's illness. [He] could feel inside of [himself his] father's abiding love and solicitude for the once-young bride he left so long ago" (Ibid. 46). In his sadness, Moore "realized that [his] father and [he] were joined together in [their] concern for [his] mother" (Ibid. 46).

In *Field of Dreams*, the protagonist, Ray Kinsella, ultimately meets and bonds with his father. Recalling the passage from Virgil's *Aeneid* when Aeneas meets his father Anchises, Moore experiences "the yearning of mortals down through the ages to remain connected to those from whom they receive life and those to whom they give life" (Ibid. 48). Moore sees in both *Field of Dreams* and the *Aeneid* the same message: "this world and the next are more closely woven together than usually imagined. The separation between these two realms is less real than the continuity between them. Therefore, the longing of the human heart for connection between the generations is not a futile yearning based on illusion, but a consoling truth grounded in reality" (Ibid. 49). This time it is the metonymic fusion of the movie and a passage from the *Aeneid* that allows Moore to take his next step: "[He] decided to follow the path of [his] own 'filial devotion'" (Ibid. 49). Moore started to collect photographs of his father in his "dress green lieutenant's uniform" and placed them on his desk and the shelves of the room where he was writing his book. Moore followed up on a memory that his father's uniform was in an old trunk in the basement of his mother's house. In the trunk, he found his father's uniform next to his mother's wedding gown. He brought his father's uniform to his study and felt that his father "was actually in the room with [him]" (Ibid. 51). Some weeks later, driving back from Richmond to Washington, Moore followed the exit sign for Quantico Marine Base, where his father had done his officer's training. He walked around the one building that was old enough to have been there in the 1940s. When he came home he confirmed from his father's graduation book that the building he had toured was indeed the Reserve Officers' Barracks, where his father had been trained. These two encounters gave Anthony Moore the trust that "there was a realm beyond the barriers of time and death where [his] father and [he] could meet" (Ibid. 52). He even "felt his healing touch" (Ibid. 52).

Moore was also helped by soldiers who knew his father. At this point in his life, Moore was ready to leave what he calls "the inner soul work" and make the pilgrimage to find people who knew his father. Following leads,

Moore met seven or eight men who revealed progressively more details about his father as a person and about the circumstances of his death. In a reunion of the Fourth Marines, an old soldier, Carl Dearborn, recognized Moore as Lt. Anthony Moore's son. Anthony Moore was struck because "No one outside [his] family had ever recognized [him] as [his] father's son" (Ibid. 57). Dearborn sent Anthony Moore a poem about a soldier falling, a woman becoming a widow, and an infant becoming an orphan. This made Moore realize that he wanted to go back to the moment when his father died. Dearborn put him in contact with Gunny Hart and Chuck Landmesser, both of whom were with his father when he died. Gunny Hart told Anthony Moore: "Your father never knew what hit him." . . . "He didn't suffer at all." . . . "You can be proud of your father. He was a good marine. Nobody can say anything against him" (Ibid. 58).

After a prolonged introduction, Chuck Landmesser told Anthony Moore: "There is something I will always remember about your dad, and that is the way he felt about your mother, Palma. Other guys might talk about their wives in a way that was not respectful, but 'A.T.' would never do that. There was only one love for your father and that was your mother" (Ibid. 63). Anthony Moore, overwhelmed with emotions could only say: "My mother returned his love; she never remarried." To which Chuck nodded: "I know" (Ibid. 63). The younger Moore heard his father speak in the words of Chuck and telling him "how much he loved [the younger Moore's] mother and by implication how much he loved him, the fruit of their love" (Ibid. 63). Moore felt that his father had this message for him: "[his] parents' love for each other and for [him] was the one truth to remember and live by, that [he] should live [his] life in the same way, letting all else in [his] life be shaped by [his] love for Michelle and the boys [his step-children]" (Ibid. 63). Moore was hereby *transforming an idealized father into a goal for his own life, an ego ideal, something he had not done as a Jesuit priest.*

Moore's journey to San Antonio for an annual meeting of the Fourth Marine Division, provided further important metonymic connections. In San Antonio, Moore was confronted with the life-size statue of the city's patron saint. His mother held a special devotion to St. Anthony because her husband had been born on that saint's feast day and also named after him. St. Anthony's statue in San Antonio "held a small boy in his arms" (Ibid. 66). Anthony Moore writes that he let the symbol speak to him. He almost felt his "father's protective arms wrapped around him" (Ibid. 66–67).

Three further pieces of information, given by his father's buddies and found in publications about the war in the Marshalls, were particularly useful for Anthony Moore. The first concerned a peccadillo committed by his father. The second provided details about his father's character which Anthony Moore could identify as his own ideals. The third furnished details about his father's concerns and the actions during the last months of his life.

INFORMATION ABOUT HIS FATHER

The first piece of information was provided by a close friend of Anthony Moore's parents during the war. His name was Walter Ridlon. Moore's father had gambled with Walt and lost all his money. Moore's mother, meeting Walt's wife, had explained how her husband had lost what remained of his month's pay to Walt. Walt's wife returned the money and later explained the situation to her husband. Walt offered to return the money and let Anthony Moore, Sr. pay his debts when he could. His wife retorted—so Walter Ridlon told the young Anthony Moore—that she had already returned the money to the Moores and that Walt would never see any of it (Ibid. 67). After telling the story, both Walt and the younger Moore broke into laughter. The story of how Moore had gambled away his family's funds had been told with such warmth by his father's close friend that the younger Moore could make use of the story for further healing. Moore tells it this way:

> I could feel my father coming to life. His human shortcomings made him more alive, more real for me. He was no longer a perfect, idealized hero, but a man of flesh and blood who could be foolish, make mistakes and get into the kind of trouble from which his wife had to rescue him.
>
> Learning about my father's peccadillos was a liberating experience. Trying to be the perfect son of an ideal father was a burden that often got in the way of my being myself. I wondered whether I inherited my incompetence as a gambler from my father. Then I thought about some of my other shortcomings and wondered whether they might also be a gift from him, and therefore something to be prized. Just thinking about my father in this way created a more balanced hero archetype for me to follow. Another gap in my fatherless childhood was being filled. (Ibid. 67–68)

For Moore, the effect of learning about his father's gambling was totally different than it had been for Freud's patient the "Ratman." For the Ratman, his father's gambling was one more reason for great ambivalence towards his father, as it was connected with stealing money from friends to pay off gambling debts (Freud, S.E., X, 151–319). For the younger Moore, his father's gambling led to a family embarrassment which was relieved by family friends. Furthermore, the story had been lovingly told by his father's friend, transforming a gambling fiasco into a charming peccadillo. This story allowed Anthony Moore to deidealize his father, without losing respect for him. Walter Ridlon's story was an exceptional gift to Anthony Moore who successfully used it to reconstruct his psychic world.

Speaking with some of his father's fellow soldiers, Moore gathered a second kind of information consisting of a series of revelations about his father's character and his interactions with other people. From Charlie Eaton, a member of his father's platoon, Anthony Moore learned that his father could joke with his friends. Eaton, who could barely speak because of his strokes, told the younger Moore: "Your father was a real man" (Ibid. 69). Burke Dixon, another soldier friend, told Anthony Moore that his "father was his favorite officer" (Ibid. 72). Burke continued by telling the younger Moore: "Your father was a great listener. . . . You could always go to him with your problem. We were just young kids away from home for the first time so you can imagine how many problems we had. Your father would always listen and try to help. After he was killed things were never quite the same for me. When the war was over, I told my wife if we ever had a son I wanted to name him Anthony after Lt. Moore" (Ibid. 72). The younger Moore felt "proud of his father. He was the kind of man other men respected and even loved. He was down-to-earth, a regular guy, someone who cared about his men and tried to help them. He was a role model who could have inspired [Anthony]" (Ibid. 73). Anthony Moore felt sad that he had missed such a father to whom he could have gone for counsel. However, at a deeper level the younger Moore recognized something. He wrote:

> I recognized in my father the kind of man that I tried to be. So much of what comes naturally to me seemed also to have been a part of him. When I heard Burke [Dixon] describe my father as a good listener, someone you could always go to with your problems, I recalled how as a new teacher at Georgetown, I would sit and listen to college freshmen as they described their struggles to adjust to college and to find a direction for their lives. I also recalled how I loved to give retreats and spiritual direction because they gave me an opportunity to connect with other people on such a deep and intimate level. I now recognized how much this natural ability that had so shaped my life was a gift from my father. I could feel him living and breathing in me as I did the work I most like to do. More importantly, I could see my father in my relationship with my sons. As I recalled sitting with my eighteen-year-old son at two in the morning discussing his problems, I realized that I had become the father my father never had a chance to be. (Ibid. 74)

Some months later, discovering an Indian belief that when a father dies, his vitality is carried over into the son, Anthony Moore made a further step in creating a dialogical identity when he writes: "I recognized in my own unique personality the secret vitality of my father's ongoing life within me. What others loved in me and what I most enjoyed about myself were gifts of his presence. If I wanted to be with my father, I only needed to live the life I had been given and to do it with enthusiasm and gratitude" (Ibid. 74).

The third type of information concerned the worries and actions taken by Lt. Moore during the last months of his life. The younger Moore became deeply engaged in his father's experience of the battle of Roi-Namur, the battle he survived. One of the facts that stood out in Lt. Moore's Roi-Namur experience was how the battle ended. Lt. Moore's mortar platoon was positioned 125 yards from the end of the island with the remaining enemy force in between (Ibid. 94). Moore possessed a firing table for the 60 mm mortar guns indicating the angle of elevation for shooting various distances. Unfortunately, the firing table did not provide the angles for distances less than two hundred yards and thus was completely useless in the final hours of the battle for Roi-Namur (Ibid. 94). This fact must have been very disturbing to Lt. Moore, as it put his men in mortal danger. When resting in Maui after the battle of Roi-Namur, Lt. Moore took corrective action. "Lt. Moore and Burke Dixon spent the afternoon of Easter Sunday firing a mortar and calculating the approximate angle of elevation for distances of 100, 125, 150, and 175 yards. The lieutenant then wrote the corresponding ranges and settings in blue ink at the top of the firing table" (Ibid. 97). Easter Sunday was the last day about which the younger Moore was able to get information about his father before he was killed in the first day of attack on Saipan. Consulting his calendar, the younger Moore dated Easter in 1944 as April 9. Moore himself was born the next Sunday, April 16, 1944. Lt. Moore died June 15, 1944. The younger Moore had always known the dates of his birth and his father's death. We know that he unconsciously interpreted the closeness of the two dates as meaning that there was no room in the world for both him and his father. The younger Moore also "felt [unconsciously] that [his] birth had caused his [father's] death" (Ibid. 98). Moore furthermore confessed that he believed fathering a child would lead to his own death (Ibid. 3). The younger Moore thus says that "the temporal sequence of April 16 and June 15, the dates respectively of my birth and my father's death [was] an inevitability that held me captive" (Ibid. 98). That temporal sequence made the younger Moore feel guilty about his existence and fear that fatherhood, for him, would entail an unconsciously announced death sentence. The younger Moore was able to use the information about his father's activity on Easter 1944, a week before his own birth, to undo the deadly grip of his own unconscious beliefs about the relationship between his birth and his father's death. Moore describes the transformation of his unconscious beliefs as follows:

> The new date, April 9, opened the possibility of an alternative temporal sequence, April 9 and April 16, a sequence that suggested a different pattern of meaning: two Sundays bracketing the First Week of Easter. Instead of associating my birth (April 16) with my father's death (June 15), I could now link my birth with a day in my father's life (April 9), an Easter Sunday celebrating our birth to new life in Christ's Resurrection. By joining our two lives together at the beginning and end of Easter Week, the dates of April 9 and April 16 provided a life-giving sequence to counterbalance the deadly sequence of April 16 and June 15. (Ibid. 98)

Moore confesses: "Learning what my father was doing on April 9 changed my attitude towards my own birth. Previously, I had viewed my birth as the prelude to my father's death. Now, I could relate my birth to a week in my father's life and, more importantly, a week that celebrated the mystery of the resurrection of the dead" (Ibid. 98). Moore gives us a description of how he made the change. He writes:

> The symbolism of the two Sundays bracketing the First Week of Easter focused my attention on the meaning of the liturgical seasons. Easter is the central feast of the Christian liturgical year, a ritual calendar of seasons that transforms secular time into sacred time by recapitulating the story of Christ's life, death and resurrection. The firing table that I held in my hand became a tangible symbol, a sacrament, that my father's life and mine were united in sacred time, a time that transcends the limitations of secular time, the First Week of Easter. By recapitulating the story of the final months of my father's journey to wholeness, I entered into sacred time where my own journey of healing came to a close. (Ibid. 98–99)

The sacred time of Easter calls upon Christians to have hope. What was the hope that the younger Moore experienced and created that could counterbalance the deadly belief that his birth caused his father's death? Moore himself gives us the answer. Meditating on his father's love letters to his mother, the younger Moore writes: "Reading about his hopes and dreams for the future—dreams that had appeared to die on the beach of Saipan—I saw clearly that the heart of those dreams had come true in my own life. I had been privileged and blessed to live the life he had dreamed of living" (Ibid. 105). The younger Moore was now able to experience himself as the realization of his father's dreams, not the cause of their destruction. He thereby liberated himself from the tyranny of the unconscious fantasy that his birth had caused the death of his father whom he missed so much.

Reflecting on the psychic work he did, Moore writes: "Telling my father's story healed the fracture that ran through my psyche at my father's death. I have now come to understand how, with simple fragments like a cardboard firing table . . . we can weave together a pattern of meaning to heal our psychic wounds. Following the guidance of the deeper self, I have learned how to re-weave the fabric of my soul and 'come home' to the wholeness I lost at my father's death" (Ibid. 101). The younger Moore understood that his deepest gifts and commitments were both his own attributes and the fulfilment of his father's dreams. Moore understood himself to be both himself and himself as a gift for his father. By the metaphor of being a gift to his father, the younger Moore was able to overcome the unconscious feeling that he had killed his father because there wasn't room in the world for the two of them. Now he feels that he is his father's dream come true. He has, at the same time, overcome the unconscious identification that was at work during his denial of the pain caused by his father's absence. Moore is now able to appreciate and commit himself to the talents and values that he feels are uniquely his own. Undoing the denial allowed the younger Moore to make the metaphoric move that set him free. From Moore's story, we learn that the tragedy of denial is that it blocks the metaphoric work necessary to become an individuated self.

2. PHILOSOPHICAL CONCLUSIONS

BUILDING BLOCKS TOWARDS EMOTIONALLY OVERCOMING THE EFFECTS OF DENIAL

Overcoming the effects of denial is an intersubjective enterprise. Moore is only able to overcome the effects of his denial with the assistance of others. The four women who helped him created a form of communion that made painful acknowledgments possible. First, there was his mother and grandmother whose "no" allowed the younger Moore to put limitations on his identification with his father. Moore wanted to be like his father but did not want to die. His psychiatrist-psychoanalyst was also instrumental in Moore's recognition and acknowledgment of his denial. Finally, there was Michelle, whose presence allowed Moore to break down near the grave of his father (Moore 6).

The six or seven soldier friends of Lt. Moore were also of invaluable help. They provided Moore with testimony about his father's characteristics. The soldiers' stories allowed the younger Moore to recognize Lt. Moore's capacity to listen, the care he took of his soldiers, and his ability to elicit his soldiers' caring. In these stories Moore found an ideal he could admire in his father and in himself.

The poems and classic pieces of literature that Moore remembered at crucial turns of his journey provided help of a more subtle kind. Moore used the writings of the prophets Elijah and Ezekiel to aid in following the advice in *Field of Dreams* that one must pay attention to the "small voice" in one's self (Ibid. 38, 39). He made use of a poem by Seamus Heaney comparing "the symbolic action of writing with the physical labor of digging" (Ibid. 41). That poetic comparison allowed Moore to accept that his call to write a book was as important as the physical labor undertaken by Ray Kinsella, who dug a baseball field in *Field of Dreams*. Moore made use of Teilhard de Chardin's letter to his impatient niece to accept the patient waiting required in what Moore calls "soul work" (Ibid. 43). Moore makes use of Virgil's description of his meeting with his father, Anchises, in order to inspire confidence that meeting between generations is possible (Ibid. 47–49). Moore makes use of Gerard Manley Hopkin's poem "Heaven-Haven" to interpret his father participation in the battle of Roi-Namur as a preparation for his death in the next battle at Saipan.

Moore received various kinds of help from a variety of sources. For example, the writer/director of *Field of Dreams* provided Moore with milestones for his inner journey. The writings of Saint Ignatius provided Moore with, among other things, the techniques for using imagination to make progress in one's inner soul work. Jung provided Moore with a psychological frame for his journey.

The symbolic system that Moore inhabited provided yet another form of help. His experience with the Jesuits gave him the opportunity to separate himself from his father by declining to become a Marine and instead to metaphorically unite himself with his father. Becoming a Jesuit was, in the symbolic system of Catholicism, becoming a "Marine of the Pope" and was also dying to "worldly life," in particularly to "marital love." The symbolic system of Catholicism provided Moore great help in another effort. Indeed, success in undoing his deadly interpretation of a causal relationship between his birth and his father's death depended heavily upon the younger Moore's belief in the symbolic system of Christianity, in particular: the hope empha-sized by the theme of Easter .

The crucial importance of saying "no." Moore does not delineate the pain he experienced growing up without a father. But he does describe the suffocating identification with his father to the point that he felt he was not himself. I therefore take his over-identification to be closely connected to the pain cov-ered over by his denial. At first glance, it is puzzling that Anthony Moore would find a solution to his unconscious belief about the cause of his father's death by way of closely identifying his life with that of his father. Indeed, the younger Moore ends his journey when he sees his life as more similar to his father's than he had realized. Why would such a realization bring healing rather than alienation? This question can be answered if we provide a more detailed phenomenological description of the end of young Moore's journey. Moore writes: "I was amazed to discover how much of my father lives in me. It felt as though the core of his soul lived on in my soul. We were so alike in the things that really mattered to us" (Moore 104); or "if I ever want to be with my father, all I have to do is look deeply in my own soul" (Ibid. 105); or "I realized that the resemblance ran down to the depth of my being" (Ibid. 104–105). I interpret these statements to mean that the younger Moore expe-rienced a self of his own that he then discovered bore a great resemblance to his father. Rather than feeling alienated, the younger Moore feels that he received a gift. He feels that he is the fulfillment of the dreams of his father. He is that by being himself. I wish to call the double identity that Moore cre-ates at the end of his journey a metaphor. The younger Moore experiences himself as his own person but at the same time as the gift to his father with whom he discovers that he has so many similarities. The younger Moore is himself and he is also something other than himself. He is both at the same time. It is this identity in nonidentity that provides Moore the healing he sought. For this healing to take place there must be a nonidentity in the iden-tity with his father. When Moore describes his adolescent experience, he writes that he identified so deeply with his father that he felt he was not himself. Between his adolescence and the healing end of his journey we have a great similarity and a great difference. The similarity is that in both cases the younger Moore deeply identifies with his father. The obvious difference is that in his adolescence Moore felt threatened and alienated by the close identification, whereas at the end of his journey the similarity he discovers with his father is experienced as a welcome gift. A less obvious difference is that Moore, as an adolescent, feels that he identifies too deeply with his father, whereas the mature Moore discovers that his deeper self is surprisingly similar to that of his father. The mature Moore thus has lived a life of his own that he discovers resembles his father's life. In the mature Moore we do not have a felt identity between the younger Moore and his father, we have a discovered similarity. Between Moore's youth and maturity something happened that allowed Moore to feel that his life was his own, not his father's. I think that the mature Moore's belief that he has lived his own life goes back to the two "no"s that he expressed toward the identification with his father. The first "no" did not stick. It was the time when he did not join the ROTC in college because he had had enough of the military. This "no" had no foundation and in time was overruled by Moore's desire to become a Marine officer. At that point a second "no" appeared. It was a "no" introduced by Moore's mother and grandmother who feared that in becoming a Marine, he might also die. Somehow the younger Moore made the "no" of his mother and grandmother his own by means of his own wish to live; he did not want to die. From then on, the young Moore had to make his own life. As we saw, the younger Moore created a life for himself in which he metaphorically incorporated the image of his father. He became a Jesuit. Even if a Jesuit is a "Marine of the Pope" and dies to marital love, it is also true that a Jesuit is not a real Marine and does not take the risk of real death. In becoming a Jesuit, the younger Moore took distance from total identification with his father and started the process of finding an identity for himself which was not a total identification with his father.

The role of metaphor in creating freedom. Identification is a powerful motive for self-worth. It is also a great source of self-alienation. The solution to this problem seems to be an unsolvable paradox. To avoid alienation one needs to give up identification. To have self-respect one needs identification with an admired model. Realistically, however, one cannot, at the same time, identify with someone and not identify with that person. Although one cannot do that realistically, one can do it metaphorically. Moore made two very important metaphoric moves in his life. The first one was his substitution of being a Jesuit for being a Marine. The second was feeling that he was a gift to his father rather than the unconsciously felt cause of his father's death.

The first metaphor proved not to be definitive. The second metaphor succeeded, according to Moore's testimony in overruling and neutralizing the deadly unconscious belief that he—the younger Moore—was the cause of his father's death. Moore was able to do so by recognizing that there was a secular time with two important dates: his birth and his father's death. There was also a sacred time with a new date: Easter Sunday, the last day of his father's life, about which the younger Moore had information. His own birthday became associated with Easter, because it was the Sunday after Easter. The sacred time connection—between Easter Sunday, when Lt. Moore used his free time to act to protect his soldiers' futures, and the Sunday after Easter, when the younger Moore was born—is at first only a new connection in time without real weight. However, in the Christian calendar, the eight days between Easter Sunday and the Sunday after Easter comprise a week in which the dominant theme is one of hope, whereby life overcomes death. When the younger Moore started to realize that his father had made an effort on Easter Sunday to better protect his soldiers, he could then begin to understand his birth as a sign of hope as well. The younger Moore began to realize that what he liked in his life, such as listening to others and loving his wife, were also the things that his father was good at. Slowly, the younger Moore was able to realize that he was the gift to his father in which the "hopes and the dreams for the future—dreams that had appeared to die on the beach of Saipan— . . . had come true in [his] own life" (Moore 105). The metaphor of gift and of hope, based around the theme of Easter hope, is the metaphor by which the younger Moore was able to override his unconscious belief that he was the cause of his father's death. The work of healing his soul ended when Moore could experience himself, not just as the son of Lt. Moore, but also as the gift to the dead Lt. Moore, a gift by which the dead father could complete his own life. It is worth noticing that the healing work relied heavily upon the younger Moore's deep belief in the symbolic system of his Christian culture. Moore did not create his metaphoric solution out of nothing. He created it with the help of and in continuity with his culture.

PHILOSOPHICAL IMPLICATIONS

The idea of a rational autonomous individual. Some authors argue that human beings are rational and autonomous. The analysis of denial and its overcoming in the case of Anthony Moore teaches us that we need to amend this theory of human beings.

Part of the denial in Anthony Moore's early life was his belief that he did not miss his father and, furthermore, that his grandfather did not have an important role, because he felt he was his own father. Rather than being a sign of autonomy in the face of a great loss, this affirmation of autonomy was an instance of self-deceit. It prevented Moore from psychological growth. Real growth depended upon Moore being able to acknowledge the truth of his deep hurt that he missed a father while growing up. As we have shown

before, healing the wound of the lost father, including healing the unconscious guilt about the loss of his father, came about when the young Moore
was able to feel that he was not just his father's son but also a gift to his father.
The young Moore healed himself by accepting that he was not only an
autonomous being but also connected with someone. The young Moore further healed himself by learning to live his life as a gift to his dead father.

Rational arguments could not override Moore's unconscious belief in
himself as the cause of his father's death. No rational argument could undo
his feeling that the short time between his birth and his father's death meant
that there was no room for both of them. The younger Moore was able to
neutralize his damaging unconscious belief but not by means of clever rational arguments. The younger Moore's healing work was not the work of rational analysis and argument; it was metaphoric work, the patient work of making a metaphor stick. Intergenerational connection and metaphoric work are
therefore ideas that must complement the claim that human beings are rational and autonomous.

Self-deception and denial. The analysis of Moore's autobiography about the
undoing of his denial can also help us clarify the concept of self-deception. In
particular, the case of Moore illustrates the idea that a self-deception can be
made in good faith and must therefore be distinguished from a lie.

The younger Moore deceived himself when he was telling himself and
others during his adolescence that he could not miss his father since he had
never had one. However, Moore made an effort to develop a form of self-conception that was in accord with this denial. First, he imagined that he was
able to be his own father. Second, he refused to acknowledge the paternal
function played by his grandfather. As long as Moore was able to maintain
these two beliefs, he could be said to have possessed important evidence for
taking as true what others were interpreting to be a self-deception. Moore
knew that he had been deceiving himself only after his psychiatrist-psychoanalyst addressed his denial and told him that you can also miss what you
never had but know that you had every right to have.[6] At that moment the
younger Moore knew that he had been deceiving himself; he knew that his
claim to have not missed a father because he had never had one was a denial.
Therefore, persons can deceive themselves without knowing that they are
doing so. Self-deception is thus, strictly speaking, not a lie.

The study of Moore's autobiography allows us to pinpoint the moment
when self-deception can become a lie. It becomes a lie after the denial has
been intellectually undone and the person refuses to do the emotional work
involved in taking the steps implied by the intellectual undoing. As Moore
was willing to do that emotional work, his self-deception never became a lie.

Explaining self-deception and denial requires that one accept at least
two layers of intentionality. In Moore's case we are able to clearly see these

two layers at work. There is first the ego which ostensibly organizes Moore's life. Moore's ego decides to go to the military school, not to enter ROTC in college, and to take the entrance exam for the Marine Corps Officer Candidate School. However, another layer of Moore—let us use the Freudian label, the unconscious—performed its own intentional acts. Long before the conscious ego made its adolescent decisions, Moore's unconscious had already interpreted the death of his father and had deeply identified with his dead father. This unconscious layer makes interpretations with a logic which is referred to by Freud as primary process. One crucial feature of the logic of unconscious interpretation is that the child gives itself a form of omnipotence. In an illusionary way, the child feels that it causes all important events around himself. Thus, when Moore's father dies a short time after he is born, the younger Moore feels, unconsciously, that he caused the death of his father. He also feels that fathering a child will guarantee imminent death for himself. Similarly, the younger Moore unconsciously idealizes and identifies with the dead father, who was so beloved by his wife. Moore's conscious ego deals with the paradox of unconscious ideations (unconscious guilt for the father's death and idealization and identification with the dead father) by, on the one hand, making decisions that allow him to be like his father and, on the other hand, by publicly denying that he misses his dead father. The healing work Moore performed starts the moment when Moore accepts that he is a multi-layered person in whom the conscious ego needs to listen to a voice beyond the ego. Furthermore, the conscious ego accepts the humility entailed in listening to that other voice. The conscious ego thereby accepts that it has to change.

An outsider may correctly ascribe self-deception to a person when he can see several forms of interpretation at work that contradict each other. Ascribing self-deception to a person at a moment when that person is not aware of self-deception is a teleological move. The expectation is that a person with multiple layers is also called upon to act as a unified person.[7] Aiding that teleological move requires that one be artful. To accuse another of self-deceit is not helpful. Rather, one should say the appropriate words so that the other can intellectually undo his own denial and thereby accept an invitation to differently address the paradox behind the self-deceit. As we have seen, that requires psychic work and the creation of appropriate metaphors.

Conclusion

1. A person who utters a denial reveals much to someone who can listen. In a denial, one reveals something that one also tries to hide. A denial is thus not just any kind of self-revelation. It is a revelation about a fault or a fracture in one's own personality. A person "in denial" is unable to deal with an emerging truth. A denial, thus, reveals not only content, but also personality structure, a kind of fracture in the person in question.

2. The revelation that occurs in a denial testifies to the fact that the person is growing in ability to name and face the truth. The need to hide what has been revealed in a denial points to a weakness in the individual. He has not been able to face the truth he is in the process of revealing. The inability to have faced the truth is not trickery. It indicates a deficiency in agency. But where there is a deficiency in agency, one needs to be careful in assigning moral blame. I argue that Freudian forms of denials should not be called lies. They should not be classified as moral failures, but rather as human deficiencies.

3. Freud teaches us that denials are frequently occurring phenomena. Appealing to Hegel's thought, I demonstrated that denials do not just occur frequently, but are unavoidable, even necessary. For Hegel, truth is not just an epistemological task. It is also an anthropological adventure. The anthropological adventure is such that emotions become involved because truth is about the meaning of one's own existence. Doubt, therefore, can become despair. Hegel also teaches us that human beings face paradoxes that can be solved only by several human beings acting jointly. In some cases the approach of no one person is satisfactory, even though it appears to the person acting that his/her approach is the only possible solution to a given problem. Facing the deficiency of one's own solution is not just a matter of doubt. It is also a matter of despair. Denials are a defensive, and thus defective way, to deal with truths that may cause one despair.

4. Even though denials are defensive moves, they are also moves towards greater freedom. Towards the end of his article on negation, Freud explicitly

connects the use of denial with the quest for freedom. He credits the use of negation with the ability to create "a first measure of freedom from . . . the compulsion of the pleasure principle" (S.E., XIX, 239). Hegel's study of the will in his *Philosophy of Right* provides a view of the different methods used by the will to create distance, and thus a degree of freedom from desires and impulses—that is, from the given. The arbitrary will creates distance from the given by denying it any importance. The arbitrary will takes as its grounds for deciding simply: "I decide." The eudemonic will, according to Hegel, creates distance and freedom from the given by submitting any given to the calculus of its contribution to a self-chosen goal, for example, happiness. Hegel argues that the method used by the eudemonic will is superior to the one used by the arbitrary will. Hegel forcefully demonstrates the deficiency of the method used by the arbitrary will. I argue that a denial can be understood as an attempt to establish distance and freedom from a given by the deficient method of the arbitrary will, that is, by an epistemological move that denies the objectively given. From Hegel, one can learn that denying the objective is not the only way to affirm one's freedom. A better and more constructive way to demonstrate one's freedom from the objectively given is to acknowledge the truth of the given, but submit the given to a calculation. Moving beyond a denial will therefore involve the two steps of, firstly, epistemologically acknowledging the given and, secondly, acquiring the emotional and intellectual capacity to submit the given to a rational evaluation of its possible contribution to one's goals. These two steps, which Freud observed and described in his article, are hereby given a logical necessity.

5. Freud describes the acquisition of the linguistic symbol of negation as the mastery of a miraculous tool. It produces the necessary distance and negativity to create freedom. The idea that human development is not linear, but proceeds by sudden spurts, is defended by Spitz. Children reach new plateaus of development because several developing areas suddenly allow the child to perform a series of previously impossible tasks. The social smile, the eight-month-anxiety, and the no-saying at fifteen months are indicators of such new spurts in development. I argue that no-saying is more than simply an indicator of that higher level of development. No-saying is the organizer, the creator of that higher level of development. Spitz recognized that no-saying creates the first unequivocal concept. I argue that no-saying creates, by itself, the distance from the caretaker required for the child's affirmation of its emerging autonomy, affirming the right to the child's own point of view, even if that point of view appears sometimes to be manifestly irrational.

6. Freud points out that undoing a denial is often a complicated and arduous task. In his article on denial he did not specify the contribution that an interlocutor can make in the overcoming of a denial. By analyzing Oedipus, we learn that Teiresias fails, while Jocasta, the messenger, and the shepherd succeed in helping Oedipus find the truth. I argue that in order to be

helpful, the interlocutor must accept that establishing the other's subjective truth is different from establishing the truth about something with which the other is not or is only marginally involved, that is, objective truth. In helping another find the truth about himself, the interlocutor must remain aware that it is the other as discourse partner who creates the meaning of his life. The interlocutor must accept that he, therefore, cannot impose a new meaning upon another. All the interlocutor can do is provide evidence that the other will be able to use in order to create a new meaning for himself. To be helpful in undoing a denial, the interlocutor must first accept the fact that truth cannot be provided to his discourse partner. The truth about oneself can only be discovered by the self. The life stories of Oedipus and Anthony Moore vividly illustrate this claim.

Notes

CHAPTER ONE. THE COMPLEX PHENOMENON OF DENIAL

1. Freud's text does allow one to identify the gender of the patient.

2. Chapter 1 will therefore analyze territory not covered by the classic commentators on Freud's "Negation (Denial)" (Freud, S.E., XIX, 235–39) such as Lacan, Spitz, Hyppolite, and Ricoeur (1970, 314–18), to name a few. For a survey of the commentaries on Freud's article see W. Ver Eecke 1984: *Saying 'No,'* 2–11. A very important recent publication is the special issue of the *Revue de Métaphysique et de Morale* (April-June 2001 [2]), with articles by Ali Benmakhlouf, Jocelyn Benoist, Antonia Soulez, and Monique David-Ménard. The above-mentioned commentators concentrate upon the crucial Freudian claim that human beings discover unpleasant truths about themselves by means of a denial. By analyzing new territory, for example, of the effort of undoing a denial, I will be able to establish a connection between the psychoanalytic concept of denial and the philosophical concept of self-deception. Curiously enough, the analytic philosophers examining the problem of self-deception do not pay attention to the function of denial as the crucial interface between unconscious self-deception and facing the truth by undoing one's self-deception as it appears in a denial. See the anthology by Brian P. McLaughlin and Amélie O. Rorty.

3. As I see it the term 'negation' refers both to the linguistic sign of negation and to the negative judgment that uses the linguistic sign of negation. The term 'denial' refers to a negative judgment that wrongly denies the truth presented in a negative judgment. A similar distinction is made in the French translation of *Verneinung* as *négation* and *dénégation*. See Hyppolite (Lacan 1988, 290), and Laplanche & Pontalis, 262.

As the meaning of the two terms "negation' and 'denial' is different in psychoanalytic theory, in contemporary linguistics, in sociology, and in logic I want to give a brief overview of the different meanings of these two terms in the different sciences. In psychoanalysis, negation refers to the logical operation in a proposition whereby one affirms that a connection in the proposition "He is not tall" does not hold. A denial refers to the use of a linguistic negation in order to affirm that a connection does not hold, whereas in fact the connection exists: "This figure in my dream is not my mother" (Wurmser 1989, 177). By extension, in psychoanalytic theory (Fenichel, Deutsch, Lewin, Jacobson) the term 'denial' is also used for nonlinguistic attitudes in which the person disregards and thus denies affects such as anxiety or guilt (Wangh 11). In a further extension of the applicability of the concept, the term denial is also used for actions of persons who behave as if a fact has no consequences, such as making plans beyond one's expected lifespan when one has terminal cancer. By such extensions, the difference between the Freudian concepts of denial (refusal to acknowledge factual reality) and disavowal (refusal to acknowledge the emotional significance of a perceived fact) is blurred (for a conceptual distinction, see Wurmser 1989, 177–78).

In contemporary linguistics the term negation is used when the assertion of the sentence is reversed (Mary is not tall). The term denial is used "if negation is directed at presuppositions, implicatures or even formal aspects of a sentence" (Geurts 274) as in "The classroom was not warm, it was boiling." Thus, in linguistics, a denial not only leaves the original affirmed connection untouched; in some cases it magnifies that connection. In the study of children's language, one makes the distinction between the acquisition of negation—"no" as refusal—and denial negation—denying that something is true. In children's language one uses the term negation for the child's "no" when it expresses refusal and denial negation when the "no" expresses an intellectual judgment that something is not the case (Hummer at al.).

The concept of denial is used also in sociology. It is used both to refer to a societal attitude and to an objective social result. Thus, there are articles that describe the social denial of death and sex in the elderly (Gussaroff), homelessness (Baum & Burnes), HIV (Hein et al.), and responsibility to disadvantaged populations such as the elderly, the handicapped, and Third World citizens (Schmitt et al.). There are also articles describing the objective fact of lack of access (denial) of, among others, Chicanos to higher education (Cortese), and of people of color to child welfare (Close).

Finally, at least some logicians point to negation as a logical operator and point to denial as an act of everyday discourse by which we "indicate that something is wrong with a proposition . . . without it being a contrary to some proposition. . . . 'No, it is not like this; rather, it is like that'" (Gabbay and Moravcsik 1978, 251).

4. Wurmser, using the research of Basch and Dorpat provides useful distinctions between denial *(Verneinung)*, repression *(Verdrängung)*, and a third term closely related to the previous two: disavowal *(Verleugnung)*. He writes that denial deals with a factual reality that might evoke painful meanings; repression with instincts whose demands are unacceptable, and disavowal with unacceptable meanings of the perceived reality. Thus, denial refuses to acknowledge factual reality; repression refuses to acknowledge instinctual demands; disavowal refuses to acknowledge emotional meanings (Wurmser 1989, 177–78). Athanassiou makes a similar distinction between repression and denial (1988).

5. The authors of the special issue of the *Revue de Métaphysique et de Morale* (April-June 2001 [2]), point out that Freud was unique among the German authors who studied negation in seeing the connection between negation and repression. In her article, Monique David-Ménard argues that the primary function of a negation is, for Freud, not the description of reality. Rather, its primary function is to deal with desired objects that are not available or disappointments and threats that are present.

By negating, a human being is able to articulate and thus to know something that is undesirable. This is much better than simply turning away from the danger. In a negation, one takes symbolic distance from disappointed desires while taking cognisance of them. Two other techniques to deal with disappointments are that of the pervert who uses a fetish to deny the absence of the phallus in the mother and that of the psychotic who can believe that as a man he is becoming a woman (Schreber). A negation is thus a creative (symbolic) way of dealing with disappointed desire. A different view was held by Frege.

In his article, Benmakhlouf points out that for Frege a negation is only a method of creating another thought. One can have the idea: red. A negation is nothing but the creation of another idea: non-red. Frege tries to eliminate the judgment present in negative sentences.

In her article, Joseleyn Benoist demonstrates that Husserl sees that something unique is happening in a negation. Husserl claims that in negation we express a deception, a deceit, even a disappointment. We expected something but it is not so. In his later years, Husserl refers to perception as the positive basis for both a positive and a negative judgment. I can expect the color of a ball to be the same on its back as it is on its front. This expected perception can be either confirmed or denied. Benoist points out that by grounding the act of negation in perception Husserl is unable to understand the contribution of the symbol of negation to the act of negation. Freud, on the contrary, saw very clearly the symbolic element in the negative judgment.

Finally, in her article, Antonia Soulez points out that Wittgenstein is puzzled about the meaning of a negation. Wittgenstein refuses to relate the meaning of a negation to an object because he denies the existence of negative facts. Wittgenstein then points out that the meaning of language and thus also of a negation is that it is a symbolic game. One can then claim that Freud understood, as Wittgenstein did, that negation is a linguistic game; he understood, as Husserl did, that negation is dealing with a disappointment. Combining the insights of Wittgenstein and Husserl, one could claim that, for Freud, negation offers the opportunity to use deceit to deal symbolically with a disappointment. It is a creative repression.

Less relevant for our study of Freud's theory of negation but still containing interesting studies about the phenomenon of negation is the special issue of *Argumentation*, 6, 1992, no. 1, 1–130, resulting from a research project at the Centre de Recherches Sémiologiques de l'Université de Neuchâtel (Denis Miéville, Guest Editor).

6. In my opinion, Freud's trick to let patients label the repressed and his later example about boasting show that Freud's usage of the concept of denial is restricted to linguistic denials. This is also observed by Litowitz (1998, 123). In German the label for denial is *"Verneinung,"* which means both denial and negation. The German label for denial thus explicitly ties denial to a linguistic act.

By comparing Freud with Frege, G. Myerson too affirms that Freud's concern was with negation in its linguistic form. He does point out correctly, however, that Freud tries to link negation "to the fundamental dynamics of the psyche" (Myerson 1995, 10).

Edith Jacobson, on the other hand, expands the meaning of denial to include nonlinguistic forms of denying the reality, such as the cancer patient who starts projects that manifestly will last beyond his expected survival time. Jacobson seems to look for nonlinguistic forms of behavior expressing the fundamental dynamics of the human psyche.

7. Freud's artifice and his examples show that his usage of the concept of denial is restricted to linguistic denials. In German the word for denial is *"Verneinung,"* which means both denial and negation. The German word for denial thus explicitly ties denial to a linguistic act. However, Jacobson is not alone in expanding the meaning of the concept of denial. In the current psychological literature, denial is used both for linguistic and nonlinguistic forms of denial. Thus, a cancer patient who starts projects that are expected to last beyond his expected survival time is said to deny his coming death, not by a linguistic statement, but by his acts (Weisman). Dorpat, on the other hand, in his important book on denial, considers denial to be a "defensive process [that] occurs at a presymbolic or prelinguistic level" (Dorpat 1985, 3). One crucial contribution of Dorpat's work is his thesis that a presymbolic denial "prevents the formation of verbal ideas" (Ibid; also 42, 247, 251, 253, 265, 267) about the denied reality. He calls this the "cognitive arrest theory of denial" (Ibid. chapter 1). Dorpat objects to Freud's usage of the word *"Verneinung"* for the defense mechanism of denial (117) because Dorpat wants to distinguish sharply between negation as a logical or grammatical concept and denial or disavowal as a defense mechanism. Notwithstanding his disagreement with Freud, I see Dorpat as providing a crucial insight for clarifying the puzzle that Freud saw in linguistic denials. The puzzle for Freud was that a linguistic denial labels that which it denies. The creative contribution of a linguistic denial is not the telling of a truth. Its creative contribution is the preparatory step of labeling the problem. Dorpat's insight is that a presymbolic denial prevents the subject from paying enough attention to the denied reality to be in a position to form the concepts necessary to properly label the denied reality. In a linguistic denial, the patient succeeds, at least partially, in overcoming the deficit pointed to by Dorpat: what was previously unknown has now been labeled (Ibid. 48, 236). Given Dorpat's clarification of the defense mechanism of denial, it makes sense that Freud pays attention to the difficulty that patients have in giving information about the unconscious. Remember that Freud reports with some pride that he invented a trap to help them describe a portion of the unconscious material (Freud, "Negation," S.E., XIX, 133).

8. Further examples of boasting can be found in Freud's study of Emmy v. N. and of Cäcilie M. (S.E., II, 76).

9. The correctness of this date is in doubt.

10. In discussing boasting Freud comes close to saying that the activity of the unconscious which is constitutive for a denial is the linguistic activity of labeling something unknown. Let me again quote the relevant text from Freud: "what was already present as a finished product in the unconscious was beginning to show through indistinctly [to consciousness]" (Freud, S.E., II, 76, n. 1). I take the expression "finished product" to mean that the unknown was labeled.

11. For an example see Ver Eecke (1984, 145). The patient deeply desires to be home when her son visits town. Yet she does not dare to ask from the nun who is director of the asylum for the permission to leave—a permission regularly granted—because: "What would that nun think of me?"

12. Some authors go further and argue that a denial demonstrates that the human being is split (Ver Eecke 1984, 19; Wurmser 1985; Wurmser 1989, 177ff).

13. Current literature often explicitly distinguishes these two phases. Authors distinguish between denial of facts or of cognition and denial of affects, responsibility, or blame (Jackson & Thomas-Peter; Levine at al.; Hoke et al.; Brenitz; Kennedy & Grubin; Winn; Wool & Goldberg). That distinction is often referred to as the distinction between a denial of the facts and the denial of the meaning of the facts. One author points to several layers hidden behind the denial of the meaning of facts. He distinguishes between the implications of facts, changes demanded if the facts are faced, and feelings related to the facts (Kearney 1996, 13–14, 43–44). Finally, another author distinguishes three forms of intensity of denial, which he labels disbelief, deferral, and dismissal (Lubinsky).

14. Freud writes that this intellectual acknowledgment without emotional acceptance is "a very important and somewhat strange variant" of that same split in a denial (Freud, S.E., XIX, 236). I understand the rest of the article to be an attempt by Freud to ponder the relation and the split between the intellectual and the affective. His main argument and contribution is the claim that, notwithstanding the split between the intellectual and the affective, it is possible to demonstrate the dependence of the intellectual upon the affective.

15. The crucial work that needs to be done in the fourth phase is well described by Dorpat: "What is denied is *disavowed*, whereas working through some denied content includes an *avowal* as part of the self of what has previously been rejected" (Dorpat 1985, 238).

16. The third and fourth phases of denial illustrate the fact that there is an intersubjective dimension to denial. Given the appropriate attitude of a partner, denial becomes unnecessary. Thus, several authors argue that a safe and accepting environment is helpful for alcoholics (Rugel & Barry), incestuous fathers (Geller et al.) and other sexual offenders to overcome their denial (Laflen & Sturm; Marshall;). The same argument is presented for overcoming denial of death (de Hennezel 1989). At the same time, certain attitudes of others promote denial. Thus, one researcher found that "The patient's need for denial . . . was in direct proportion to the doctor's need for denial" (Dorpat 1989, 19). Dorpat calls this the "interactional perspective" of denial. I will explicitly address this puzzle in chapter 6 when I ask the question of why Teiresias provokes a denial in Oedipus, whereas Jocasta, the shepherd, and the messenger help Oedipus undo his previous denial. I will address the problem of helping others undo a denial in my analysis of A. Moore autobiography, in which he describes overcoming a profound denial.

17. Hyppolite indicates the complexity of such undoing by using Hegel's concept of *aufheben*, 'to overcome,' as a matrix for such undoing (Ver Eecke 1984, 25–27). Later on I will be able to do more than indicate the complexity of undoing a denial. I will provide a careful phenomenological description of that process as a basis for a number of anthropological conclusions.

18. In cognitive science, one would call that an emergent property.

19. I therefore agree with A.O. Rorty when she stresses that human beings organize their psychic life at different levels. She makes that claim a precondition for the

possibility of self-deception: "Relying on the details of modular theories of all kinds, the second picture (of multiple layers of self-organization) explains our hospitality to self-deception and other forms of irrationality" (Rorty 23). Freud's thesis is one step stronger than Rorty's in that Freud argues that the different layers in a human being follow a different logic in their interpretation of events: the logic of primary processes and of the pleasure-ego (as in dreams, jokes, or fantasies) or, on the contrary, the logic of secondary processes and of the reality-ego (rational arguments). One can therefore expect that the effort of unification in a person will not be achieved solely by the logic used in secondary processes. The secondary process logic might be able to recognize a self-deception (Rorty 25). However, one cannot expect that the secondary processes will have the resources to undo a self-deception or a denial since these phenomena are also controlled by the logic of primary processes. In fact, Anthony Moore's case will teach us that undoing self-deception or denial owes a lot, among other factors that might be mentioned, to metaphoric work.

One can make a similar argument in the technical language of Lacan when he argues that the challenge to human beings is that they must master the experience of the real. They can do so by the totally different logics of the imaginary or the symbolic. The imaginary is not identical to Freud's primary processes, nor is the symbolic identical to Freud's secondary processes or the philosophical concept of the rational. Since the symbolic is closely connected with language, we can understand Lacan's symbolic to subsume the rational or secondary processes of Freud. I have argued elsewhere (Ver Eecke 2001), that therapeutic interventions with mentally ill people, such as schizophrenics, must take into account the fact that the schizophrenic has deficiencies in both the imaginary and the symbolic register. Furthermore, a different logic applies to the two registers. Failure to respect the distinction between these two registers or failure to respect the difference in logic between them makes the therapeutic intervention ineffective or counterproductive. The Lacanian framework, just like the Freudian, confirms Rorty's idea that human beings have different layers of interpretation while making the stronger claim that these interpretations obey different logics.

20. Oedipus becomes aggressive towards Teiresias when the latter tells him an unpleasant truth. Forced to recognize, at the end of the play, the unpleasant truth announced by Teiresias, Oedipus mourns even his existence. In Ibsen's *Ghosts*, at the end of the play, Mrs. Alving mourns the fact that she brought no brightness into the home of her husband and child but instead believed obstinately in duty and thus contributed to the despair of her own son (Ibsen, *Collected Works*, VII, 277–78). See chapters 3 and 6 in this book for further comments on how these tragedies can clarify the problematic of denial.

21. It is curious that Freud draws explicit attention to the great importance of the acquisition of the linguistic function of negation but does not further conceptualize the negative moment postulated by his claim that the object of a judgment of existence must first have been lost. In the following pages, I will argue that acts of separation and the obvious or hidden forms of aggression accompanying such acts of separation will have to play an important role in the development of a person and thus also in undoing a denial and thereby restoring wholesomeness in that person.

22. Freud himself has given a survey of the development of his theory about this problem (Freud, *S.E.*, XXI, 117–22). For an extensive discussion of this same problem, see *S.E.*, XIV, 113–16.

23. One can find in the writings of Donald Winnicott (1971, 86–94) confirmation of such a psychoanalytic interpretation of the development of the child. Winnicott argues that the child has the need to have the illusion or the experience of fusion with the mother. He also argues that the aggression of the child against the mother is necessary for the child to have confidence in the mother. The child, so Winnicott argues, believes in the omnipotence of its aggression. The child thus fears that its aggression will kill the mother. If the mother responds to the aggression of the child with rejection then the child will feel that its aggression is able to destroy the good object. If the mother continues to relate warmly to the child, the child feels that its aggression is not effective. The good object, the good mother, survives the aggression of the child. Such a mother is not the product of the imagination. Such a mother really exists. In such a view of child development, fusion precedes separation. Between the two stands aggression. This aggression can take many forms such as biting when nursing, or saying "no" to the mother's offer of something the child obviously likes.

24. Elsewhere Freud refers to two authors who studied this phenomenon: Bleuler and Gross (Freud, *S.E.*, VIII, 175, n.2).

25. One can find texts in Freud's "Negation" where Freud seems to touch on the two dimensions I discuss below. But touching on a subject matter is not the same as highlighting its importance.

26. These and other of Hegel's ideas will be used in chapters 3 and 4 to further clarify the phenomenon of denial.

27. I am, of course, not arguing that Hegel already discovered the Lacanian understanding that all mental illnesses can be articulated in their structure by their relative success or failure with respect to the paternal metaphor. I am arguing that Hegel's requirement of elevating feelings and needs to 'ideality' has great similarities with Lacan's requirement that human beings must accept their insertion into the world of language or into the symbolic system. Hegel gives us an example of a mentally derailed person who was not able to elevate his desire to 'ideality'; "an Englishman who had hanged himself, on being cut down by his servant not only regained the desire to live but also the disease of avarice; for when discharging the servant, he deducted twopence from his wages because the man had acted without instructions in cutting the rope with which his master had hanged himself" (Hegel, *Philosophy of Mind*, 134).

28. Spitz acknowledges his debt to Anna Freud's work, *The Ego and the Mechanisms of Defense*, for this idea (Spitz, 45–48).

29. I will use Spitz's ideas more abundantly in chapter 5 to clarify the liberating function of negation.

30. Authors other than Spitz have made us aware of the constitutive function of aggression in the development of human infants. For instance, Melanie Klein makes the paranoid-schizoid position a necessary phase in the child's development (Hanna

Segal, *Klein*, 112–21) . Winnicott, on the other hand, points to the function of aggression in establishing the trustworthiness of the caring person. As mentioned before, Winnicott argues that the experience of one's own aggression and the experience of the benign reaction of the mother allows the child to establish that the caring mother is not subject to the effects of its own aggression, which the child feels to be all-powerful. The child feels that its aggression is not able to destroy the good mother. Such a mother acquires the status of an independent and thus trustworthy object (i.e., a person) (Winnicott 1971, 90).

31. The importance of this idea for the young Moore is obvious since within the space of two pages he repeats it several times. Thus, he writes: "I needed to distinguish my own identity from my father's so I could live my own life" (Moore 4) and "By allowing my grandfather to assume a role within my conscious identity, I was able to establish some sense of identity distinct from my father" (Ibid. 4–5) and finally "Some separation from my father's identity was necessary for me to be free to lead my own life" (Ibid. 5).

32. A metaphoric move is a move whereby a subject accepts a different identity while still feeling himself to be the same person, because a word is able to express the great similarity between the two identities (Evans 111–13).

33. Moore seems to understand that unconscious forces were at work in his decision to become a Jesuit when he writes: "When I entered the Jesuits, I was twenty-three years old. Only years later did I realize that was the same age my father was when he died" (Moore 3).

34. The metaphorical power hidden in being a Jesuit was insufficient to unify the life of the young Moore. He left the Jesuits and spent more than a decade creating a new metaphor. I will analyze that effort in chapter 7.

35. Rorty proposes a similar thesis when she writes: "We certainly think we can recognize self-deception in others, and we strongly suspect it in ourselves, even *retrospectively attributing it to our past selves*" (Rorty 22, italics mine).

36. The claim that self-deception and denial are not lies will be further argued for in chapters 2 and 7.

CHAPTER TWO. THE EPISTEMOLOGICAL PROBLEM
OF SELF-DESCRIPTION IN FREUDIAN PSYCHOANALYSIS

1. *S.E.*, XXI, 12. Another such colloquial usage can be found in *S.E.*, VI, 221: "my being scarcely able to tell lies anymore . . ."

2. The first date is the date of analysis. The second is the publication date.

3. Laplanche and Pontalis (1973, 333ff) and De Waelhens (1978, 53ff) further clarified this concept.

4. This will be one of the themes of chapter 6 where I analyze Sophocles' *Oedipus, the King*. The same distinction between immorality and impotence is aptly made by Berthold-Bond when he discusses Hegel's analysis of the Greek tragedy. The first leads to moral guilt. The second leads to ontological guilt, which has nothing to do

with moral responsibility. Still, ontological guilt points to a deficiency, an incompleteness (Berthold-Bond, 171; Applied to Creon and Ajax, Ibid. 159).

5. Surveying cognitive psychology studies, Greenwald presents two models to explain apparent self-deceptions. Both models allow for apparent self-deceptions that are quite different from lies. His first model is the hierarchical model of information processing. Information is processed at a lower level. There one decides whether or not to process the information in greater depth. Greenwald illustrates that model by using the example of a person processing mail. What looks like junk mail is thrown away without analyzing whether it is important. One guesses that the information might not be worth the trouble. Similarly, a cancer patient might detect some symptoms and feel that studying the symptoms will only provide unpleasant information. Therefore, the patient might decide to treat it as someone treats junk mail (Greenwald, 57–58). Greenwald's second model is the neural network model which argues that one single piece of information can be processed in two or more parallel ways without the one being related to the other. He illustrates that model with Claparède's observation of a memory deficiency in a Korsakoff-syndrome patient. Claparède's patient "was unable to recognize Claparède from one visit to the next. During one visit, Claparède deliberately pricked the patient's finger with a hatpin when they were shaking hands. On the next visit, the patient hesitated to shake hands with Claparède—whom, as usual, the patient did not recognize as a familiar figure" (Ibid. 65). Even though Greenwald's theory agrees with my position that not all apparent forms of self-deception are active lies, his theory abandons some essential features of the Freudian concept of denial. Freud maintains the possibility of some form of the person's unification: Freud's patient, by saying that the figure in her dream was not her mother, simultaneously labels the figure in her dream and confesses that there are unconscious forces in her objecting to such labeling. Greenwald's neural network model of picturing apparent forms of self-deception allows for one part of the person not knowing what the other part knows. Freud, however, maintains that consciousness can label the unconscious. In Greenwald's hierarchical model it is possible for a lower-level information process to decide not to learn about the phenomenon beyond the superficial information, thereby creating the motivation for refusing to invest more energy in information processing. Once the junk mail is thrown away, it might not be possible to know what had been written. Freud points out that a denial labels the unknown repressed. Thus, it is difficult to see how Greenwald's models could explain Freud's cases of denial. However, Greenwald's models show us that apparent self-deception is different from a lie in many more cases than Freud's denials.

6. Dorpat expands on the Freudian notion that denial involves a lack of inscription at a higher level of consciousness. He argues that "denial reactions prevent the subject from fully and accurately symbolizing in words whatever it is that he has defensively negated" (Dorpat 1983, 229; Dorpat 1988).

7. Our thesis should not be construed as meaning that psychoanalysis would make the moral dimension superfluous. The psychoanalytic point of view is valid only when responsibility for the real is somehow taken into account. This is the case with children who are protected and guarded by their parents. This is also the case with psychoanalytic patients who promise the therapist that they will not make important decisions during therapy.

136 NOTES TO CHAPTER THREE

CHAPTER THREE. DENIAL AND
HEGEL'S PHILOSOPHICAL ANTHROPOLOGY

1. For Freud's claim regarding the universality of denial to be true, denials must appear in many circumstances. Research has in fact documented denial as an attitude or as a linguistic expression in terminally ill patients reacting to their impending deaths (de Hennezel 1991; Morita et al.; Baider & Edelstein; Beilin; Strelzer et al.; Connor); in cancer patients (Wool; Jelicic et al.; Morita et al.; Weisman); in patients with Alzheimers disease (Weinstein et al.; Sevush & Leve); in patients with multiple sclerosis (Finger); in patients with a heart disease such as myocardinal infarction (Fukiniski et al.; Pruneti et al.), or angina pectoris (Levenson et al.) and in candidates for heart transplants (Young et al.); in patients with disabling diseases (Stewart); in persons with eating disorders (Jackson & Davidson; Vitousek et al.); in cases of transplant failures (Streltzer et al.); in infertility resulting from Hodgkin's disease (Cella & Najavits); in mothers of children and adolescents with malignant and terminal cancer (Freitas); in sex offenders (Stevenson et al; Kennedy & Grubin; Winn; Marshall) and in incestuous families (Hoke et al.); in drug and alcohol addiction (Krestan & Bepko; Wing; Amodea & Liftik; Liebeskind; Wiseman et al.; Kearney); in pregnant mothers (Van der Hart et al.; Miller; Green & Manohar; Berns; Finnegan et al.; Milden et al.; Atkins et al.; Moyer & Levine). We further have descriptions of fathers whose wives are in the last three months of their first pregnancy who are in denial in order to deal with their ambivalent feelings (Gerzi et al.); in whole cultures when they are dealing with a national defeat such as the Japanese after WWII (Grandjean); in those dealing with genocide, as was the case with the Holocaust (Klein & Kogan; Davidson; Solomon; Vidal-Naquet) or the Armenian genocide (Boyajian & Grigorian). There is thus empirical evidence for the plausibility of denial being a widespread, or perhaps universal, phenomenon. To analyze that claim of universality is a philosophical task.

2. Philosophical theories have been helpful for the clarification of psychodynamic processes. Thus, Louis Sass uses Wittgenstein's criticism of the solipsist and the solipsist's unavoidable contradictions to explain a curious phenomenon observed in schizophrenics: They experience themselves as the absolute source of their experiences, thereby denying the independence of the world and the existence of other minds. They simultaneously experience their thoughts as being controlled by others, similar to the solipsist who needs to create another consciousness who can take his own consciousness as an object so as to give existence to his own ego (Sass 1994, 67–73; 51–85). John Muller uses Peirce's semiotic to demonstrate the importance of semiotic activity between mother and child and the failure of semiotic activity in psychotics (For an analysis of Muller's argument see Ver Eecke 1997).

Several authors have used Hegel specifically to clarify unconscious processes. Lacan relied on Hegel's *Phenomenology* to construct his mirror stage theory and to create the logical connection between the imaginary and aggressivity (For an exposition of the Hegel-Lacan connection, see Ver Eecke 1983a). Opatow uses Hegel's ideas about the transition from consciousness to self-consciousness to clarify the psychoanalytic claim that the infant needs to make a transition from hallucinating the world to accepting reality. From Hegel, Opatow borrows the idea that consciousness and self-consciousness are characterized by some form of negativity. For Opatow, a child overcomes hallucination as a method of creating the world by negating the notion that, as consciousness, it is tied to this form of awareness. Instead, reacting to the pain and displeasure resulting from the lack of satisfaction provided by hallucination, the infant has the option to leave hallucination behind and accept that, first, there is an independent reality; and second that it—the infant—is in need of that independent reality (Opatow 1988, 622–24, 626, 628–29, 635; 1989, 651–55; 1993, 443–46). André Green, in his book *The Work of the Negative*, devotes a whole chapter to the fruitfulness of connecting the ideas of Hegel and Freud (Green 1999, 26–49). In particular, so Green argues, both thinkers understand "the work of the negative. (Ibid. 4). Using two previously published articles (Green 1997; 1998), Green reinterprets Winnicott's ideas about the function of transitional objects (Green 1999, 7) and Bion's reflections on the "fundamental intolerance of frustration" (Ibid. 7–10). He sees in the work of these two psychoanalysts a deep understanding of the work of the negative. Several reasons justify using Hegel to clarify the logical structure of Freudian insights. First, there are similarities in Hegel's and Freud's conceptions of madness (Berthold-Bond, 26–28, 39,54). Freud of course provides multiple detailed analyses, where Hegel offers one general ontological structure. But Hegel's general ontological structure is useful in preventing us from losing sight of the overall structure of mental illness. A second reason to rely on Hegel for insights into psychodynamic processes is Hegel's insight into the similarity between some of consciousness's structures and madness. Thus, Berthold-Bond points out that, for Hegel, "the healthy mind is still grappling with the same sorts of contradictions and feelings of alienation, the same 'infinite pain' . . . which characterizes insanity" (Ibid. 3; see also Ibid. 51–54). A third reason to consult Hegel is to deepen our understanding of the structure of denial. Indeed, Hegel insists, as Freud does, that both the insane person and the normal person have two psychic centers: the life of feelings and the life of rationality (Ibid. 34, 41). Having two psychic centers in a person is the ontological condition for the possibility of a denial. Finally, both Hegel and Freud recognize the importance of the negative (stressed by Lacan 1988, 52–61; Hyppolyte 1988, 289–99; Opatow op.cit). One way Freud does so is through his theory of overcoming hallucination. Another way is by introducing the concept of the death drive. Hegel stresses the negative's importance by making the negative the motor of his philosophical system and by stressing negative experiences such as despair, contradiction, and disappointment (Berthold-Bond 45–48). As a denial is—in Freud's mind—a defective form of negating, it might clarify matters to look at Hegel's theory for conceptual explanations of the expressive form the negative takes in a denial.

3. The case of Oedipus will be examined in detail in chapter 6.

4. Here and throughout this chapter we are using Grene and Lattimore, 1959.

5. One could argue that Lacan holds such a view when he writes that the human world has an ontological structure similar to that of paranoiac knowledge (Lacan 1977, 2)

6. When two people look at a modern painting, it is possible for one to be greatly impressed by it, while the other is completely indifferent. The first person might encourage the second one and say: look closely and you will like it. The second person might respond: the more I look at the painting, the more I feel that it is a stu-

pid painting. In this conversation these two persons discover that looking more closely does not lead to agreement. The object is not what divides these two persons. It is the way they perceive the object. Thus, both people become aware of being different from the other. They become self-aware.

7. Douglass describes his willingness to face death and to fight Mr. Covey, the slave breaker, as the turning point in his life as a slave: "Mr. Covey entered the stable with a long rope; and just as I was half out of the loft, he caught hold of my legs, and was about tying me. . . . I resolved to fight; and, suiting my action to the resolution, I seized Covey hard by the throat; and as I did so, I rose. He held on to me, and I to him. My resistance was so entirely unexpected, that Covey seemed taken all aback. He trembled like a leaf. This gave me assurance, and I held him uneasy, causing the blood to run where I touched with the ends of my fingers. . . . He asked me if I meant to persist in my resistance. I told him I did, come what might; that he had used me like a brute for six months, and that I was determined to be used so no longer. . . . This battle with Mr. Covey was the turning-point in my career as a slave. It rekindled the few expiring embers of freedom, and revived within me a sense of my own manhood. It recalled the departed self-confidence, and inspired me again with a determination to be free. . . . It was a glorious resurrection, from the tomb of slavery, to the heaven of freedom. My long-crushed spirit rose, cowardice departed, bold defiance took its place; and I now resolved that, however long I might remain a slave in form, the day had passed forever when I could be a slave in fact. I did not hesitate to let it be known of me, that the white man who expected to succeed in whipping, must also succeed in killing me" (Douglass 79–81).

8. When deliberating as to whether they would try to escape, Frederick Douglass and his companions saw the alternative. Some chose to risk death. One at least is reported to have feared death too much to risk freedom: "Here were the difficulties, real or imagined—the good to be sought, and the evil to be shunned. On the one hand, there stood slavery, a stern reality, glaring frightfully upon us,—its robes already crimsoned with the blood of millions, and even now feasting itself greedily upon our own flesh. On the other hand, away back in the dim distance, under the flickering light of the north star, behind some craggy hill or snow-covered mountain, stood a doubtful freedom—half frozen—beckoning us to come and share its hospitality. This in itself was sometimes enough to stagger us; but when we permitted ourselves to survey the road, we were frequently appalled. Upon either side we saw grim death, assuming the most horrid shapes. Now it was starvation, carving us to eat our own flesh;— now we were contending with the waves, and were drowned;—now we were overtaken, and torn to pieces by the fangs of the terrible bloodhound. . . . With us it was a doubtful liberty at most, and almost certain death if we failed. For my part, I should prefer death to hopeless bondage. Sandy, one of our number, gave up the notion, but still encouraged us" (Douglass 90–91).

9. In the *Narrative of the Life of Fredrick Douglass* we find a beautiful description of how far the slaveholder will go in order to enforce his right to give orders and to make his slaves obey. "Very near Mr. Freeland lived the Rev. Daniel Weeden, and in the same neighborhood lived the Rev. Rigby Hopkins. These were members and ministers in the Reformed Methodist Church. Mr. Weeden owned, among others, a woman slave, whose name I have forgotten. This woman's back, for weeks, was kept

literally raw, made so by the lash of this merciless, *religious* wretch. He used to hire hands. His maxim was, behave well or behave ill, it is the duty of a master occasionally to whip a slave, to remind him of his master's authority. Such was his theory, and such his practice. Mr. Hopkins was even worse than Mr. Weeden. His chief boast was his ability to manage slaves. The peculiar feature of his government was that of whipping slaves in advance of deserving it. He always managed to have one or more of his slaves to whip every Monday morning. He did this to alarm their fears, and strike terror into those who escaped. His plan was to whip for the smallest offences, to prevent the commission of large ones. Mr. Hopkins could always find some excuse for whipping a slave. It would astonish one, unaccustomed to a slaveholding life, to see with what wonderful ease a slaveholder can find things, of which to make occasion to whip a slave. A mere look, a word, or motion,—a mistake, accident, or want of power,—are all matters for which a slave may be whipped at any time. Does a slave look dissatisfied? It is said, he has the devil in him, and it must be whipped out. Does he speak loudly when spoken to by his master? Then he is getting high-minded, and should be taken down a button-hole lower. Does he forget to pull off his hat at the approach of a white person? Then he is wanting in reverence, and should be whipped for it. Does he venture to vindicate his conduct when censured for it? Then he is guilty of impudence,—one of the greatest crimes of which a slave can be guilty. Does he ever venture to suggest a different mode of doing things from that pointed out by his master? He is indeed presumptuous, and getting above himself; and nothing less than a flogging will do for him" (Douglass 85–86).

10. When Frerick Douglass describes how he becomes an experienced caulker, one can feel his great pride: "He [the Master] then took me into the ship-yard of which he was foreman, in the employment of Mr. Walter Price. There I was immediately set to calking, and very soon learned the art of using my mallet and irons. In the course of one year from the time I left Mr. Gardner's, I was able to command the highest wages given to the most experienced calkers [sic]. I was now of some importance to my master. I was bringing home from six to seven dollars per week. I sometimes brought him nine dollars per week: my wages were a dollar and a half a day. After learning how to caulk, I sought my own employment, made my own contracts, and collected the money which I earned" (Douglass 101).

11. In other passages, too, Hegel demonstrates that a human being needs another person to embody a contrary point of view in order for him or her to discover the full meaning of existence. This is beautifully elaborated in at least two other passages: "The Law of the Heart" and "The Beautiful Soul." (Hegel 1966, 390–600, 642–79). For Kristeva's rejection of Hegel's master/slave paradigm and its use of binary opposition see Van Buren, 1995.

12. Hegel's concept of the will is more thoroughly analyzed in chapter 4.

13. We find an indirect confirmation for this Hegelian thought in the memoirs of Frederick Douglass when he points out that the life of the master shows puzzling aspects. Slaveholders become monsters (Douglass 22–23, 27, 32–33, 36–38, 85–86); a kind-hearted woman who marries a slaveholder becomes vicious; religious slave holders turn into hypocrites (Douglass 65, 84–85). A Hegelian explanation for these observations by Douglass could be: slaveholders lead a life that is not giving them

what they had hoped for. Hence, slaveholders become human monsters and cannot but distort profound truths, including religious truths. Let me quote the description Douglass gives of a decent woman's transformation: "It was at least necessary for her to have some training in the exercise of irresponsible power, to make her equal to the task of treating me as though I were a brute. My mistress was, as I have said, a kind and tender-hearted woman; and in the simplicity of her soul she commenced, when I first went to live with her, to treat me as she supposed one human being ought to treat another. In entering upon the duties of a slaveholder, she did not seem to perceive that I sustained to her the relation of a mere chattel, and that for her to treat me as human being was not only wrong, but dangerously so. Slavery proved as injurious to her as it did to me. When I went there, she was a pious, warm, and tender-hearted woman. There was no sorrow or suffering for which she did not have a tear. She had bread for the hungry, clothes for the naked, and comfort for every mourner that came within her reach. Slavery soon proved its ability to divest her of these heavenly qualities. Under its influence, the tender heart became stone, and the lamblike disposition gave way to one of tiger-like fierceness. The first step in her downward course was in her ceasing to instruct me. She now commenced to practice her husband's precepts. She finally became even more violent in her opposition than her husband himself. She was not satisfied with simply doing as well as he had commanded; she seemed anxious to do better. Nothing seemed to make her more angry than to see me with a newspaper. She seemed to think that here lay the danger. I have had her rush at me with a face made all up of fury, and snatch from me a newspaper, in a manner that fully revealed her apprehension. She was an apt woman; and a little experience soon demonstrated, to her satisfaction, that education and slavery were incompatible with each other" (Douglass 50–51).

14. Michael Roth wrote a beautiful book *Psycho-Analysis as History: Negation and Freedom in Freud.* The subtitle makes it clear that the book is addressing the problematic addressed in this book. One, if not the most important, thesis of Roth's book is closely connected to the idea in the text just mentioned by Hegel: when human beings discover the truth about themselves it is painful; it involves despair. Thus, about transference, Roth writes: "Not that transference love is in itself a qualitatively new way of being: it certainly does not manifest a radically changed way of life. In fact, it is the very opposite of such a life, since it displays the repetitions, defenses, and frustrations that characterize the 'pathological' facets of 'normal' living. It is by being this manifestation, though, that the transference offers the analysand the prospects of negation, that is of freedom through the creative acknowledging of one's history" (Roth 1987, 26). He further specifies that improvement, higher freedom, and greater truth demand the acceptance of sacrifice: "The degree of contradiction between the person's desires and the world that confronts them is the key to whether the opportunity for negation found in the transference is to be realized. In other words, radical activity is initiated as the result of struggle, and this only when the person sees that the sacrifice necessary to make the radical change is outweighed by the potential gratification of the change" (Ibid. 100). Finally, Roth makes a direct comparison between Hegel and Freud by means of the idea of pain. "For Hegel, as for Freud, the mind preserving itself in contradiction is in pain. The psycho-analytic investigation of the contradiction of 'knowing yet not knowing' is an

investigation of a mind in pain and an attempt to understand that pain. The mind in this immediate (unreflective) state of contradiction is free only implicitly, according to Hegel. The reading of Freud that has been presented here has no difficulty with this notion" (Ibid. 125).

15. If change in self-conception is unavoidable and if such a change involves a loss of hope, we have discovered a theoretical possibility that denial sometimes has a positive and constructive function. Joel Shanan argues that human development demands a constant change in engagement and disengagement. Without using my concept of self-conception, but instead using the concept of ego-structure, Shanan argues that denial allows the ego to withdraw and reinvest energy in new objects with less conflict. He thus points to the great use of denial in moments of developmental change (Shanan 114–15; Lazarus). This is precisely the argument I derive from my reading of Hegel: change requires the force of the negative. Denial is one path open to the forces of the negative.

16. The proof that the master needs to defend a role that Hegel has shown to be false presents us with a deduction of the unavoidability of self-deception within a Hegelian philosophical anthropology. I will prove that denial follows self-deception. In a survey article, Agassi demonstrates that classical rationalism also unavoidably leads to self-deception. Classical rationalism rejected the idea, coming out of various religious traditions, that self-deception is unavoidable, and that therefore tradition and authority are necessary as guides to a good life. Rather, classical rationalism argues that self-deception should be avoided and can be avoided if one is self-reliant. Such self-reliance requires not accepting any proposition except those proven by the facts as they show themselves to a mind without preconceptions. For Bacon, the father of classical rationalism, this meant that science rests on "the rejection of all preconceived opinions and [that] the accumulation of a vast collection of items of factual information [would] lead rapidly to the full growth of theoretical science" (Agassi 35). Agassi then points out that belief in such a view is a self-deception for two reasons. First, scientific theory requires the formulation of hypotheses for the development of theories. Second, the Gödel theorem demonstrates that "all effective proof procedures are limited" (Ibid. 41). Thus, classical rationalism, which rejected the religious idea that human beings are subject to self-deception, shows itself to be a self-deception. Agassi thus demonstrates philosophically that self-deception is unavoidable, even outside a Hegelian anthropology. The argument for self-deception derived from Hegel therefore seems to have broad general validity. We need to keep in mind, though, that denial is more than just self-deception. It is a form of self-deception that also reveals truth.

17. Psychologists also provide us with such examples. In one case they use a conceptualization close to my own to report their findings. They compare perceived risk for contracting a sexually transmitted disease or becoming pregnant with reported sexual behavior and divide the group into people with realistic low risk, realistic high risk, and illusionary low risk. This latter group tended to avoid exposure to risk information, deny its relevance, and experienced no increase in negative emotions when facing contraceptive information. The authors interpret such denial as "ego-protective" (Wiebe & Black).

CHAPTER FOUR. DENIAL AND
HEGEL'S THEORY OF THE WILL

1. References to the *Philosophy of Right* will almost always be by numbered paragraphs (Hegel 1967b; or Hegel 1991).

2. I will make use of Hegel in a different way than the four authors referenced in chapter 3. Berthold-Bond emphasizes that Hegel's theory of consciousness has a similar structure to his theory of mad consciousness. Rather than arguing that similarity, I will presuppose such a similarity and search for an explanation of the phenomenon of denial by understanding it as a deficient solution to structural challenges to the human will as articulated by Hegel. Hyppolyte concentrates on overcoming a denial and uses Hegel's concept of *"aufheben"* (to deny, to suppress, and to conserve) (Hyppolyte 1988, 291) in order to clarify the process of overcoming a denial and to stress the presence of negation in "the fundamental attitude of symbolicity rendered explicit" (Ibid. 296). I will not concentrate, in this chapter, on explaining the overcoming of negation. Rather, I will try to understand why a denial itself is created. Lacan and Opatow focus on the distinction between perception and hallucination and the function of negativity in the emergence of one or the other. For Opatow, perception requires the force of the negative capable of rejecting hallucination (see footnote 1 in chapter 3). For Lacan, adult hallucination results from a different form of negativity than negation and denial. It involves a rejection of the symbolic system (Lacan 1988, 58). My reflections concern the function of the negative after hallucination has been overcome and after the symbolic system has been accepted. I want to clarify the difficulties faced by a person who utters a denial because he is already able to face the reality or is already willing to accept the symbolic system. I further want to clarify the deficiencies in the way such a person confronts these difficulties.

3. One can find a brief commentary on these three paragraphs using Hegel's concepts of universality, particularity, and individuality in Westphal 1992, 5–7. For a book-length commentary on the Preface of the *Philosophy of Right* see Peperzak 1987. There are a number of useful publications on Hegel's concept of freedom or the implications of his concept of freedom for his views on property, morality, and different ethical institutions: Angehrn 1977; Avineri 1972; Chamley 1963; Cullen 1979; Denis 1984; Dubouchet 1995; Fleischmann 1964; Harada 1989; Hardimon 1994; Henrich & Horstmann 1982; Jarczyk & Labarrière 1986; Jermann 1987; Kainz 1974: Kraus 1931/1932; Lucas & Pöggeler 1986; Lukacs 1973; Maker 1987; Marx 1977; Pelczynski 1984; Reyburn 1967; Riedel 1974; Roth 1989; Seeberger 1961; Smith 1989; Steinberger 1988; Waszek 1988; Westphal 1992; Whitebook 1977; Winfield 1988; Winfield 1990; Wood 1990.

4. I am aware that some excellent Hegel scholars reject the idea that Hegel's thought can be molded in a thesis-antithesis-synthesis schema. Thus, Allen Wood writes: "Some of those who discourse on Hegel with the greatest sophistication know him only through warped, inaccurate or bowdlerized second-hand accounts (for instance, accounts of the Hegelian dialectic as 'thesis-antithesis-synthesis'" (Hegel 1991, xxvii) or "This particular triadic piece of jargon was actually used by both Fichte and Schelling (each for his own purposes), but to my knowledge it was never used, not even once, by Hegel. We owe this way of presenting the Hegelian dialectic to Hein-

rich Moritz Chalybäus, a bowdlerizer of German idealist philosophy. . . . To use this jargon in expounding Hegel is almost always an unwitting confession that the expositor has little or no first-hand knowledge of Hegel" (Ibid. xxxii). My view is that a philosopher sometimes uses a method without reflectively discussing it or without labeling it in a scholarly fashion. Nevertheless, in the electronic version of Bailley's translation of the *Phenomenology* there were 17 hits for the word 'anti-thesis,' 2 hits for 'synthesis,' 1 for 'synthesizing,' and 10 for 'synthetic.' Also, Hegel frequently uses the word '*aber*' (but) to signal a turn in the argument. Furthermore, the word '*aber*' signals an upward spiral in the argumentation because it introduces facets of reality not taken into account by the view under discussion or because it introduces a new way of looking at the world which embraces previously overlooked facets of reality. (Hegel 1952, 147). I therefore feel justified in trying to put Hegel's argument, at least for pedagogical purposes, in the form of theses, anti-theses, and syntheses. It will be up to the reader to judge whether or not my effort creates clarity.

5. The full paragraph reads as follows: "The will contains (α) the element of pure indeterminacy or that pure reflection of the ego into itself which involves the dissipation of every restriction and every content either immediately presented by nature, by needs, desires, and impulses, or given and determined by any means whatever. This is the unrestricted infinity of absolute abstraction or universality, the pure thought of oneself."

6. Hegel defends a similar idea in his *Phenomenology* when he defines self-consciousness as: "primarily simple existence for self, self-identity by exclusion of every other from itself. It takes its essential nature and absolute object to be Ego; and in this immediacy, in this bare fact of its self-existence, it is individual. That which for it is other stands as unessential object, as object with the impress and character of negation" (Hegel 1967, 231).

7. The full text of the paragraph reads: " (β) At the same time, the ego is also the transition from undifferentiated indeterminacy to differentiation, determination, and positing of a determinacy as a content and object. Now further, this content may either be given by nature or engendered by the concept of mind. Through this positing of itself as something determinate, the ego steps in principle into determinate existence. This is the absolute moment, the finitude or particularization of the ego."

8. Again, Hegel makes a similar claim in his *Phenomenology* when he argues that life is essential for the life of self-consciousness. Self-consciousness discovers that in the fear of death. Hegel writes it this way:"In this experience [the life-and-death struggle which produces fear of death] self-consciousness becomes aware that life is as essential to it as pure self-consciousness. In immediate self-consciousness the simple ego is absolute object, which, however, is for us or in itself absolute mediation, and has as its essential moment substantial and solid independence" (Hegel 1967, 234).

9. The full text of this paragraph reads: "(γ) The will is the unity of both these moments. It is particularity reflected into itself and so brought back to universality, i.e. it is individuality. It is the self-determination of the ego, which means that at one and the same time the ego posits itself as its own negative, i.e. as restricted and determinate, and yet remains by itself, i.e. in its self-identity and universality. It determines itself yet at the same time binds itself together with itself. The ego determines itself

in so far as it is the relating of negativity to itself. As this self-relation, it is indifferent to this determinacy: it knows it as something which is its own, something which is only ideal, a mere possibility by which it is not constrained and in which it is confined only because it has put itself in it.—This is the freedom of the will and it constitutes the concept or substantiality of the will, its weight, so to speak, just as weight constitutes the substantiality of a body."

10. See Hegel 1975, 226 ff, #163–65; Hegel 1989, 600–22; Léonard 1974, 324–31. Several authors have reflected on the relation of Hegel's *Philosophy of Right* and his *Logic*. The definitive article, surveying also previous research is Richardson 1989.

11. At a certain age, children present a nice illustration of this development of the will. If one asks them the question: "why did you do that?," they answer: "because." To the further question: "because what?," they answer again: "because." With the help of Hegel's categories we can paraphrase the child's statements as follows: there is a because, namely the fact that the child decided. There is no object of the 'because,' since the child is not bound to have reasons, it is satisfactory that it so decided.

12. The great demands made upon thought for satisfying the strategy of happiness are clearly present in act utilitarianism. Thus, according to Bentham the pursuit of happiness requires one to calculate the value of each pleasure and each pain. The extent of calculation required becomes imaginable when one quotes the circumstances that must be taken into account to calculate an act's value. They are: its intensity, its duration, its certainty or uncertainty, its propinquity or remoteness, its fecundity, its purity, and its extent. These calculations have to be repeated for each person affected by the act under consideration (J. Bentham. *An Introduction to the Principles of Morals and Legislation*. Quoted in *Introductory Readings in Ethics*. W. K. Frankena and J. T. Granrose, eds. 134–37). The reference in this and the next footnote comes from my colleague T.L.Beauchamp.

13. One could see in rule utilitarianism an attempt to reach this level. Thus, in his article "Towards a Credible Form of Utilitarianism" R. B. Brandt's first proposal reads: "An act is right if and only if it conforms with that learnable set of rules, the adoption of which by everyone would maximize intrinsic value." (Quoted from *Introductory Readings in Ethics*, edited by W. K. Frankena and J. T. Granrose 160.) Commenting on his own principle he writes: "Presumably, then, it would contain rules rather similar to W. D. Ross's list of prima facie obligations" (Ibid. 160). Clearly, Brandt's thinking is different from Hegel's. The results too are different. However, both require from thought that it be able to specify a small number of things that have, unconditionally, to be done. Specifying what has to be done in order to reach freedom is the task that Hegel sets himself in his *Philosophy of Right*.

14. Ethical life in turn has three subdivisions which correspond to the three subdivisions of the third syllogism: the syllogism of necessity. The state is the third form of ethical life and thus corresponds to the third and last form of the syllogism of necessity: the disjunctive syllogism. Hegel's method is such that every level of the dialectic prepares the next step or that the next step relates to the problems of the previous step. Thus, the analysis of the disjunctive syllogism ends with the concept "objectivity"

(Hegel 1989, 704), which is the topic of analysis in the next section of Hegel's *Logic*, whose first chapter is "Mechanism." Richardson uses this consideration for his mapping of the *Logic* onto the *Philosophy of Right* (Richardson 1989, 65), which includes the state relating to both the disjunctive syllogism of necessity and mechanism.

15. The 1985 symposium in Jerusalem "Denial: A clarification of Theoretical Issues and Research" was very much concerned with this double possibility of denial. On the one hand, denial is potentially a maladaptive reaction as in the case of the Warsaw Ghetto where the Jews denied that they were in imminent danger of extermination by the Nazis. "They convinced themselves that only those Jews who had been communists were murdered in revenge by the Nazis" (Wangh 14). On the other hand, some who saw the danger and did not deny it committed suicide such "as the chairman of the Judenrat (Jewish Council) Adam Cherniakow" (Ibid. 14; Klein & Kogan; Davidson).

CHAPTER FIVE. A CHILD'S NO-SAYING: A STEP TOWARD INDEPENDENCE

1. In stressing that anxiety is caused by seeing a stranger, Spitz emphasizes the function of attachment to a familiar figure who was expected but turns out not to be there. In stressing that anxiety is caused by being seen by a stranger, I will argue that being seen, particularly by a stranger, has a disorganizing effect on the child. I will be using Sartre's theory to articulate the disorganizing effect of being seen.

2. Thus, the absence of eight-month-anxiety would not by itself justify the prediction of a later deficiency in interpersonal relations, because eight-month-anxiety is an organizer in the weak sense. The absence of no-saying would justify the prediction of later emotional deficiencies, because no-saying is, in my theory, an organizer in the strong sense.

3. In the first part of the chapter I will refer to the child as she and in the second part as he. However, for the purpose of the argument, sexual difference can be overlooked. I am simply following recommendations for gender neutral description.

4. It is worthwhile to look at the two figures mentioned in the quotation, pp.146 and 147.

5. For a relevant survey article see John Bowlby, 1982, particularly 667–70.

6. This is also the interpretation Konner attributed to the attachment theorists, referring to Bowlby and Ainsworth, writing that fear of strangers indicates "a deepening of the emotional bond" or "signalling the onset of the capacity for attachment" (Konner 1982, 149).

7. The concepts of indicator and organizer are concepts used by Spitz. Lacan uses the expressions: "The mirror stage as formative of the function of the I" (Lacan 1977, 1); "We have only to understand the mirror stage as an *identification*, in the full sense that analysis gives to the term: namely, the transformation that takes place in the subject when he assumes an image" (Ibid. 2). Both expressions indicate that, for Lacan, the mirror stage is creating something new. It is thus more than an indicator; it is an organizer.

8. In philosophical language, one can call a weak organizer a sufficient condition for the presence of a new and higher function in the child. It is not a necessary condition, however. On the contrary, a strong organizer is both a sufficient and a necessary condition for the new and higher function.

9. In Décarie et al.,1974, in the conclusion, one finds the following: "The findings of Goulet and Brossard raise serious doubts about the universality of the negative response" (192). In another study of the Montrèal group (Solomon and Décarie) one finds the statement: "It would also cast doubt upon theories which hold that stranger fear is an essential phase in normal development, and that the absence of stranger fear is pathogenic" (352).

10. The three publications and the relevant quotations are: "However, when a stranger approaches the eight-month-old, he is disappointed in his wish to have his mother. The anxiety he displays [. . .] is a response to his perception that the stranger's face is not identical with the memory traces of the mother's face" (Spitz 1965, 155). "In psychoanalytic terms we say: this is a response to the intrapsychic perception of the reactivated wishful tension and the ensuing disappointment" (Ibid. 155–56). Also, "The realization that it cannot be rediscovered in the given instance provokes a response of unpleasure. In terms of the eight-month anxiety, what we observe can be understood as follows: the stranger's face is compared to the memory traces of the mother's face and found wanting. This is not mother, she is still lost. Unpleasure is experienced and manifested" (Spitz 1957, 55). And third, "When a stranger approaches an infant, then the infant finds itself disappointed in its desire to see again the mother. And thus the anxiety which the infant manifests is not a reaction to a perception which revives a memory of a painful experience with the stranger. The infant is concerned with the nonidentity of the stranger with the mother, which the infant misses. Hence, we are here in the presence of a response to an intra-psychic perception, of a reactivation of a desire" (Spitz 1963, 155 [translation mine]).

11. Elsewhere, I formulate the new problem faced by the eight-month-old child as one of living with the body that he has appropriated. That body has an interiority and an exteriority. The child has the task of unifying those two aspects. Seeing seems to be the privileged sense with which to do so. But hearing and touching might be able to do so too. As these three senses synthesize the interiority and the exteriority of the body in different ways one could predict that persons who lack one of these senses will literally have to live with another body in as much as the lived body is not the physical body but the body as synthesized and as psychologically appropriated. Thus, children born blind or deaf can be expected to relate differently to their bodies. And indeed, deaf persons show a higher incidence of paranoic characteristics (Ver Eecke 1984, 61ff).

12. It is important to reflect on the relation between an *indicator* and an *organizer* and to keep in mind the distinction between a weak and a strong organizer.

For Spitz, the eight-month-anxiety is both an indicator and an organizer. First, the eight-month-anxiety is an *indicator* of a higher psychic structure because it indicates that the child has created libidinal object relations (she differentiates between the mother and a stranger), that she has the capability of experiencing a new affect (anxiety), and that she has achieved a higher integration of the ego (she can make judgments about the external world and take, if she so decides, defensive measures).

The eight-month-anxiety is also an *organizer of developments in several areas*. The eight-month-anxiety requires a psychic development which permits the child to discharge affective tensions in an intentional, directed, and volitional manner. The child must also possess a mental apparatus in which a number of memory traces can be stored such that she can distinguish between mother and stranger. Finally, many of the child's psychic and mental achievements require a somatic development which includes myelinization of the neural pathways such that the diacritic function of the sensory apparatus and the control of groups of skeletal muscles which permit directed action are possible.

An achievement in a critical period does not just organize developments of the past, it also makes the child ready for new achievements. Anxiety induced by the presence of a stranger demonstrates that the child has endowed the familiar person (the mother) with unique object attributes (Spitz 1957, 161–62). This allows the child to establish a kind of secure and exclusive relation with the mother. According to Spitz, this process requires differentiation and integration or a fusion of aggressive and libidinal drives. Seen in this way, the anxiety at eight months is an indicator of a highly complex emotional process that leads to the creation of a love object. This in turn, Spitz claims, will permit the development of identification as a defense mechanism. More precisely: the eight-month-anxiety can be seen as the organizer of a future achievement: identification.

But as the eight-month-anxiety does not by itself create future achievement, but only points to the presence of the necessary preconditions for that achievement, it is evident that one can call the eight-month-anxiety an organizer only in the weak sense of the term as defined above.

13. A somewhat longer summary of the development of Lacan's thought can be found in John P. Muller and William J. Richardson, *Lacan and Language*, 1–25.

14. By the concept of intrusion complex Lacan refers to the fact that siblings have difficulty tolerating other siblings. Lacan interprets sibling rivalry as a defensive reaction of one sibling to another sibling who is experienced as intruding into the cozy relation he or she has with the mother figure.

15. The difference between the drive model and the object relations model is the main concern of Jay R. Greenberg and Stephen A. Mitchell in their superb book, *Object Relations in Psychoanalytic Theory*. One can find references to their summaries on the mother-child relationship in various psychoanalytic theories by looking in the index under the concepts: attachment; deprivation, maternal; mother; mothering; symbiosis; separation-individuation.

16. Lacan's theory of the function of vision will allow me to explain eight-month-anxiety in a more satisfactory way. Of course, that makes my explanation dependent upon the validity of Lacan's theory. However, I will introduce a correction to Lacan's theory which should make my explanation not totally dependent upon Lacan. The correction I will introduce is that the child, in my reading, needs to appropriate his body as a totality. To use other language, one could say that the child needs to conquer his body by the construction of a body image. Seeing is an important sense

for such an image construction, but other senses can make a contribution too. When seeing is not available, as in children born blind, other senses can be thought of as capable of replacing the function of seeing to some extent. It is my hypothesis that the final result for the child will be different if he constructed his body image mainly by the sense of seeing, or used other senses as well, or constructed his body image by senses other than seeing. My hypothesis would find a tentative confirmation in the fact that deaf mutes tend statistically to have more paranoiac traits than the average population. My theory would also possibly provide a theoretical framework to think about the fact that hyperactive children interact more physically with people than the average child and thus must use the sense of touch more than other children, even for the construction of their own body image.

17. The expressions: "to appropriate one's body" or "the appropriation of one's body" have been coined to refer to a psychological act postulated in the child's development as a genetic counterpart to a philosophical idea. The philosophical idea is that the will and the body are not identical, yet are closely related. One way of understanding the coming to be of that close relation is to say that the will takes possession of the body. Let me quote the original philosophical text from which I took the idea: "In so far as the body is an immediate existent, it is not in conformity with mind. If it is to be the willing organ and soul-endowed instrument of mind, it must first be taken into possession by mind" (Hegel 1952, #48). The expressions "to appropriate one's body" or "the appropriation of one's body" are identical with the expressions: "to take possession of one's body" or "the taking possession of one's body." It is my understanding that the child takes possession of his body in many steps. Learning to walk is an example of such a step. I understand the mirror stage to be such a step as well. If my understanding of the mirror stage theory is correct, then it provides the child for the first time with the psychological sense of the unity of its body. For this reason I understand the mirror stage to be a crucial step in the psychological process of taking possession of one's body, of appropriating one's body.

Clearly such an interpretation of the concept "appropriation of one's body" is akin to the process other authors capture when they talk about the importance of the body image. In anorexia nervosa, for example, the body image is distorted. In the language I propose, one would say that the appropriation of the body is defective.

18. Specialists in child language distinguish between two forms of using "no": rejection and denial. Rejection refers to what we have called refusal. "No" as denial is the intellectual activity of disagreeing with the truth of a statement: "Is this a picture of a dog?" "No, it is a picture of a cat" (Hummer et al. 607). Specialists in child language observe that the capability to perform the rejection or refusal "no" emerges first. At least one group of authors argues for the so-called continuity thesis such that capability for using the denial "no" both benefits and depends upon the capability for using the rejection "no" (Ibid. 616). As a consequence, the child is better positioned to learn to correctly use the pair yes/no than to use the pair more/less or the pair before/after, and so on (Ibid. 608). Thus, one can claim that, for correctly using pairs of opposite terms, the child is initially helped by the emotional development which allowed him to use the refusal "no." The linguistic spill-over effects of the acquisition of "no" might therefore be greater than Spitz expected. It lays the groundwork for intellectually understanding opposite terms just as it also lays the groundwork for the

correct use of the pronouns (Ver Eecke 1984, 77–78). This foundational function of "no" as a rejection (refusal) is cross-culturally validated by a developmental study in child language which distinguishes nine forms of negation which emerge in three phases across three languages (English, French, and Korean). Rejection, judgment of nonexistence, prohibition, and indication of failure emerge in the first phase. Denial negation, epistemic negation, and expression of inability emerge in the second phase. Inferential and normative negation emerge in the third phase (Choi 525, 529). In some cases an old form of negation was used to express a new function—thus rejection negation (the refusal "no" discussed by Spitz) was used later as denial negation (intellectual judgment) (Ibid. 529). Bonnie Litowitz, in a remarkable survey article, defends the thesis that there are developmentally three forms of taking distance, each form dependant upon the prior form: rejection, refusal, and denial. Litowitz uses the vocabulary of object relations theory to define them: "what is rejected are 'bad' parts of others or oneself; what is refused is the impingement of an other's demand; what is denied is a statement from a separate other. Nevertheless, in all cases self and other are intrapsychic representation" (Litowitz 1998, 143).

19. This form of no-saying has an obvious dialogical character. It is then also not surprising that several studies noticed that negations occur more frequently in spoken language than in writing (Tottie; Stenstrom).

20. If the exercise of no-saying creates the beginning of autonomy, then we have a psychological argument for Freud's thesis that the acquisition—in the sense of mastery and usage—of the linguistic symbol of negation is a precondition of human freedom. Two linguists present arguments that are different from mine but do not contradict my thesis. Rather, their arguments reinforce the claim of negation's importance for human beings. Thus, Horn points out the opportunities that linguistic negation makes available to human beings. He writes: "All human systems of communication contain a representation of negation. No animal communication system includes negative utterances, and consequently none possesses a means for assigning truth utterances, and consequently none possesses a means for assigning truth value, for lying, for irony, or for coping with false or contradictory statements. The distinction between the largely digital nature of linguistic representation in human language and the purely analog mechanisms of animal communication can be argued to result directly from the essential use humans make of negation and opposition" (Horn xiii). Another linguist, Falkenberg, analyzes the three attempts to define a negation: the syntactic-morphological, the semantic-logical, and the pragmatic or action-theoretic one. He concludes that none succeeds in satisfactorily defining the negation. He then infers that negation is fundamental for the human world: "Reality cannot be created completely by affirmation alone, reality is really constituted in speech, in affirmative and negative speech" (Falkenberg, 148; my translation).

21. A more obvious example of the importance of emotional relations in helping the child live with his hurting body is the case of children who have teething pains. Sometimes their crying diminishes or even stops when they are cuddled by the mother or by a familiar figure. In my conceptual framework I would say that the child learns to live and to accept his hurting and thus unacceptable body *when* and *because* he is cuddled and thus loved or cared for. Living with one's body thus requires specific emotional relations with others. As historical sedimentation, others can therefore be presumed to be present in the relation I have developed to my body.

In my view, the child's emotional relations to others are crucial for accepting his body around the age of the mirror stage (about six months). It is an age that is included in the ages of the children studied by Spitz in his study on hospitalism.

22. An example (Ver Eecke 1984, 79–80) will be summarized in the next page.

23. This happy formula was coined after reading Muller and Richardson's summary statement about the function of language (1982, 9ff).

24. Eva Brann stresses several of the ideas developed above when she writes: "But meanwhile, in the terrible twos, there is also the *no* that is a mere manifesto of independence. It shows a cleavage in the child's ego, for while the child is saying *no*, it is, as was observed, often doing what the adult demands. The naysaying does not concern the objective issue but the ownership of the will: 'I have a will of my own and even when it is the same as yours, it is different because it is won. I am doing this because *I* want it and I am not doing what *you* want'" (Brann 13).

25. For a more complete treatment of the problem see Ver Eecke 1984.

26. The parallelism between Hegel and Freud might seem surprising at first. However, Hegel, as much as Freud and much more than, for instance, Kant, insisted on the fact that desires, wishes, and even vices are forces contributing to human action. In his theory of morality, Hegel will not insist on obedience to a universal law as Kant did, but to the need for mutual forgiving between human beings. Freud too is modest with reference to the moral demands he makes of human beings. Thus, Freud wrote in a letter to Putnam: "It is therefore more humane to establish this principle: 'Be as moral as you can honestly be and do not strive for an ethical perfection for which you are not destined'" (Hale 1971a, 122).

CHAPTER SIX. OEDIPUS, THE KING: HOW AND HOW NOT TO UNDO A DENIAL

1. The translated verses throughout this chapter are from Grene and Lattimore 1959.

2. Telling the truth, like warning people about preventable disasters, is often met, not with gratitude, but with irritation or denial. Thus, a study, dealing with the problem of how to overcome denial and negation of death, explicitly argues that one must avoid taking an opposite attitude as Teiresias did (de Hennezel 1989). Another author shows how arguments between a helper and a denier (called a"helpee") transform an intrapersonal struggle of denial into an interpersonal one of accusation and rejection. This happens because the denier is pushed by the helper to face frightening facts; the denier then defends herself against the threatening facts by denying them. The helper robs the denier of this defense. What a helper should do is provide support so that the denier can slowly learn to face frightening facts (Kearney 1996, 9–10). The helper should join the denier "(client) within the wall of denial" (Ibid. 114 ff). In short, the failure of Teiresias was his inability to understand that "denial does not yield to truth; it is a protection against it" (Ibid.).

3. Marie Kurrik prefers to underline a different role played by Jocasta. She lets the queen be the voice of warning that a tragic hero cannot listen to (Kurrik 1979,

243). She then also describes the cruel self-punishment of Oedipus as an act of freedom (Ibid. 259–60).

4. One might say that Oedipus repressed nothing, but simply did not know the
real meaning of certain events. (For example, he knew he committed a murder, but he
did not know the identity of the victim.) This observation could then support the
claim that what was needed was not "the return of the repressed" but a "revelation of
the truth." I prefer to maintain my usage of the idea of repression and to counter this
objection by referring to the definition of 'repression' in Jean Laplanche and J.B. Pontalis 1973, 2. The authors claim that repression can be considered a universal phenomenon in so far as it constitutes the unconscious as a domain that is separated from
consciousness, and that amnesia is to be understood as the result of "the incapability
to register meaningfully certain experiences." Undoing repression and amnesia would
therefore always involve an effort of interpretation in the sense of a search for the
"real meaning" of past events. According to psychoanalytic theory, the therapist is the
person who must present possible interpretative schemas and fulfill the role of revealer
of truth. Thus, the concept of repression still allows for "revelation of truth." I am
grateful to Dr. James Thomasson for having brought this objection to my attention,
and for the reference to Kierkegaard (see note 7).

5. As my colleague R. Curtis Bristol, MD pointed out to me, the stage directions
at the beginning of the play almost pictorially support this interpretation. The stage
directions demand that "Oedipus comes forward, *majestic* but for a *telltale limp*"
(emphasis mine). How can the audience not expect the story of this telltale limp?

6. Remember the stage instructions at the beginning of the play: "Oedipus
comes forward, majestic but for a telltale limp, and *slowly views the condition of his people*" (emphasis mine).

7. There is a succinct way to formulate this difference within a Lacanian framework. In order to help someone else-—for example, a patient in analysis-—it is necessary to allow imaginary projection prior to introducing a discordant element. Furthermore, the discordant remark must be introduced in such a way as not to
completely break the imaginary relationship. Jocasta, the messenger, and the shepherd
permitted Oedipus's imaginary identification. Teiresias makes such identification
impossible (Schema L in Lacan 1977). A non-Lacanian analyst, Dorpat, has described
two of his interventions which illustrate the difference. His first intervention was a
failure. The patient threatened to stop psychotherapy in order to go to an alcohol
counselor. Dorpat, just as Teiresias, lectured his dialogue partner. He lectured his
patient "about the differences between psychoanalytic psychotherapy and alcoholism
counseling" (Dorpat 1985, 232). Dorpat confessed that he acted out. And indeed, in
the next session the patient said: "you really did manipulate me last time by the way
you talked to me about psychotherapy" (Ibid.). With another patient, Dorpat inter-
vened successfully. The patient presented herself as helpless and asked Dorpat what
she should do about her infant son: Should she give up work in order to stay at home
with her infant or not? Dorpat answered: "You are turning over to me your own abil-
ities for thinking and deciding" (Ibid. 233). The patient answered that, as a child, she
felt that she only received attention when she presented a problem. Her father then
eagerly gave her advice. After the intervention,"The patient was relieved and grati-

fied that she could use her own mind in her relations with [Dorpat] and that she did not have to turn over the 'good' parts of herself to [Dorpat] (Ibid. 233). Dorpat here did not position himself as opposed to the patient. Rather, he provided the patient with words by which the patient could redescribe to herself her own situation. She thus was given the means to recreate herself.

Similar ideas are found in the psychological literature when addressing the question of how to help people in denial. The idea that people in denial must first be allowed imaginary identification with the interlocutor is formulated by several authors. Indeed, we find arguments to the effect that the interlocutor should avoid adopting an attitude opposite to that of the patient (de Hennezel 1989)—as Teiresias did; or that approaches other than direct confrontation are needed (Forchuk & Westwell); or that a degree of nurturance is required that creates a safe and accepting environment in the therapeutic relationship (Laflen & Sturm); or that acceptance in group therapy decreases denial because it allows identification (Rugel & Barry); or that avoidance of rejection and assurance of continued support and help improves the process of overcoming denial (Marshall); or that empathic understanding and a noncondemnatory attitude are crucial for moving from denial to acknowledgment of the denied facts (Geller et al.). Finally, in reviewing three methods for overcoming denial, Kearney stresses that in each method a positive climate has to be created. Thus, he writes that, when using the method of "Bursting the Bubble," "Participants must be willing and able to state their affection for the abuser" (Kearney 1996, 119); when using the method of "Peeling the Denial Onion," "a relationship with the user behind the wall of denial" (Ibid.) needs to be established which can become "a force of growth from within" (Ibid.). Kearney calls his third method for overcoming denial ENUF: "Empathizing Non-judgmentally and Unconditionally, and Focusing on feelings" (Ibid. 155).

Current authors are also aware that the interlocutor must not collude with denials and that the introduction of a discordant note is unavoidable. Identification and sympathy should therefore, not be the last step in one's relationship with deniers. Some argue that the underlying problem should be named (Berenson & Schrier); another author argues that the severity of the underlying problem should not be minimized; rather, in the case of patients denying death, the caregivers should acknowledge the patient's situation and the tragic violence of death (de Hennezel 1989). In the three methods surveyed to deal with denial, Kearney argues that the patient should be confronted either forcefully (bursting the bubble), step by step (peeling the onion), or should be refused the false comfort of merger (Kearney 1996, 152–53). One could argue that Jocasta, the messenger, and the shepherd—by their reluctance to speak—indirectly acknowledged the difficulty that Oedipus found himself in.

8. The thesis that truth can only be communicated indirectly can also be found in Søren Kierkegaard (1941), particularly in the section "Theses Possibly or Actually Attributable to Lessing," 67–113.

9. In Lacanian terminology one can say that the positions of Jocasta, the messenger, and the shepherd avoid imaginary identification with the discourse partner (Lacan 1977, 332–33). Avoidance of imaginary identification with one's discourse partner is necessary in order to be helpful to that partner.

10. The therapist is not supposed to talk to the relatives of the patient to confirm the truth of the information provided by the patient.

11. The patient is not supposed to make decisions that would fundamentally alter his/her life.

12. The psychoanalyst's task is to help a patient find the truth about himself. In the drama of *Oedipus*, however, we learn that Jocasta is more helpful than Teiresias in bringing about Oedipus's true self-knowledge. She is more helpful even though she was deceitful. Does this suggest that the psychoanalyst, in order to perform his task, must be deceitful? The answer seems to be affirmative; even the technical rules of the therapeutic discourse suggest this answer. The psychoanalyst is forbidden to gather information about the real-life situation of the patient. One could argue that such a rule forces the psychoanalyst into the position of having to do *as if* the account given by the patient about his life is true. But acting *as if* is the essence of deceitfulness.

A more constructive interpretation of the psychoanalyst's role is that the refusal to search for information beyond the discourse of the patient is the psychoanalyst's expression that he trusts the word of the patient as a tool towards discovery of the truth. Looking for evidence beyond the discourse would indicate that the therapist does not believe. The drama of Oedipus demonstrates that Oedipus himself must discover the truth about himself. *His* word must bring it about.

This interpretation of the role of the psychoanalyst finds confirmation in another rule of the therapeutic situation: that is, the psychoanalyst should not confirm the false beliefs of the patient. Instead, he should respond to the patient's story about himself by silence or by questions for further interpretation.

Thus we are in the presence of a crucial element in the discovery of truth about oneself: it is that *one's own word* must be respected as being capable of finding the truth about oneself. Sophocles gets this idea across by putting into opposition the attitudes of Teiresias and Jocasta towards Oedipus's own discourse. In telling the truth, Teiresias shows disrespect for Oedipus's own search. Jocasta's method of encouraging Oedipus to hold to false beliefs is a method which repects the capability of Oedipus to discover the truth about himself. In hindsight—that is, by means of a comparison with psychoanalysis—one can argue that it is not Jocasta's deceitfulness, but her respect for the power of Oedipus's own discourse, that helps Oedipus discover the truth about himself.

CHAPTER SEVEN. DENIAL, METAPHOR, THE SYMBOLIC, AND FREEDOM: THE ONTOLOGICAL DIMENSIONS OF DENIAL

1. In this chapter I will start by summarizing the analyses made in chapter 1 of this book and then proceed with a much more detailed analysis of the steps and processes involved in overcoming a denial. I will pay close attention to the steps that lead to a constructive outcome, compared with the tragic outcome portrayed in the case of Oedipus.

2. Freud, S.E., 236: "In the course of analytic work we often produce a further, very important and somewhat strange variant of this situation. We succeed in conquering the negation as well, and in bringing about a full intellectual acceptance of the repressed; *but the repressive process itself is not yet removed by this*" (emphasis mine).

3. Freud, *S.E.*, XIX, 235–36: "Thus the content of a repressed image or idea can make its way into consciousness, on condition that it is *negated*. Negation is a way of taking cognizance of what is repressed; indeed it is already a lifting of the repression, though not, of course, an acceptance of what is repressed."

4. In footnote 9 of chapter 1 of this book I explain how the just mentioned observation can be used to show my agreement and my disagreement with A.O. Rorty's interpretation of self-deception. Although concepts of self-deception and denial are not identical they are obviously related.

5. It is my contention that young Moore could understand the significance of his not participating in ROTC in college only after he had intellectually unmasked the denial of the importance of losing his father.

6. Rorty proposes a similar thesis when she writes: "We certainly think we can recognize self-deception in others, and we strongly suspect it in ourselves, even *retrospectively attributing it to our past selves*" (Rorty 22, emphasis mine).

7. Contrary to Rorty, I see self-deception as the result of a person having at least two layers of intentionality and these layers following each a different logic in their interpretation of experience. Rorty proposes a further condition for self-deception when she writes: "Not everyone has the special talents and capacities for self-deception. It is a disease only the presumptively strong minded can suffer" (Rorty 25). Rorty interprets strong-mindedness as the capability to superimpose on a multilayered intentionality the will to rational unity. I want to argue that the will to rational unity leads to a denial, not a self-deception. Furthermore, Moore's case, as I analyzed it, demonstrates that the ability to formulate a denial as opposed to simply living in self-deception should not be called strong-mindedness. Rather, it is the result of the help of another, who in this case spoke the proper words so that Moore could accept the pain that had necessitated the self-deception. By relating the concept of denial to that of self-deception, I am forced to disagree twice with Rorty's understanding of self-deception. To put it in a different way: for me it seems that many people can and do deceive themselves; fewer are able to articulate the deception in the form of a denial; fewer still are able to intellectually undo such denials and come to understand that they denied something and were thus subject to self-deception; fewer still are able to do the psychic work demanded to face up to the implications of the discovery of their denial or self-deception.

Bibliography

Agassi, J. (1997). Self-Deception: A View from the Rationalist Perspective. In M. S. Myslobodsky (Ed.), *The Mythomanias: The Nature of Deception and Self-Deception*. Mahwah, NJ: Lawrence Erlbaum Associates.

Amadeo, M., & Liftik, J. (1990). Working Through Denial in Alcoholism. *Families in Society*, 71(3), 131–35.

Angehrn, E. (1977). *Freiheit und System bei Hegel*. Berlin: de Gruyter.

Athanassiou, C. (1995). *Introduction á l'Étude du Surmoi*. Lyon: Césura.

Atkins, E. L., Grimes, J. P., Gregory, W., & Liebman, J. (1999). Denial of Pregnancy and Neonaticide During Adolescence: Forensic and Clinical Issues. *American Journal of Forensic Psychology*, 17(1), 5–33.

Avineri, S. (1968). *The Social and Political Thought of Karl Marx*. London and New York: Cambridge University Press.

Baider, L., & Edelstein, E. (1989). Beyond Denial: Replacement Fantasies in Patients with Life-Threatening Illness. In E. Edelstein, D. L. Nathanson & A. M. Stone (Eds.), *Denial: A Clarification of Concepts and Research*. New York: Plenum Press.

Baum, A. S., & Burnes, D. W. (1993). *A Nation in Denial: The Truth about Homelessness*. Boulder, Co: Westview Press.

Beilin, R. (1981–82). Social Functions of Denial of Death. *Omega: Journal of Death and Dying*, 12(1), 25–35.

Benmakhlouf, A. (2001). G. Frege sur la Négation comme Opposition sans Force. *Revue de Métaphysique et de Morale* (2), 7–19.

Benoist, J. (2001). La Théorie Phénoménologique de la Négation, entre Acte et Sens. *Revue de Métaphysique et de Morale* (2), 21–35.

Berns, J. (1982). Denial of Pregnancy in Single Women. *Health and Social Work*, 7(4), 314–19.

Berthold-Bond, D. (1995). *Hegel's Theory of Madness*. Albany, NY: State University of New York Press.

Bowlby, J. (1982). Attachment and Loss: Retrospect and Prospect. *American Journal of Orthopsychiatry*, 52, 664–78.

Boyajian, L. Z., & Grigorian, H. M. (1998). Reflections on the Denial of the Armenian Genocide. *Psychoanalytic Review*, 85(4), 505–16.

Brann, E. (2001). *The Ways of Naysaying*. Lanham: Rowman & Littlefield Publishers.

Brenitz, S. (1988). The Seven Kinds of Denial. In P. Defares et al. (Eds.), *Stress and Anxiety, Vol. 11. The Series in Clinical and Community Psychology*. Washington, D.C.: Hemisphere Publishing Corp/ Harper & Row.

Cella, D. F., & Najavits, L. (1987). Denial of Infertility in Patients with Hodgkin's Disease. *Psychosomatics*, 27(1), 71.

Chamley, P. (1963). *Economie politique et philosphie chez Steuart et Hegel*. Paris: Dalloz.

Chauvin, R. (1941). Contibutions à l'étude physiologique du criquet pélerin et du déterminisme des phénomènes grégaires. *Annales de la Société entologique de France*, 110, 133–272.

Choi, S. (1988). The Semantic Development of Negation. *Journal of Child Language*, 15(3), 517–31.

Close, M. M. (1983). Child Welfare and People of Color: Denial of Equal Access. *Social Work Research and Abstracts*, 19(4), 13–20.

Connor, S. R. (1988). Measurement of Denial in the Terminally Ill: A Critical Review. *Hospice Journal*, 2(4), 51–68.

Cortese, A. J. (1987). The Denial of Access: Chicanos in Higher Education. *Cornell Journal of Social Relations*, 18(2), 28–39.

Cullen, B. (1979). *Hegel's Social and Political Thought: An Introduction*. New York: St. Martin's Press.

David-Ménard, M. (2001). La Négation comme sortie de l'Ontologie. *Revue de Métaphysique et de Morale* (2), 59–67.

Davidson, S. (1989). Avoidance and Denial in the Life Cycle of Holocaust Survivors. In E. Edelstein, D. L. Nathanson & A. M. Stone (Eds.), *Denial: A Clarification of Concepts and Research*. New York: Plenum.

Décarie, T. G., Goulet, J., Brossard, M. D., & Shaffran, R. (1974). *The Infant's Reaction to Strangers* (J. Diamanti, Trans.). New York: International Universities Press.

Denis, H. (1984). *Logique Hegelienne et systèmes économiques*. Paris: Presses Universitaires de France.

de Hennezel, M. (1989). Denial and Imminent Death. *Jounal of Palliative Care*, 5(3), 27–31.

———. (1991). La Dimension du Déni à l'Aproche de la Mort. *Psychologie Medicale*, 23(2), 149–53.

de Saussure, F. (1959). *Course in General Linguistics* (C. Bally & A. Sechehaye, Eds.) (W. Baskin, Trans.). New York: Philosophical Library.

De Waelhens, A. (1978). *Schizophrenia: A Philosophical Reflection on the Structuralist Interpretation of J. Lacan* [Introduction, Explanatory Footnotes and a Bibliography by W.Ver Eecke] (W. Ver Eecke, Trans.). Pittsburgh: Duquesne University Press.

Dorpat, T. L. (1983). The Cognitive Arrest Hypothesis of Denial. *International Journal of Psychoanalysis*, 64, 47–59.

———. (1985). *Denial and Defense in the Therapeutic Situation*. New York: Aronson.

———. (1988). A New Look at Denial and Defense. *Annual of Psychoanalysis*, 15, 23–47.

———. (1989). Interactional Perspective on Denial and Defense. In E. Edelstein, D. L. Nathanson & A. M. Stone (Eds.), *Denial: A Clarification of Concepts and Research*. New York: Plenum.

Douglass, F. (1997). *Narrative of the Life of Frederick Douglass*. New York: Signet Classic.

Dubouchet, P. (1995). *La Philosophie du Droit de Hegel: Essay de Lecture des "Principes."* Lyon: L'Hermes.

Evans, D. (1996). *An Introductory Dictionary of Lacanian Psychoanalysis*. London and New York: Routledge.

Falkenberg, G. (1985). Negation und Verneinung. In W. Kürschner & R. Vogt (Eds.), *Sprachtheorie, Pragmatik, Interdisciplinäres*, 141–50. Tübingen: Max Niemeyer Verlag.

Finger, S. (1998). A Happy State of Mind: A History of Mild Elation, Denial of Disability, Optimism, and Laughing in Multiple Sclerosis. *Archives of Neurology*, 55(2), 241–50.

Forchuk, C., & Westwell, J. (1987). Denial. *Journal of Psychosocial and Mental Health Services*, 25(6), 9–13.

Forrester, J. (1980). *Language and the Origins of Psychoanalysis*. New York: Columbia University Press.

Fraiberg, S., & Adelson, E. (1973). Self-Representation in Language and Play: Observations of Blind Children. *Psychoanalytic Quarterly*, 42, 539–62.

Frankena, W., & Granrose, J. T. (1974). *Introductory Readings in Ethics*. Englewood Cliffs: Prentice-Hall.

Freitas, N. K. (1982). Um Estudo sobre a Negacao Maniaca e a Depresssao nas maes de Pacientes Cancerosos Terminais. *Psico*, 5(2), 94–131.

Freud, S. (1953–74). *The Standard Edition of the Complete Psychological Works of Sigmund Freud* (J. Strachey, Ed. and Trans.) (Vol. 1–24). London: Hogarth Press.

———. (1963). *Three Case Histories*. New York: Collier.

Fukunishi, I., Numatas, Y., & Hattori, M. (1994). Alexithymia and Defense Mechanisms in Myocardial Infarction. *Psychological Reports*, 75(1), 219–23.

Gabbay, D., & Moravsick, J. (1978). Negation and Denial. In F. Guenther & C. Roher (Eds.), *Studies in Formal Semantics*, 251–65. Amsterdam: North Holland.

Geller, M., Devlin, M., Flynn, T., & Kaliski, J. (1985). Confrontation of Denial in a Fathers' Incest Group. *International Journal of Group Psychotherapy*, 35(4), 545–67.

Gerzi, S., & Berman, E. (1981). Emotional Reactions of Expectant Fathers to their Wives' First Pregnancy. *British Journal of Medical Psychology*, 54(3), 259–65.

Geurts, B. (1998). The Mechanism of Denial. *Language*, 74(2), 274–307.

Green, A. (1997). The Intuition of the Negative in Playing and Reality. *International Journal of Psycho-Analysis*, 78, 1071–84.

———. (1998). The Primordial Mind and the Work of the Negative. *International Journal of Psycho-Analysis*, 79, 649–65.

———. (1999). *The Work of the Negative* (A. Weller, Trans.). London, New York: Free Association Books.

Green, C. M., & Manohar, S. V. (1990). Neonaticide and Hysterical Denial of Pregnancy. *British Journal of Psychiatry*, 156, 121–23.

Greenberg, J. R., & Mitchell, S. A. (1983). *Object Relations in Psychoanalytic Theory*. Cambridge, Mass.: Harvard University Press.

Greenwald, A. G. (1997). Self-Knowledge and Self-Deception: Further Consideration. In M. S. Myslobodsky (Ed.), *The Mythomanias: The Nature of Deception and Self-deception*, 51–71. Mahwah, NJ: Lawrence Erlbaum Associates.

Grene, D., & Lattimore, R. (Eds.). (1959). *The Complete Greek Tragedies. 4 Volumes. Vol 2: Sophocles*. Chicago: University of Chicago Press.

Gussaroff, E. (1998). Denial of Death and Sexuality in the Treatment of Elderly Patients. *Psychoanalysis and Psychotherapy*, 15(1), 77–91.

Hale, N. G. (1971). *Freud and the Americans: The Beginnings of Psychoanalysis in the United States, 1876–1917*. Oxford: Oxford University Press.

Harada, T. (1989). *Politische Ökonomie des Idealismus und der Romantik: Korporatismus von Fichte, Muller und Hegel*. Berlin: Duncker & Humblot.

Hardimon, M. O. (1994). *Hegel's Social Philosophy: The Project of Reconciliation*. Cambridge: Cambridge University Press.

Hegel, G. (1952). *Phänomenologie des Geistes* (J. Hoffmeister, Ed.). Hamburg: Felix Meiner.

———. (1967). *Jenaer Realphilosophie. Vorlesungsmanuskripte zur Philosophie der Natur und des Geistes von 1805–1806*. In *Philosophische Bibliothek* 47 [Reprint of "Jenenser Realphilosophie II"] (J.Hoffmeister, Ed.). Hamburg: Felix Meiner.

———. (1967). *The Phenomenology of Mind* (J. B. Baillie, Trans.). New York: Harper Torchbooks.

———. (1967b). *Hegel's Philosophy of Right* (T. Knox, Trans.). Oxford: Oxford University Press.

———. (1971). *Hegel's Philosophy of Mind* (W. Wallace & A. Miller, Trans.). Oxford: Clarendon Press.

———. (1971). *Philosophy of Mind* (T. Knox, Trans.). Oxford: Oxford University Press.

———. (1975). *Aesthetics: Lectures on Fine Art. Vol. I–II* (T. Knox, Trans.). Oxford: Clarendon Press.

———. (1977). *Early Theological Writings* (T. M. Knox, Trans.). Philadelphia: University of Pennsylvania Press.

———. (1977b). *Phenomenology of Spirit* (A. Miller, Trans.). Oxford: Oxford University Press.

———. (1989). *Hegel's Science of Logic* (A. Miller, Trans.). Atlantic Highlands, NJ: Humanities Press International.

———. (1990). *The Phenomenology of Mind* [Machine readable version] (J. Baillie, Trans.). Washington, D.C.: Georgetown University.

———. (1991). *Elements of the Philosophy of Right* (A. Wood, Ed.) (N. Nisbet, Trans.). Cambridge: Cambridge University Press.

Hein, K. K., Blair, J. F., Ratzan, S. C., & Dyson, D. E. (1993). Adolescents and HIV: Two Decades of Denial. In S. C. Ratzan et al. (Eds.), *AIDS: Effective Health Communication for the 90s*. Philadelphia: Taylor & Francis.

Henrich, D., & Horstmann, R. (Eds.). (1982). *Hegels Philosophie des Rechts: Die Theorie der Rechtsformen und ihre Logik*. Stuttgart: Klett-Cotta.

Hoke, S. L., Sykes, C., & Winn, M. (1989). Systemic /Strategic Interventions Targeting Denial in the Incestuous Family. *Journal of Strategic and Systemic Therapies*, 8(4), 44–51.

Horn, L. R. (1989). *A Natural History of Negation*. Chicago: University of Chicago Press.

Hummer, P., Wimmer, H., & Antes, G. (1993). On the Origins of Denial Negation. *Journal of Child Language*, 20(3), 607–18.

Hyppolite, J. (1988). A Spoken Commentary on Freud's "Verneinung" (J. Forrester, Trans.). In J. Miller (Ed.), *The Seminar of Jacques Lacan. Book I . Freud's Papers on Technique. 1953–1954*. New York: W.W. Norton.

Ibsen, H. (1908). *The Collected Works. 11 Vols. Vol. VII: Ghosts* (W. Archer, Ed.). New York: Scribners.

Jackson, C., & Davidson, G. P. (1997). The Anorexic Patient as a Survivor: The Denial of Death and Death Themes in the Literature on Anorexia Nervosa. *International Journal of Eating Disorders*, 5(5), 821–35.

Jackson, C., & Thomas-Peter, B. A. (1994). Denial in Sex Offenders: Workers' Perceptions. *Criminal Behavior and Mental Health*, 4(1), 21–32.

Jacobson, E. (1957). Denial and Repression. *Journal of the American Psychoanalytic Association*, 5, 61–92.

Jakobson, R., & Halle, M. (1956). Two Aspects of Language and Two Types of Aphasic Disturbances. In *Fundamentals of Language*. The Hague: Mouton.

Jarczyk, G., & Labarrière, P. (1986). *Hegeliana*. Paris: Presses Universitaires de France.

Jelicic, M., Bonke, B., & Millar, K. (1993). Clinical Note on the Use of Denial in Patients Undergoing Surgery for Breast Cancer. *Psychological Reports*, 72(3, Pt.1), 952–54.

Jermann, C. (Ed.). (1987). *Anspruch und Leistung von Hegels Rechtsphilososphie*. Stuttgart-Bad Cannstatt: Frommann-Holzboog.

Kagan, J. (1976). Emergent Themes in Human Development. *American Scientist*, 64(2), 186–96.

Kainz, H. (1974). *Hegel's Philosophy of Right, with Marx's Commentary: A Handbook for Students*. The Hague: Martinus Nijhoff.

Kearney, R. (1988). *The Wake of Imagination: Toward a Postmodern Culture*. Minneapolis, MN: University of Minnesota Press.

———. (1996). *Within the Wall of Denial: Conquering Addictive Behaviors*. New York: W.W. Norton and Co.

Kennedy, H., & Grubin, D. (1992). Patterns of Denial in Sex Offenders. *Psychological Medicine*, 22(1), 191–96.

Kernberg, O. F. (1974). Further Contributions to the Treatment of Narcissistic Personalities. *International Journal of Psycho-Analysis*, 55, 215–40.

Kierkegaard, S. (1941). *Concluding Unscientific Postscript* (D. F. Swenson & W. Lowrie, Trans.). Princeton: Princeton University Press.

Klein, H., & Kogan, I. (1989). Some Observations on Denial and Avoidance in Jewish Holocaust and Post-Holocaust Experience. In E. Edelstein, D. L. Nathanson & A. M. Stone (Eds.), *Denial: A Clarification of Concepts and Research*. New York: Plenum.

Klein, M. (1948). The Early Development of Conscience in the Child. In *Contributions to Psycho-analysis. 1921–1945*. London: Hogarth Press.

———. (1957). *Envy and Gratitude: A Study of Unconscious Sources*. New York: Basic Books.

Kojève, A. (1969). *Introduction to the Reading of Hegel, Abridged* (J. Nichols, Trans.). New York: Basic Books.

Konner, M. (1982). Biological Aspects of the Mother-Infant Bond. In R. Emde & R. Harmon (Eds.), *The Development of Attachment and Affiliate Systems*, 137–59. New York and London: Plenum Press.

Kraus, J. B. (1931/1932). Wirtschaft und Gesellschaft bei Hegel. *Archiv für Rechts-und Wirstschaftsphilosophie*, 25.

Krestan, J., & Bepko, C. (1993). On Lies, Secrets, and Silence: The Multiple Levels of Denial in Addictive Families. In E. Imber-Black, al. (Ed.), *Secrets in Families and Family Therapy* (141–59). New York: W.W. Norton & Co.

Kurrik, M. J. (1979). *Literature and Negation*. New York: Columbia University Press.

Lacan, J. (1977). *Écrits: A Selection* (A. Sheridan, Trans.). New York: W.W. Norton & Co.

———. (1981). *Séminaire III. Les Psychoses*. Paris: Éditions du Seuil.

———. (1984). *Les complexes Familiaux*. Paris: Navarin.

———. (1988). Introduction and Reply to Jean Hyppolite's Presentation of Freud's "Verneinung" (J. Forrester, Trans.). In J. Miller (Ed.), *The Seminar of Jacques Lacan Book I: Freud's Papers on Technique 1953–1954*. New York: W.W. Norton & Co.

———. (1988). *The Seminar of Jacques Lacan Book I: Freud's Papers on Technique. 1953–1954* (J. Miller, Ed.) (J. Forrester, Trans.). New York: W.W. Norton & Co.

———. (1993). *Seminar III. The Psychoses*. New York: W.W. Norton & Co.

Lacoue-Labarthe, P., & Nancy, J. L. (1992). *The Title of the Letter: A Reading of Lacan* (F. Raffoul & D. Pettigrew, Trans.). New York: State University of New York Press.

Laflen, B., & Sturm, W. R. (1994). Understanding and Working with Denial in Sexual Offenders. *Journal of Child Sexual Abuse*, 3(4), 19–36.

Lakoff, G., & Johnson, M. (1980). *The Metaphors We Live By*. Chicago: University of Chicago Press.

———. (1999). *Philosophy in the Flesh: The Embodied Mind*. New York: Basic Books.

Laplanche, J., & Leclaire S. (1970). The Unconscious: A Psychoanalytic Study (P. Coleman, Trans.). *Yale French Studies* 1972, 48, 118–75.

Laplanche, J., & Pontalis J-B. (1973). *The Language of Psychoanalysis* (D. Nicholson-Smith, Trans.). New York: W.W. Norton & Co.

Léonard, A. (1974). *Commentaire Litteréral de la Logique de Hegel*. Louvain: Institut Supérieur de Philosophie. Éditions Peeters.

Lévi-Strauss, C. (1949). The Effectiveness of Symbols (C. Jacobson & B. Schoepf, Trans.). In *Structural Anthropology*, 186–205. New York: Basic Books, 1963.

———. (1949). Language and the Analysis of Social Laws (C. Jacobson, & B. Schoepf, Trans.). In *Structural Anthropology*, 55–66. New York: Basic Books.

Levenson, J. L., Kay, R., Monteferrante, J., & Herman, M. V. (1984). Denial Predicts Favorable Outcome in Unstable Angina Pectoris. *Psychosomatic Medicine*, 46(1), 25–32.

Levine, J., Rudy, T., & Kerns, R. (1994). A Two Factor Model of Denial of Illness: A Confirmatory Factor Analysis. *Journal of Psychosomatic Research*, 38(2), 99–110.

Liebeskind, A. S. (1991). Chemical Dependency and the Denial of the Need for Intimacy. In A. Smaldino et al. (Eds.), *Psychoanalytic Approaches to Addiction*. New York: Brunner/Mazel.

Litowitz, B. E. (1998). An Expanded Developmental Line for Negation: Rejection, Refusal, Denial. *Journal of the American Psychoanalytic Association*, 46(1), 121–48.

Lubinsky, M. S. (1994). Bearing Bad News: Dealing with the Mimics of Denial. *Journal of Genetic Counseling*, 3(1), 5–12.

Lucas, H., & Pöggeler, O. (Eds.). (1986). *Hegels Rechtsphilosophie im Zusammenhang der Europäischen Verfassungsgeschichte*. Stuttgart-Bad Cannstatt: Frommann-Holzboog.

Lukacs, G. (1973). *Der junge Hegel*. Frankfurt am Main: Suhrkamp.

Maker, W. (Ed.). (1987). *Hegel on Economics and Freedom*. Macon: Mercer University Press.

Mannoni, M. (1972). *The Backward Child and his Mother* (A. M. Sheridan Smith, Trans.). New York: Random House.

Marshall, W. (1994). Treatment Effects on Denial and Minimization in Incarcerated Sex Offenders. *Behaviour Research and Therapy*, 32(5), 559–64.

Marx, K. (1977). *Critique of Hegel's Philosophy of Right* (J. O'Malley, Trans.). Cambridge: Cambridge University Press.

Matthews, L. (1938–39). Visual Stimulation and Ovulation in Pigeons. In *Proceedings of the Royal Society of London, Series B 126*, 557–60.

McLaughlin, B. P., & Rorty, A. O. (Eds.). (1988). *Perspectives on Self-Deception*. Berkeley: University of California Press.

Miéville, D. (Guest Editor). (1992). *Argumentation*, 6(1). Negation.

Milden, R., Rosenthal, M., Winegardner, J., & Smith, D. (1985). Denial of Pregnancy: An Exploratory Investigation. *Journal of Psychosomatic Obstretrics and Gynecology*, 4(4), 255–61.

Miller, L. J. (1990). Psychotic Denial of Pregnancy: Phenomenology and Clinical Management. *Hospital and Community Psychiatry*, 41(11), 1233–37.

Moeschler, J. (1992). The Pragmatic Aspects of Linguistic Negation: Speech Act, Argumentation and Pragmatic Inference. *Argumentation*, 6(1), 51–76.

Moore, A. (2000). *Father, Son, and Healing Ghosts*. Gainesville, Fl: Center for Applications of Psychological Type.

Morita, T., Inoue, S., & Chihara, S. (1997). Denial of Terminal Patients with Advanced Cancer. *Seishin Igaku Clinical Psychiatry*, 39(2), 173–80.

Moyer, A., & Levine, E. G. (1998). Clarification of the Conceptualization and Measurement of Denial in Psychosocial Oncology Research. *Annals of Behavioral Medicine*, 20(3), 149–60.

Muller, J. P., & Richardson, W. J. (1982). *Lacan and Language. A Reader's Guide to Écrits*. New York: International Universities Press.

Myerson, G. (1994). *Rhetoric, Reason, and Society: Rationality as Dialogue*. London: Sage.

Opatow, B. (1988). The Self as Desire: A Freudian Dialectic. *Psychoanalysis and Contemporary Thought*, 11(4), 615–37.

———. (1989). Drive Theory and the Metapsychology of Experience. *International Journal of Psycho-Analysis*, 70, 645–60.

———. (1993). On the Drive-Rootedness of Psychoanalytic Ego Psychology. *International Journal of Psycho-Analysis*, 74, 437–57.

———. (1997). The Real Unconscious: Psychoanalysis as a Theory of Consciousness. *Journal of the American Psychoanalytic Association*, 45(3), 865–90.

Ornstein, P. (1976). A Discussion of the Paper by Otto F. Kernberg on "Further Contributions to the Treatment of Narcissistic Personalities." *International Journal of Psycho-Analysis*, 55, 241–47.

Pelczynski, Z. (Ed.). (1984). *The State & Civil Society*. Cambridge: University of Cambridge Press.

Peperzak, A. (1960). *Le Jeune Hegel et la Vision Morale du Monde*. La Haye: Nijhoff.

———. (1987). *Philosophy and Politics: A Commentary on the Preface to Hegel's Philosophy of Right*. Dordrecht: Martinus Nijhoff.

Pruneti, C., L'Abbate, A., & Steptoe, A. (1993). Personality and Behavioral Changes in Patients after Myocardial Infarction. *Research Communications in Psychology, Psychiatry and Behavior*, 18(1–2), 37–51.

Reyburn, H. A. (1967). *The Ethical Theory of Hegel: A Study of the Philosophy of Right*. Oxford: Clarendon Press.

Richardson, H. (1989, January). The Logical Structure of Sittlichkeit: A Reading of Hegel's Philosophy of Right. *Idealistic Studies*, 19(7), 62–78.

Richardson, W. J. (1987). Ethics and Desire. *The American Journal of Psychoanalysis*, 47(4), 296–301.

———. (1988). Lacan and the Problem of Psychosis. In D. B. Allison, P. de Oliveira, M. S. Roberts & A. S. Weiss (Eds.), *Psychosis and Sexual Identity: Toward a Post-Analytic View of the Schreber Case*. Albany: State University of New York Press.

Riedel, M. (1973). *System und Geschichte. Studien zum historischen Standort von Hegels Philosophie*. Frankfurt am Main: Suhrkamp Verlag.

———. (Ed.). (1975). *Materialien zu Hegels Rechtsphilosophie* (Vols. I–II). Frankfurt am Main: Suhrkamp Verlag.

Rorty, A. O. (1988). The Deceptive Self: Liars, Layers, and Lairs. In B. P. McLaughlin & A. O. Rorty (Eds.), *Perspectives on Self-Deception*. Berkeley: University of California Press.

Roth, K. (1989). *Freiheit und Institutionen in der politischen Philosophie Hegels*. Rheinfelden: Schauble.

Roth, M. S. (1987). *Psycho-Analysis as History. Negation and Freedom in Freud*. Ithaca: Cornell University Press.

Rugel, R. P., & Barry, D. (1990). Overcoming Denial through the Group: A Test of Acceptance Theory. *Small Group Research*, 21(1), 45–58.

Sartre, J. P. (1966). *Being and Nothingness: An Essay in Phenomenological Ontology* (H. E. Barnes, Trans.). New York: Washington Square Press.

Sass, L. (1994). *Paradoxes of Delusion: Wittgenstein, Schreber, and the Schizophrenic Mind*. Ithaca: Cornell Uiversity Press.

Schmitt, M., Montada, L., & Dalbert, C. (1992). Struktur und Funktion der Verantwortlichkeitsabwher. *Zeitschrift für Differentielle und Diagnostische Psychologie*, 12(4), 203–14.

Seeberger, W. (1961). *Hegel oder die Entwicklung des Geistes zur Freiheit*. Stuttgart: Ernst Klett.

Segal, H. (1989). *Klein*. London: Karnac Books.

Sevush, S., & Leve, N. (1993). Denial of Memory Deficit in Alzheimer's Disease. *American Journal of Psychiatry*, 150(5), 748–51.

Shanan, J. (1989). The Place of Denial in Adult Development. In E. Edelstein, D. L. Nathanson & A. M. Sone (Eds.), *Denial: A Clarification of Concepts and Research*, 107–18. New York: Plenum Press.

Smith, S. B. (1989). *Hegel's Critique of Liberalism: Rights in Context*. Chicago: University of Chicago Press.

Solomon, Z. (1995). From Denial to Recognition: Attitudes towards Holocaust Survivors from World War II to the Present. *Journal of Traumatic Stress*, 8(2), 215–28.

Sophocles. (1959). *The Complete Greek Tragedies. 4 Volumes* (D. Grene & R. Lattimore, Eds.) (Vol. 1). Chicago: University of Chicago Press.

Soulez, A. (2001). De la Négation à la Dénégation chez Wittgenstein: Une Enquête Limitée sur la Source de l'Aveuglement au Symbolisme. *Revue de Métaphysique et de Morale* (2), 37–58.

———. (2001). Présentation. *Revue de Métaphysique et de Morale* (2), 3–6.

Spitz, R. A. (1957). *No and Yes: On the Genesis of Human Communication*. New York: International Universities Press.

———. (1958). On the Genesis of the Super-Ego Components. *Psychoanalytic Study of the Child*, 13, 375–404.

———. (1965). *The First Year of Life*. New York: International Universities Press.

———. (1963). *La Première Annèe de lavie de l'Enfant*. Paris: Presses Universitaires de France.

Steinberger, P. J. (1988). *Logic and Politics: Hegel's Philosophy of Right*. New Haven: Yale University Press.

Stenstrom, A. B. (1985). English in Speech and Writing: A Project Report. *Papers and Studies in Contrastive Linguistics*, 19, 115–30.

Stevenson, H. C., Castillo, E., & Sefarbi, R. (1989). Treatment of Denial in Adolescent Sex Offenders and their Families. *Journal of Offender Counseling Services and Rehabilitation*, 14(1), 37–50.

Stewart, J. R. (1995). Denial of Disabling Conditions and Specific Interventions in the Rehabilitation Counseling Setting. *Journal of Applied Rehabilitation Counseling*, 25(3), 7–15.

Strelzer, J., Moe, M., Yanagida, E., & Siemsen, A. (1984). Coping with Transplant Failure: Grief vs. Denial. *International Journal of Psychiatry in Medicine*, 13(2), 97–106.

Tottie, G. (1982). Where Do Negative Sentences Come From? *Studia Linguistica*, 36(1), 88–105.

Van Buren, J. (1995). Postmodernism: Feminism and the Deconstruction of the Feminine: Kristeva and Irigaray. *American Journal of Psychoanalysis*, 55(3), 231–43.

Van der Hart, O., Faure, H., Van Gerven, M., & Goodwin, J. (1991). Unawareness and Denial of Pregnancy in Patients with MPD. *Dissociation: Progress in the Dissociative Disorders*, 4(2), 65–73.

Ver Eecke, W. (1975). The Look, the Body, and the Other. In D. Ihde and R. M. Zaner (Eds.), *Selected Studies in Phenomenology and Existential Philosophy. Vol 5: Dialogues in Existential Philosophy*. The Hague: Nyhoff.

———. (1981). Epistemological Consequences of Freud's Theory of Negation. *Man and World*, 14, 111–25.

———. (1983). Hegel as Lacan's Source for Necessity in Psychoanalytic Theory. In *Interpreting Lacan*. In J. H. Smith and W. Kerrigan (Eds.), 113–38. New Haven: Yale University Press.

———. (1983). Negation and Desire in Freud and Hegel. *Owl of Minerva*, 15, 11–22.

———. (1984). *Saying 'No.'* Pittsburgh: Duquesne University Press.

———. (1988). Saying 'No':The Special Status of the Word 'No.' *Psychanalyse*, 5, 94–97.

———. (1989). Seeing and Saying 'No' Within the Theories of Spitz and Lacan. *Psychoanalysis and Contemporary Thought*, 12(3), 383–431.

———. (1997, Spring). Jean Cocteau: Word and Image. In C. A. Tsakiridou (Ed.), *Bucknell Review. Vol 41: Reviewing Orpheus: Essays on the Cinema and Art of Jean Cocteau* (1, Vol. 41, pp. 57–77). Lewisburg: Bucknell University Press.

———. (2001). Lacan's theory, Karon's Psychoanalytic Treatment of Schizophrenics. *Psychoanalysis and Contemporary Thought*, 24(1), 79–105.

———. (2004). Ontology of Denial. In J. Mills (Ed.), *Rereading Freud: Psychoanalysis through Philosophy*, 103–25. Albany, NY: State University of New York Press.

Vidal-Naquet, P. (1992). *Assassins of Memory: Essays on the Denial of the Holocaust* (J. Mehlman, Trans.). New York: Columbia University Press.

Vitousek, K. B., Daly, J., & Heiser, C. (1991). Reconstructing the Internal World of the Eating Disordered Individual: Overcoming Denial and Distortion in Self-report. *International Journal of Eating Disorders*, 10(6), 647–66.

Wangh, M. (1989). The Evolution of Psychoanalytic Thought on Negation and Denial. In E. Edelstein, D. L. Nathanson & A. M. Stone (Eds.), *Denial: A Clarification of Concepts and Research*. New York: Plenum.

Waszek, N. (1988). *The Scottish Enlightment and Hegel's Account of "Civil Society."* Dordrecht: Kluwer Academic Publishers.

Weinstein, E. A., Friedland, R. P., & Wagner, E. E. (1995). Denial/Unawareness of Impairment and Symbolic Behavior in Alzheimer's Disease. *Neuropsychiatry, Neuropsychology, and Behavioral Neurology*, 7(3), 176–84.

Weisman, A. D. (1989). Denial, Coping, and Cancer. In E. Edelstein, D. L. Nathanson, & A. M. Stone (Eds.), *Denial: A Clarification of Concepts and Research*. New York: Plenum Press.

Westphal, K. (1991, Fall). Hegel's Critique of Kant's Moral World View. *Philosophical Topics*, 19(2), 133–76.

Westphal, M. (1992). *Hegel, Freedom, and Modernity*. Albany, NY: State University of New York.

Whitebook, J. (1977). *Economics and Ethical Life: A Study of Aristotle and Hegel*. Ann Arbor, MI: University Microfilms.

Wiebe, D., & Black, D. (1997). Illusional Beliefs in the Context of Risky Sexual Behaviors. *Journal of Applied Social Psychology*, 27(19), 1727–49.

Winfield, R. D. (1988). *Reason and Justice*. Albany, NY: State University of New York Press.

———. (1990). *The Just Economy*. New York: Routledge.

Wing, D. M. (1995). Transcending Alcoholic Denial. *Image: Journal of Nursing Scholarship*, 2(2), 121–26.

Winn, M. E. (1996). The Strategic and Systematic Management of Denial in the Cognitive/Behavioral Treatment of Sexual Offenders. *Sexual Abuse: Journal of Research and Treatment*, 8(1), 25–36.

Winnicott, D. W. (1971). The Use of an Object and Relating through Identifications. In *Playing and Reality*, 86–94. London and New York: Routledge.

Wiseman, E. J., Souder, E., & O'Sullivan, P. (1996). Age and Denial of Alcoholism Severity. *Clinical Gerontologist*, 17(1), 55–58.

Wood, A. (1990). *Hegel's Ethical Thought*. Cambridge: Cambridge University Press.

Wool, M. S. (1986). Extreme Denial in Breast Cancer Patients and Capacity for Object Relations. *Psychotherapy and Psychosomatics*, 46(4), 196–204.

Wool, M. S., & Goldberg, R. J. (1986). Assesment of Denial in Cancer Patients: Implications for Intervention. *Journal of Psychosocial Oncology*, 4(3), 1–14.

Wurmser, L. (1985). Denial and Split Identity: Timely Issues in the Psychoanalytic Psychotherapy of Compulsive Users. *Journal of Substance Abuse Treatment*, 2(2), 89–96.

———. (1989). Blinding the Eye of the Mind: Denial, Impulsive Action, and Split Identity. In E. Edelstein, D. L. Nathanson & A. M. Stone (Eds.), *Denial: A Clarification of Concepts and Research*. New York: Plenum.

Young, L. D., Schweiger, J., Beitzinger, J., McManus, R. et al. (1991). Denial in Heart Transplant Candidates. *Psychotherapy and Psychosomatics*, 55(2–4), 141–44.

Author Index

Subject Index

abandon, 43, 51, 135
absence, 33, 63, 69, 78, 82, 86, 106, 111, 116, 129, 145, 146
absent, 62, 69, 80, 103, 118
absolute, 98, 136, 143
abuser, 152
acceded, 87
accept, xi, 2, 3, 10, 12, 13, 14, 15, 16, 17, 21, 33, 40, 42, 43, 44, 45, 46, 49, 50, 51, 52, 53, 54, 55, 58, 59, 63, 66, 69, 73, 78, 86, 91, 92, 93, 96, 97, 99, 102, 103, 105, 108, 110, 117, 121, 122, 125, 131, 133, 134, 136, 137, 142, 149, 150, 152, 154
acceptance, xi, 2, 13, 14, 43, 51, 59, 86, 92, 94, 131, 140, 152, 153, 154
accomplish, 35, 54, 85
accord, 108, 121
accusation, 38, 94, 95, 150
accuse, 93, 94, 95, 122
achieve, 2, 14, 30, 35, 50, 51, 59, 68, 69, 77, 79, 85, 88, 132, 147
achievement, 4, 27, 34, 53, 56, 69, 82, 84, 85, 88, 101, 147
acknowledge, 2, 5, 25, 27, 46, 53, 56, 57, 58, 59, 63, 66, 77, 102, 105, 108, 109, 120, 121, 124, 128, 133, 140, 152
acknowledgment, 14, 53, 105, 117, 131, 152
acquire, 10, 18, 19, 20, 54, 84, 124, 134
acquisition, 3, 16, 18, 19, 61, 64, 82, 84, 85, 88, 124, 128, 132, 148, 149

act, 8, 16, 18, 19, 20, 26, 27, 28, 33, 34, 35, 36, 46, 48, 50, 51, 52, 53, 57, 58, 59, 64, 65, 73, 75, 83, 85, 86, 88, 92, 96, 106, 122, 123, 128, 129, 130, 133, 144, 148, 151, 153
action, xi, 17, 32, 45, 49, 52, 53, 56, 57, 58, 59, 60, 72, 83, 84, 97, 107, 109, 110, 112, 114, 115, 117, 120, 128, 138, 147, 149, 150
activate, 80, 82
active, 16, 40, 65, 75, 79, 80, 82, 91, 95, 96, 101, 135
activity, 8, 9, 10, 15, 33, 40, 42, 45, 61, 69, 75, 76, 83, 88, 110, 115, 130, 136, 140, 148
actors, 123
acts, 4, 7, 8, 20, 22, 33, 41, 46, 52, 70, 122, 129, 130, 132
actualize, 41
adapted, ix
addiction, 136
address, 3, 9, 15, 18, 22, 35, 36, 40, 57, 73, 81, 86, 96, 121, 122, 131, 140, 152
adjust, 19, 114
admire, 27, 107, 117, 119
admission, 9, 27
admit, 15, 27, 28
admonish, 110
adored, 27
advice, advise, 26, 63, 117, 151
affect, 66, 69, 70, 77, 128, 131, 146

attributable, 63
attribute, 22, 31, 55, 71, 116, 134, 145, 147, 154
attributive, 14, 15, 16, 31
aufheben, 131
authentic, 22
autonomous, 101, 120, 121
autonomy, 4, 81, 85, 86, 120, 124, 149
avarice, 133
avenge, 92, 96
avoid, 2, 21, 22, 37, 40, 45, 55, 57, 60, 74, 91, 96, 99, 102, 106, 119, 141, 150, 152
avoidable, 115
avoidance, 10, 107, 152
avowal, 131
aware, 11, 12, 13, 27, 40, 55, 72, 73, 79, 94, 99, 106, 109, 110, 122, 125, 133, 138, 142, 143, 152
awareness, 26, 33, 97, 104, 137

baby, 65, 66, 71, 72, 76, 77, 79
barriers, 111
become, xi, 4, 12, 21, 22, 27, 28, 29, 31, 32, 33, 36, 40, 41, 42, 43, 44, 45, 49, 50, 51, 53, 54, 55, 59, 65, 67, 68, 69, 70, 72, 73, 75, 77, 78, 81, 82, 84, 85, 91, 94, 97, 99, 104, 105, 106, 107, 108, 109, 112, 114, 116, 117, 118, 119, 120, 121, 123, 129, 131, 132, 134, 138, 139, 140, 141, 143, 144, 152
blind, 68, 73, 82, 146, 148, 157
boast, 7, 10, 11, 12, 37, 129, 130, 139
body, 2, 4, 40, 51, 65, 72, 73, 74, 75, 76, 78, 79, 82, 85, 87, 88, 144, 146, 147, 148, 149, 150
body-disintegration, 76
bond, 63, 67, 69, 83, 111, 145
bondage, 45, 138
bondsman, 45
boring, 49, 82
bowdlerizer, 142, 143
breast, 14, 15, 103
brother, 38, 93, 94
brute, 138, 140
burden, 38, 58, 113

Cäcilie, 11, 130
capability, 11, 31, 51, 52, 56, 82, 99, 124, 146, 148, 153, 154
capacity, 31, 82, 84, 117, 145, 154
care, 4, 7, 22, 41, 77, 83, 92, 114, 117, 120, 124, 134, 149, 152
caretaker, 64, 68
castration, 10, 75
Catholicism, 118
censorship, 29
censured, 139
character, 39, 73, 79, 105, 112, 113, 143, 149
child, 3, 4, 14, 17, 18, 19, 20, 21, 27, 33, 38, 39, 61, 62, 63, 64, 65, 66, 67, 68, 69, 70, 71, 72, 73, 74, 75, 76, 77, 78, 79, 80, 81, 82, 83, 84, 85, 86, 87, 88, 89, 93, 103, 104, 111, 115, 122, 124, 128, 132, 133, 134, 136, 144, 145, 146, 147, 148, 149, 150, 151
childhood, 21, 101, 103, 107, 113
childish, 4
children, 3, 26, 27, 38, 48, 62, 65, 67, 68, 69, 74, 77, 80, 81, 82, 93, 128, 135, 136, 144, 146, 148, 149, 150, 157
chimpanzee, 76
Christ, 108, 115, 116
Christian, 55, 116, 120
Christianity, 55, 118
circumcision, 75
cleavage, 20, 150
client, 150
clinical, 18
cognition, 131
cognitive, 81, 129, 130, 131, 135
cognizance, 9, 12, 13, 129, 154
command, 83, 86, 139, 140
comment, 8, 16, 43, 78, 84, 87, 132
commentary, 127, 142, 160
commentators, 127
commit, 49, 95, 96, 106, 116, 145, 151
communicate, 82, 84, 85, 88, 149, 152
complain, 11, 38
complement, 32, 62, 66, 71, 73, 77, 80, 121

liberate, 113, 116, 133
liberty, 8, 138
libidinal, 18, 32, 33, 36, 64, 69, 83, 84, 85, 146, 147
libido, 16, 17, 18, 33, 76
lie, 2, 22, 25, 26, 27, 28, 33, 34, 35, 36, 40, 77, 97, 121, 123, 134, 135
life, 2, 5, 14, 18, 19, 21, 22, 26, 31, 38, 39, 40, 41, 44, 48, 51, 54, 55, 57, 62, 64, 65, 68, 70, 75, 78, 85, 92, 93, 94, 97, 98, 99, 102, 103, 104, 105, 106, 107, 108, 110, 111, 112, 113, 114, 115, 116, 118, 119, 120, 121, 122, 125, 128, 131, 134, 137, 138, 139, 140, 141, 143, 144, 153
life-and-death, 143
life-giving, 115
lifeless, 45
life-size, 112
life-span, 128

man, 29, 55, 96, 105, 113, 114, 115, 129, 133, 138, 146
mankind, 40, 51, 53
marital, 21, 104, 108, 118, 119
marriage, 92
marry, 29, 48, 92, 95, 139
mask, 64
master, 2, 33, 37, 41, 42, 43, 44, 45, 46, 51, 53, 73, 74, 79, 132, 133, 139, 141
mastered, 87
mastering, 70
master-slave, 2, 37, 42, 43, 44, 74
mastery, 124, 149
maternal, 4, 20, 74, 78, 80, 83, 84, 85, 88, 104, 147
maturation, 70, 81, 82
maturational, 81, 82
mature, 81, 110, 119
matured, 81
maturity, 59, 60, 119
mean, xi, 4, 8, 9, 10, 16, 17, 19, 20, 27, 30, 31, 32, 33, 36, 37, 39, 41, 42, 44, 45, 48, 49, 50, 54, 56, 59, 60, 61, 63, 64, 65, 68, 69, 78, 80, 82, 84, 85, 86, 87, 97, 99, 105, 119, 121, 127, 129, 130, 138, 140, 141, 143, 149, 152, 153

meaning, 9, 10, 21, 26, 27, 28, 42, 51, 54, 62, 64, 76, 84, 86, 91, 93, 97, 98, 99, 115, 116, 123, 125, 127, 128, 129, 130, 131, 135, 139, 151
meaningful, 46, 91, 99, 151
meaningless, 105
mediate, 74, 81
mediation, 143
meditation, 108
meditative, 110
mental, 19, 37, 62, 76, 132, 133, 137, 147
mentality, 55
metaphor, 8, 20, 22, 74, 101, 107, 109, 116, 118, 119, 120, 121, 122, 133, 134
metaphoric, 4, 7, 17, 20, 21, 22, 107, 108, 117, 118, 119, 120, 121, 132, 134
metapsychological, 8
metonymy, 74, 101, 110, 111, 112
mind, 2, 8, 9, 10, 14, 15, 16, 54, 94, 137, 140, 141, 143, 146, 148, 152
minded, 139, 154
mindedness, 154
minds, 29, 136
mine, 29, 39, 70, 80, 81, 85, 116, 134, 149, 151
mineness, 52
mirror, 4, 65, 68, 72, 74, 75, 76, 77, 78, 79, 80, 81, 82, 83, 85, 87, 88, 136, 145, 148, 150
mirror-image, 65
mirror-stage, 4, 74, 78, 83, 85, 88
misfortune, 92
moral, 2, 28, 89, 96, 123, 134, 135, 150
moralistic, 96
morality, 48, 54, 57, 142, 150
morally, 26, 27, 28, 33, 49
mortal, 55, 111
mortality, 77, 78
mother, xi, 7, 8, 9, 13, 14, 15, 19, 20, 21, 33, 45, 56, 57, 58, 59, 63, 64, 65, 66, 67, 68, 69, 70, 71, 72, 74, 76, 77, 78, 79, 80, 81, 82, 83, 84, 85, 86, 87, 88, 92, 95, 102, 103, 107, 108, 109, 110, 111, 112, 113, 116, 117, 119, 128, 129, 133, 134, 135, 136, 146, 147, 149